Mastering SQLite with Python

From Basics to Advanced Techniques

Robert Johnson

Published by HiTeX Press

For permissions and other inquiries, write to:
P.O. Box 3132, Framingham, MA 01701, USA

Contents

Introduction

SQLite, a software library that provides a relational database management system, is a cornerstone for developers seeking a lightweight database solution. It is unique in its design, being a self-contained, serverless, and zero-configuration database engine. With widespread adoption across various platforms, including mobile devices, desktop applications, and even embedded systems, SQLite is notably versatile and efficient. Its implementation is seamless in diverse programming environments, making it a popular choice among developers.

This book, "Mastering SQLite with Python: From Basics to Advanced Techniques," serves as a comprehensive guide for those aspiring to harness the full potential of SQLite using Python. Python's ease of use and powerful libraries make it an ideal companion for SQLite, providing robust tools to manage and manipulate databases with simplicity and elegance.

The contents of this book are structured to lead the reader from fundamental concepts to advanced techniques. The early chapters introduce SQLite's basic features and setup processes. As the reader progresses, the book explores sophisticated SQL operations, integration strategies with Python, and effective database management practices. Additionally, it covers critical topics like performance optimization, security, and handling large datasets.

Furthermore, the book integrates real-world applications and case studies to provide practical insights into the application of SQLite in various domains. This approach ensures that readers not only understand theoretical concepts but also appreciate their practical applicability.

By the end of this journey, readers will have acquired a solid understanding of how to utilize SQLite effectively within Python applications. Whether you are a student, a software developer, or an IT professional, this book provides the knowledge necessary to leverage SQLite's powerful features to their fullest extent.

Aspiring to cater to a diverse audience, this book ensures accessibility by explaining concepts with clarity, supported by examples and exercises. Its aim is to demystify the complexities associated with database management, offering you the tools to become proficient in utilizing SQLite alongside Python.

In conclusion, "Mastering SQLite with Python: From Basics to Advanced Techniques" is more than just a technical manual. It is a resource designed to equip you with the skills needed to navigate the increasingly data-driven world we live in. Its structured approach guarantees a thorough understanding of both SQLite and its integration with Python, empowering you to tackle real-world data challenges with confidence and competence.

Chapter 1

Introduction to SQLite and Python

SQLite is a lightweight, self-contained database engine favored for its simplicity and efficiency across diverse platforms. This chapter covers its fundamental features, the benefits of using SQLite, and compares it to other relational databases. The basics of Python's relevance for SQLite integration are discussed, along with key considerations for selecting SQLite for projects and understanding its file-based architecture.

1.1. What is SQLite?

SQLite is a relational database management system characterized by its lightweight design and its ability to operate without the need for a separate server process. This embedded database engine is self-contained, requiring minimal setup and configuration, which distinguishes it from many other database systems. SQLite stores its entire database as a single ordinary disk file, making it portable and ideal for applications that require a simple, reliable, and fast database solution integrated directly into the software.

The inception of SQLite dates back to the late 1990s, when its creator, D. Richard Hipp, sought to provide a mechanism for handling persistent storage without the complexity of a client-server database system. This design philosophy has led to SQLite becoming one of the most widely deployed database systems in both desktop and mobile environments. Over time, its development has focused on ensuring reliability, efficiency, and ease of use, which, coupled with its public domain status, has contributed to its broad adoption in various software projects ranging from web browsers to embedded systems.

Fundamental to SQLite's architecture is its serverless design. Traditional database management systems often operate based on a client-server model, where multiple clients communicate with a centralized server that handles queries and data management. In contrast, SQLite operates directly on the disk file, allowing applications to perform database operations using a standardized SQL interface without interprocess communication. This eliminates the overhead associated with network protocols and simplifies the deployment process.

One of the key features of SQLite is its self-contained nature. The entire SQLite engine is embedded within the application itself, meaning that the application does not rely on a separate database server. This results in a smaller memory footprint and reduces the potential for configuration errors because the database engine is distributed alongside the application. Applications using SQLite can be deployed in environments where installing and maintaining a dedicated database server is impractical.

SQLite implements most of the SQL standard while incorporating a subset of SQL functionalities that balance performance with resource constraints. It supports transactions with Atomicity, Consistency, Isolation, and Durability (ACID) properties, ensuring that database operations are processed reliably. Despite being lightweight, SQLite is designed to handle a considerable amount of data and complex queries. Its support for indexing, triggers, and views enables developers to optimize performance and enforce data integrity rules even in resource-constrained scenarios.

The file-based architecture of SQLite brings with it several implications for application design. Since the database exists as a single file, filesystem features such as permissions and file locks become central to its operation. SQLite employs file locking mechanisms to manage concurrent access to the database file, ensuring that data remains consistent even when accessed by multiple threads or processes. This design simplifies backup and copying operations, as the entire database can be encapsulated in one file. However, developers must be aware of the limitations that file-based storage imposes when dealing with extremely high levels of concurrent write operations.

Performance optimization within SQLite is achieved through a combination of compiler-level optimizations and an efficient query engine. The internal design of SQLite minimizes the amount of memory used for data structures, which is crucial for operating in environments with limited computational resources. Furthermore, SQLite adopts a dynamic optimization strategy that compiles SQL queries into a bytecode representation that can be executed by its virtual machine. The seamless integration of these optimizations contributes to SQLite's reputation for speed, even when handling typical relational database workloads.

A notable strength of SQLite is its ease of integration with programming languages, particularly in scenarios where a full-blown database server would be excessive. The integration with Python is a prime example, as the Python standard library includes the `sqlite3` module, which provides a straightforward and efficient interface to SQLite databases. This module allows developers to execute SQL commands, manage transactions, and interact with database records using Python data structures. For instance, the following example demonstrates how to establish a connection to an SQLite database, create a table, and insert data:

```python
import sqlite3

# Establish a connection to the SQLite database file
connection = sqlite3.connect('example.db')

# Create a cursor object for executing SQL commands
cursor = connection.cursor()

# Create a table named 'users'
cursor.execute('''
CREATE TABLE IF NOT EXISTS users (
    id INTEGER PRIMARY KEY,
    name TEXT NOT NULL,
    email TEXT UNIQUE NOT NULL
)
''')

# Insert sample data into the 'users' table
cursor.execute('''
INSERT INTO users (name, email)
VALUES ('Alice Smith', 'alice.smith@example.com')
''')

# Commit the changes and close the connection
connection.commit()
connection.close()
```

The ability to integrate SQLite seamlessly with Python not only enhances development efficiency but also supports rapid prototyping and testing. By leveraging the simplicity of SQLite, application developers can build and iterate over database-driven features without the overhead of setting up and managing a server-based database.

Beyond its performance characteristics and ease of use, SQLite is also distinguished by its robust reliability and simplicity in deployment. The absence of a server component eliminates many common points of failure that can be encountered in distributed database systems. This quality, combined with extensive testing and a focus on correctness, makes SQLite a dependable choice for a wide range of applications from small-scale utilities to embedded systems in consumer electronics.

Furthermore, the history and evolution of SQLite have fostered a rich ecosystem of tools and libraries that enhance its capabilities. Various third-party tools are available for database administration, backup, and optimization, which further extend the functionality of SQLite while maintaining its lightweight footprint. This ecosystem supports advanced features such as full-text search and spatial data management through extensions and modules, enabling applications to leverage specialized database functions when needed.

The design philosophy behind SQLite emphasizes minimalism and universality. Its public domain status allows organizations to incorporate it within proprietary projects without concerns of licensing or distribution limitations. This has proven particularly important in industries where cost, performance, and integration flexibility are paramount. SQLite's simplicity does not come at the expense of its functionality; rather, the deliberate selection of features ensures that every operation, from query execution to database modification, is handled in an optimal and predictable manner.

SQLite's evolution over the years can be seen in the way it has maintained backward compatibility while incorporating modern database features. Advanced querying capabilities, enhanced security, and improved support for concurrent operations have been added over successive versions. In each iteration, the focus remains on delivering a reliable and consistent engine that can reliably operate in environments where resources may be limited. These improvements have not only broadened the scope of SQLite's applications but also solidified its role in scenarios where consistent performance and data integrity are critical.

The educational value of SQLite lies in its simplicity and the clarity of its operational model. For learners, SQLite offers an accessible entry point into relational database concepts without the complexity found in larger, server-based systems. The single-file database structure, coupled with a straightforward SQL interface, makes it an ideal tool for understanding fundamental database principles including table creation, data manipulation, and query optimization. This reduced complexity facilitates the rapid uptake of relational database concepts, serving as a foundation for exploring more complex systems in the future.

SQLite also serves as an effective teaching tool for demonstrating the principles of transaction management, error handling, and performance tuning. By studying SQLite, learners can gain insights into how file-level locking mechanisms operate to ensure data consistency, how internal query optimizers work, and how the balance between functionality and performance is achieved in modern database systems. The compact and readable source code of SQLite is also available for study, allowing advanced learners to explore its internal mechanisms and better understand the implementation of a sophisticated yet accessible database engine.

The integration with various programming languages and environments further demonstrates SQLite's versatility. Its minimalist configuration allows it to be embedded in mobile applications, IoT devices, and web applications, where the demands of high availability and scalability are balanced against the need for a lightweight, self-contained database system. This adaptability has spurred an active community of developers and researchers who continue to refine and extend SQLite's capabilities.

The emphasis on a small footprint does not compromise its robustness or its ability to handle complex queries. Features such as triggers, views, and compound SQL statements enable the construction of sophisticated database schemas and interactions. Additionally, SQLite supports various numeric, string, and date/time functions, providing the necessary tools to implement a broad range of data manipulation and analysis tasks. Its adherence to SQL standards, while customized for a lightweight environment, ensures that developers can leverage their existing SQL knowledge to build and maintain reliable database applications.

Overall, SQLite stands as an exemplar of efficient database design through careful prioritization of key features over extraneous functionality. Its self-contained nature, file-based approach, and focus on reliability make it highly suited for modern applications that require a balance between performance, simplicity, and ease of deployment. The practical examples of integrating SQLite with Python further illustrate how developers can leverage its simplicity and power to create dynamic, database-driven applications with minimal overhead.

1.2. Benefits of Using SQLite

SQLite offers several advantages in scenarios where simplicity, reliability, and ease of deployment are critical. One significant benefit is its serverless architecture, which eliminates the need for a separate database server process. This feature reduces the overhead associated with installing, configuring, and maintaining a dedicated server. Developers can thus embed SQLite directly into their applications, which simplifies the deployment process. Applications that rely on SQLite typically experience faster startup times and a lower overall system resource consumption.

Another prominent advantage is SQLite's file-based storage model.

Instead of managing multiple files or complex directory structures, SQLite stores the entire database in a single file. This design simplifies tasks such as backup, transport, and sharing of data. The single-file approach enables effortless replication and version control using standard filesystem tools. Considering the use case where an application is distributed across different devices, the portability afforded by a single database file proves invaluable. Moreover, file-based architecture allows for the use of file system security features to protect the data.

SQLite's minimal configuration requirement further enhances its appeal. Unlike traditional database systems that may require extensive configuration files and environment setup, SQLite requires no installation or administrative tasks. This low barrier to entry is particularly useful for developers working on small-scale projects, rapid prototyping, or mobile applications. The reduced configuration complexity results in fewer issues related to deployment and maintenance, enabling developers to focus on application logic rather than database administration.

The integration of SQLite with programming languages such as Python is another notable benefit. The Python standard library includes the `sqlite3` module, which offers a straightforward interface for interacting with SQLite databases. This direct integration streamlines database operations and minimizes the overhead normally associated with more complex client-server database systems. The following example demonstrates the simplicity of establishing a connection, creating a table, and executing basic CRUD operations:

```
import sqlite3

# Connect to SQLite database file; it will be created if it does not
    exist
conn = sqlite3.connect('benefits_example.db')
cursor = conn.cursor()

# Create a table to store sample data
cursor.execute('''
```

```
CREATE TABLE IF NOT EXISTS products (
    id INTEGER PRIMARY KEY,
    name TEXT NOT NULL,
    price REAL NOT NULL
)
''')

# Insert sample data into the table
cursor.execute("INSERT INTO products (name, price) VALUES ('Widget',
    19.99)")
conn.commit()

# Fetch and display the inserted record
cursor.execute("SELECT * FROM products")
print(cursor.fetchall())  % This would display the output in the
    console

conn.close()
```

This example illustrates the ease with which SQLite can be embedded in Python applications. Developers can execute standard SQL commands without the need to manage a separate database server, resulting in a more streamlined development and deployment cycle. The simplicity of interaction offered by SQLite encourages rapid prototyping and testing, thereby cutting down on development time.

The performance of SQLite, particularly in single-user or low- to moderate-concurrency environments, is another benefit that many developers find attractive. SQLite is designed to handle a significant number of read operations efficiently, making it an excellent choice for applications where read speed is critical. Its optimization strategies, such as caching frequently accessed data and compiling SQL queries into efficient bytecode, contribute to its overall speed. Even though SQLite uses file locks for concurrency control, these mechanisms are optimized to work efficiently for many applications where heavy write concurrency is not a primary concern.

For applications that do not require robust concurrent write operations, SQLite provides an optimal balance between speed and simplicity. Its transactional capabilities guarantee the Atomicity, Consistency, Isolation, and Durability (ACID) properties for database transactions. This level of reliability ensures that applications maintain data integrity, even in scenarios where interruptions occur unexpectedly. The ACID compliance is a critical factor in industries where data reliability is paramount, yet the required scale does not justify the overhead of a full-fledged server-based solution.

The licensing of SQLite further exemplifies its benefits. Being in the public domain, SQLite can be freely used in both open-source and proprietary applications without concerns over licensing fees or restrictions. This flexibility has encouraged widespread adoption across various industries, from mobile application development to embedded systems in consumer electronics. Organizations benefit from the security of knowing that they are not subject to licensing limitations or potential legal complications related to proprietary software.

The lightweight nature of SQLite, in terms of both disk space and memory usage, is another compelling reason for its selection over other database systems. In environments with limited system resources, such as IoT devices or mobile platforms, the small footprint of SQLite allows for efficient use of multimedia storage. The reduced resource consumption translates into lower power requirements and improved performance in resource-constrained settings. For developers targeting such platforms, SQLite offers a database solution that aligns with the need for minimal overhead without sacrificing essential database functionalities.

Additionally, SQLite features a relatively simple and clean code base due to its focus on providing reliable performance without unnecessary complexity. This simplicity translates into fewer bugs and a lower chance of security vulnerabilities. Developers can inspect and understand the inner workings of SQLite more readily than those of larger, more complex database systems. This transparency is beneficial for applications that require a high degree of customization or that operate in environments where security is critical.

SQLite's robustness in handling diverse workloads is another advantage. While it may not be the ideal solution for high-write concurrency in large-scale web applications, its performance and reliability for small to medium-sized projects are well documented. The ease of setting up, managing, and deploying an SQLite database allows developers to efficiently manage data operations without the need for extensive infrastructure. This feature is particularly advantageous for startups and independent developers, where ease of maintenance and low overhead can significantly reduce costs and streamline development processes.

From an educational standpoint, SQLite serves as an excellent platform for teaching fundamental database operations. Its minimalist design and straightforward integration with common programming languages allow learners to focus on understanding SQL concepts without the distractions of server management. In classroom settings and tutorials, SQLite is frequently used as an introductory tool to demonstrate database design, query formulation, and transactional integrity. It lays a sound foundation for exploring more advanced database systems later in the learning progression.

The availability of extensive documentation and community-driven support further enhances the benefits of using SQLite. Developers can leverage a wealth of resources that provide insights into best practices, optimization techniques, and troubleshooting methods. The active community around SQLite contributes to a continuously evolving knowledge base, ensuring that practitioners can find solutions to diverse challenges with relative ease. This robust support network is crucial for fostering long-term adoption and confidence in the technology.

The versatility of SQLite also makes it suitable for various application domains. Whether it is for mobile apps, desktop applications, or embedded systems, SQLite's ability to provide a complete relational database solution in a compact and efficient manner sets it apart from other database systems. The flexibility to use SQLite in both development and production environments simplifies many aspects of application lifecycle management, including testing, deployment, and maintenance. Applications that start with SQLite in the early stages might continue to use it throughout the product lifecycle, thereby avoiding potentially disruptive migrations to other systems.

The combined benefits of low resource consumption, ease of use, reliability, and broad compatibility with multiple platforms and programming environments make SQLite a preferred choice for many developers. When contrasted with heavier, more complex client-server databases, SQLite often provides all the necessary functionality for a fraction of the operational overhead. By leveraging SQLite, developers can focus on the core application logic rather than being burdened by infrastructure complexities.

SQLite's performance optimization, simple integration model, and minimal footprint are attributes that collectively reduce both development time and maintenance requirements. These qualities make SQLite not only an effective solution for small to medium-sized applications but also a robust platform to handle challenging resource constraints. The decision to choose SQLite often hinges on the need to balance performance with simplicity, and in many cases, SQLite meets this criterion more effectively than its larger counterparts.

The practical benefits of SQLite, evidenced by its adoption across a variety of industries, underscore its value as a database system. The combination of ease of installation, minimal configuration, file portability, and robust ACID compliance provides an attractive package for projects where ease of management and reliability are more critical than handling extreme concurrent transactional loads. Through careful consideration of these advantages, developers may choose SQLite to accelerate the development process, reduce operational complexity, and ultimately deliver efficient, reliable software solutions.

1.3. Basics of Python

Python is a versatile, high-level programming language celebrated for its clarity and ease of use. Its simple syntax and dynamic typing make it accessible for beginners while being robust enough for advanced programming paradigms. This section introduces the core concepts of Python and illustrates its relevance to SQLite integration by highlighting its inherent readability, extensive standard library, and ability to bridge application logic with database operations.

At its core, Python uses indentation to define blocks of code rather than traditional braces or keywords found in other languages. This design choice enforces readability and uniformity, reducing syntactic clutter. Code blocks for functions, loops, and conditionals are created upon indenting, which enforces logical grouping and eases maintenance. For example, a basic function in Python is defined as follows:

```
def greet(name):
    if name:
        print("Hello, " + name)
    else:
        print("Hello, World!")

greet("Alice")
```

The function greet accepts one parameter, and its block is identified by consistent indentation, which is critical for Python's interpretation of code structure. Comments in Python are initiated using the # symbol, allowing developers to annotate code without affecting execution.

Python's dynamic typing eliminates the need for explicit variable declarations. Variables are created upon assignment and can change type

23

over their lifetime. This characteristic allows developers to write concise code, though it requires careful attention to variable usage to prevent runtime errors. Consider the following example:

```
x = 42
print("The value of x is:", x)
x = "Forty-two"
print("Now, x is:", x)
```

The flexibility of dynamic typing, coupled with Python's robust standard library, streamlines the process of integrating different functionalities into a coherent program.

In the context of database integration, Python excels because of its well-maintained and documented modules, such as sqlite3, which facilitates the incorporation of SQLite databases in applications. The sqlite3 module, part of the Python standard library, provides a straightforward approach to interact with SQLite databases using simple and familiar SQL commands. This module abstracts away much of the complexity behind connecting to and operating on a SQLite database, thereby enabling developers to perform common operations with minimal code. An illustrative example is demonstrated below:

```
import sqlite3

def get_database_connection(db_file):
    try:
        connection = sqlite3.connect(db_file)
        return connection
    except sqlite3.Error as error:
        print("Error while connecting to database:", error)
        return None

conn = get_database_connection('python_sqlite.db')
if conn:
    cursor = conn.cursor()
    cursor.execute('CREATE TABLE IF NOT EXISTS employees (id INTEGER
     PRIMARY KEY, name TEXT, department TEXT)')
    cursor.execute("INSERT INTO employees (name, department) VALUES
     ('John Doe', 'Engineering')")
    conn.commit()
```

24

```
cursor.execute('SELECT * FROM employees')
for record in cursor.fetchall():
    print(record)
conn.close()
```

In this example, a connection to an SQLite database is established using the `sqlite3.connect` function. After confirming a successful connection, the code creates a table, inserts a record, and queries the database. The use of error handling via try-except blocks further enforces robust programming practices, ensuring that any issues are caught and reported without causing abrupt program termination.

Python's syntax supports both procedural and object-oriented programming paradigms. Object-oriented features allow developers to model real-world scenarios with classes and objects, leading to code that is modular and easier to manage. The object-oriented approach is particularly beneficial when developing larger applications that require interaction with databases. For example, developers may encapsulate database connection logic and query operations within a class, thereby promoting reusability and maintainability. An example of a simple class-based encapsulation for SQLite operations is provided below:

```
class SQLiteDB:
    def __init__(self, db_file):
        self.connection = sqlite3.connect(db_file)
        self.cursor = self.connection.cursor()

    def execute_query(self, query, params=()):
        try:
            self.cursor.execute(query, params)
            self.connection.commit()
        except sqlite3.Error as error:
            print("Query failed:", error)

    def fetch_all(self, query, params=()):
        self.cursor.execute(query, params)
        return self.cursor.fetchall()

    def close(self):
        self.connection.close()
```

25

```
# Usage of the SQLiteDB class
db = SQLiteDB('object_oriented.db')
db.execute_query('''
CREATE TABLE IF NOT EXISTS projects (
    id INTEGER PRIMARY KEY,
    title TEXT,
    status TEXT
)
''')
db.execute_query("INSERT INTO projects (title, status) VALUES ('
    SQLite Project', 'Active')")
records = db.fetch_all('SELECT * FROM projects')
for record in records:
    print(record)
db.close()
```

This class, SQLiteDB, provides a structured framework for managing SQLite connections and operations. By encapsulating database functionality within a dedicated class, Python enables developers to adhere to principles of abstraction and modularity, which are essential for scalable application development.

Beyond its expressive syntax and programming paradigms, Python is known for its extensive ecosystem of packages and community support. Libraries like pandas for data analysis, numpy for numerical computations, and matplotlib for data visualization extend Python's core capabilities. In database management, these libraries can often be used together with SQLite to perform complex data manipulation and analysis, streamlining workflows that integrate data retrieval, processing, and visualization. For example, a typical workflow might involve querying data from a SQLite database, using pandas to manipulate the dataset, and plotting the data with matplotlib. Consider the following integrated example:

```
import sqlite3
import pandas as pd
import matplotlib.pyplot as plt

# Connect to SQLite database
conn = sqlite3.connect('data_analysis.db')
```

```
query = "SELECT id, sales FROM monthly_sales"
df = pd.read_sql_query(query, conn)

# Plot sales data
plt.plot(df['id'], df['sales'], marker='o')
plt.title('Monthly Sales')
plt.xlabel('Month ID')
plt.ylabel('Sales')
plt.show()

conn.close()
```

In this scenario, Python acts as an orchestrator that ties together data extraction, transformation, and visualization with minimal code. The seamless cooperation between SQLite and other Python libraries underscores the role of Python as a unifying framework for various stages of application development.

Error handling in Python is an essential aspect, particularly when integrating with external systems such as databases. Python's exception-handling mechanism employs try, except, else, and finally blocks, providing developers with the tools needed to gracefully manage runtime errors. For database operations, this means that potential issues like connection failures, execution errors, or data integrity problems can be captured and addressed without causing the application to crash. This improves reliability and aids in maintaining consistent application behavior. An example of enhanced error handling in database interactions is illustrated below:

```
def execute_safe_query(db_file, query, params=()):
    try:
        with sqlite3.connect(db_file) as conn:
            cursor = conn.cursor()
            cursor.execute(query, params)
            conn.commit()
            return cursor.fetchall()
    except sqlite3.Error as error:
        print("Error encountered:", error)
        return None

results = execute_safe_query('secure.db', 'SELECT * FROM
```

```
        sensitive_table')
if results is not None:
    for row in results:
        print(row)
```

This snippet leverages Python's context management via the with statement to manage database connections, ensuring that resources are properly released even if an error occurs.

Python also supports the creation of virtual environments which isolate project dependencies and ensure that applications run with the correct library versions. This is particularly useful when multiple projects require different versions of the same packages. Virtual environments can be created and managed with tools like venv or virtualenv, thereby enabling developers to experiment with database integrations, libraries, and code without interference from other projects. The following command line instructions demonstrate how to set up a virtual environment:

```
python -m venv myenv
source myenv/bin/activate   % On Windows, use: myenv\Scripts\activate
pip install sqlite3  % Although sqlite3 comes with Python, additional
        libraries for processing may be installed
```

The creation of virtual environments promotes reproducibility and isolation, ensuring that projects remain self-contained and mitigating potential version conflicts.

Modern Python development practices also emphasize testing and documentation. The unittest framework, integrated with Python's standard library, supports systematic testing of application modules, including database operations. Well-written tests can validate that SQL queries return the expected results and that database state modifications behave as intended. An example of a simple test case for database operations may be structured as follows:

```
import sqlite3
import unittest
```

28

```
class TestDatabaseOperations(unittest.TestCase):
    def setUp(self):
        self.conn = sqlite3.connect(':memory:')   % Use an in-memory
    database for testing
        self.cursor = self.conn.cursor()
        self.cursor.execute('CREATE TABLE test (id INTEGER PRIMARY
    KEY, value TEXT)')

    def test_insert_and_select(self):
        self.cursor.execute("INSERT INTO test (value) VALUES ('sample
    ')")
        self.conn.commit()
        self.cursor.execute('SELECT value FROM test WHERE id=1')
        result = self.cursor.fetchone()[0]
        self.assertEqual(result, 'sample')

    def tearDown(self):
        self.conn.close()

if __name__ == '__main__':
    unittest.main()
```

This test harness utilizes an in-memory SQLite database to validate CRUD operations without the overhead of managing a physical database file. The practice of implementing unit tests is fundamental to ensuring that database integrations behave reliably across iterations of development.

Python's simplicity in syntax coupled with its powerful libraries makes it an ideal companion for SQLite. By focusing on readability and ease of integration, the language allows developers to construct reliable, maintainable applications without excessive overhead. The practical examples provided herein illustrate the direct application of Python's syntax and programming paradigms in performing database operations. The interplay between Python's dynamic structure and SQLite's lightweight, file-based database model forms the backbone of many modern applications, demonstrating how these tools can work in tandem to offer practical, effective solutions in software development.

1.4.   Choosing SQLite for Your Projects

When deciding on a database solution, the selection of SQLite should be based on a careful evaluation of the project's requirements, architectural constraints, and scalability expectations. SQLite is particularly well-suited for applications where ease of deployment, minimal configuration, and low resource overhead are of paramount importance. Several factors can guide the decision to leverage SQLite over more complex client-server database systems.

A primary criterion for choosing SQLite is its self-contained, file-based architecture. Projects that require a lightweight, embedded database benefit from the simplicity of a single-file storage model. This design encapsulates the entire database within one file on disk, which simplifies backup, replication, and even version control. For example, small desktop applications, mobile apps, and embedded systems typically do not require the extensive features provided by server-based databases. In these contexts, SQLite's compact nature minimizes installation and operational overhead, thereby streamlining the deployment process across various platforms.

When operating on resource-constrained devices, such as Internet of Things (IoT) gadgets or low-power mobile devices, the small memory and processing footprint of SQLite are critical. In these cases, the reduced resource requirements contribute to faster startup times and lower energy consumption. Developers targeting these platforms can rely on SQLite to offer reliable data persistence without necessitating the infrastructure needed for heavier relational database management systems.

Another aspect to consider is the expected level of concurrency and transaction volume. SQLite implements locking mechanisms that suffice for many use cases, especially those dominated by read operations. It handles multiple concurrent reads efficiently, but its write operations are serialized. Hence, projects with low- to moderate-write concurrency or applications where high levels of simultaneous write activity are not central to the application's functionality stand to gain from SQLite's simplicity. In scenarios requiring high transactional throughput with frequent writes from multiple clients, alternatives like MySQL or PostgreSQL might be more appropriate due to their client-server architectures that handle concurrent connections more effectively.

The ease of integration with programming languages, notably Python, serves as another critical factor in the decision to choose SQLite. As covered in previous sections, the availability of the sqlite3 module in Python's standard library provides a straightforward interface that allows developers to execute SQL commands, manage transactions, and handle the database with minimal boilerplate code. This facilitates rapid prototyping and development cycles. For instance, consider a developer working on a prototype of a mobile application. They can quickly set up an SQLite database and start building features without the burden of installing and configuring a separate database server.

A practical example that illustrates this quick integration can be observed in the following code snippet:

```python
import sqlite3

def create_database(db_name):
    connection = sqlite3.connect(db_name)
    cursor = connection.cursor()
    cursor.execute('''
        CREATE TABLE IF NOT EXISTS sessions (
            id INTEGER PRIMARY KEY,
            user TEXT NOT NULL,
            timestamp DATETIME DEFAULT CURRENT_TIMESTAMP
        )
    ''')
    connection.commit()
    connection.close()

def insert_session(db_name, user):
    connection = sqlite3.connect(db_name)
    cursor = connection.cursor()
```

31

```
    cursor.execute('INSERT INTO sessions (user) VALUES (?)', (user,))
    connection.commit()
    connection.close()

# Setup database and insert a session
db_file = 'app_data.db'
create_database(db_file)
insert_session(db_file, 'test_user')
```

This example demonstrates how quickly a database schema can be created and manipulated within an application using SQLite coupled with Python. The simplified workflow minimizes the learning curve and accelerates the development process—a key benefit when time-to-market is a crucial factor.

For projects that are intended to evolve from prototype to production without significant migration overhead, starting with SQLite can be a sensible decision. During early stages of development, applications often benefit from the simplicity and quick setup provided by SQLite. As the application matures, developers might choose to retain SQLite for production if the performance and scalability of the database continue to meet the project's needs. Alternatively, if future demands require a more robust system, the initial design can facilitate a migration path. The familiarity with SQL and adherence to ACID properties in SQLite reduce the cognitive load during such transitions, since many of the underlying principles remain consistent across different database systems.

Another critical factor is the licensing and cost considerations. SQLite is released into the public domain, meaning it can be used freely in both open-source and commercial projects without incurring licensing fees or facing distribution constraints. This unrestricted usage model is particularly advantageous for startups and small- to medium-sized enterprises that might be constrained by budget or concerned about vendor lock-in. The public domain status also encourages widespread adoption, leading to a strong community support network and a wealth of documentation, tutorials, and third-party tools that can further simplify development tasks.

Developers should also consider the long-term maintenance and deployment aspects of their projects. SQLite's minimal configuration and operational simplicity reduce the burden on system administrators and developers alike. Since SQLite does not depend on a separate server process, there is no need to manage network connections or perform intricate user privilege configurations that are common with server-based databases. This ease of maintenance can be particularly beneficial in environments where technical support resources are limited. Moreover, its self-contained nature simplifies the testing process. Development teams can use in-memory databases for unit testing, which accelerates automated test suites and enhances development workflows.

Evaluating the use of SQLite does require being mindful of its limitations. For instance, scenarios that involve extremely high levels of concurrent writes or require complex multi-user management might expose SQLite's serialization of write operations as a bottleneck. Additionally, for applications that demand advanced database features such as stored procedures, extensive replication, or complex sharding capabilities, more feature-rich systems could be a better fit. Thus, the decision to use SQLite should be balanced with an honest appraisal of the application's performance requirements and scalability targets.

In planning your project, consider how frequently data is accessed and modified, and whether the advantages of a single-file database outweigh the benefits offered by distributed database systems. Projects that involve significant offline capabilities benefit from SQLite's portability across multiple platforms and environments. This is particularly relevant for mobile applications, where local data storage is necessary for offline functionality and quick, responsive user interfaces.

The decision-making process for utilizing SQLite can be structured around key parameters such as data volume, performance objectives, hardware constraints, concurrency needs, and future scalability. When data volume is moderate, the performance gains provided by the lightweight nature of SQLite are often sufficient. Equally, when the majority of interactions with the database are read-heavy, SQLite's ability to efficiently handle concurrent read operations makes it a compelling choice.

The conceptual simplicity of SQLite also aids in reducing cognitive complexity for developers. Since the entire database system is embedded into the application, the typical challenges associated with system administration, connectivity, and network security are mitigated. This not only accelerates development but also reduces the overall risk of errors and vulnerabilities arising from misconfigured database servers.

From an architectural perspective, SQLite fits well in microservices and modular applications where each component may manage its own small-scale data store. In such architectures, the overhead of maintaining a separate database system for every microservice could be prohibitive. SQLite's integration as an embedded database ensures that each service can operate independently without extensive external dependencies, thereby enhancing overall system resilience and simplifying deployment pipelines.

When evaluating project requirements, consider also the learning curve associated with new technology adoption. SQLite's straightforward implementation aligns well with projects that aim to reduce technical debt and focus on rapid development. For educational purposes and smaller scale applications, utilizing SQLite can provide tangible benefits without sacrificing performance or reliability.

Choosing SQLite for your projects ultimately boils down to aligning project constraints and goals with the inherent characteristics of the database system. Its ease of integration with programming languages, cross-platform compatibility, and minimal administrative overhead make it particularly attractive for projects that require agility and simplicity. By carefully assessing the scale, concurrency, and performance needs of your application, you can make an informed decision on whether SQLite is the optimal choice. This deliberate approach in selecting SQLite allows developers to leverage a dependable, lightweight database system that not only streamlines development but also supports a robust, maintainable, and scalable application lifecycle.

1.5. Comparison with Other Database Systems

When evaluating relational database systems for application development, it is essential to consider the distinctive architectural and operational characteristics of each system. SQLite, MySQL, and PostgreSQL represent three prominent choices within the relational database ecosystem. The comparison among these systems centers on differences in deployment models, performance under varying load conditions, feature sets, and administrative overhead.

SQLite distinguishes itself with its serverless, file-based architecture. As described in previous sections, the entire database resides in a single disk file, allowing for straightforward deployment and minimal configuration. This embedded model simplifies development for small-scale applications, desktop utilities, mobile applications, and scenarios where installation of a full server is not feasible. In contrast, MySQL and PostgreSQL follow a client-server architecture. They run as independent server processes that manage databases, which facilitates centralized administration, high availability, and robust concurrent access options. This difference in architecture means that while SQLite excels in simplicity and minimal resource consumption, MySQL and

35

PostgreSQL offer more extensive features suited for scaling and handling simultaneous multi-user transactions.

From a performance perspective, SQLite is optimized for scenarios where read operations dominate and write concurrency is limited. Its internal locking mechanism, though robust for many applications, serializes writes to prevent data corruption. Thus, in high-write environments that require handling of bulk insertions or simultaneous write operations from numerous clients, a server-based system like MySQL or PostgreSQL can outperform SQLite by distributing the load over multiple connections and leveraging advanced concurrency controls. PostgreSQL, for instance, has a sophisticated multi-version concurrency control (MVCC) mechanism, which provides high levels of isolation and reduces locking conflicts, thereby supporting environments with heavy transactional workloads. MySQL, when configured with the InnoDB storage engine, also offers robust transactional support and row-level locking, making it suitable for web applications with high concurrent access.

Feature support is another critical dimension of the comparison. SQLite implements a large subset of the SQL standard, including support for ACID-compliant transactions. However, some advanced features are either absent or implemented in a simplified manner in SQLite. MySQL and PostgreSQL provide a broader range of features, such as stored procedures, user-defined functions, complex join operations, and extensive indexing options. PostgreSQL is recognized for its adherence to SQL standards and support for advanced data types like JSON, arrays, and custom types, which allow developers to perform complex queries and data manipulations directly within the database engine. On the other hand, MySQL is noted for its ease of use and performance improvements in read-heavy environments, although it can lag behind PostgreSQL in terms of certain advanced features and standards compliance.

The ease of management also varies significantly. SQLite requires virtually no administration since it is a single-file system with embedded logic. This makes it extremely attractive for rapid prototyping, development, and applications where database administration resources are limited. In contrast, both MySQL and PostgreSQL require more comprehensive configuration and management. They offer rich command-line utilities and graphical interfaces for database administration, backup, replication, and performance tuning. However, this complexity may impose an additional administrative overhead, particularly for developers or organizations that do not have dedicated database administrators.

A useful coding example illustrates the difference in setup between SQLite and MySQL. The following Python snippet demonstrates a simple database insertion using SQLite's embedded system:

```
import sqlite3

# Connect to SQLite database file; database is created if not exists.
conn = sqlite3.connect('example_sqlite.db')
cursor = conn.cursor()

# Create a table
cursor.execute('''
CREATE TABLE IF NOT EXISTS users (
    id INTEGER PRIMARY KEY,
    username TEXT NOT NULL,
    email TEXT NOT NULL
)
''')

# Insert a record
cursor.execute("INSERT INTO users (username, email) VALUES (?, ?)",
    ("alice", "alice@example.com"))
conn.commit()
conn.close()
```

In contrast, establishing a connection to a MySQL database requires additional configuration, such as specifying host details, user credentials, and port numbers. The following code snippet uses the `mysql.connector` module to illustrate these differences:

```
import mysql.connector

# Connect to MySQL database server
conn = mysql.connector.connect(
    host="localhost",
    user="your_username",
    password="your_password",
    database="example_mysql"
)
cursor = conn.cursor()

# Create a table
cursor.execute('''
CREATE TABLE IF NOT EXISTS users (
    id INT AUTO_INCREMENT PRIMARY KEY,
    username VARCHAR(50) NOT NULL,
    email VARCHAR(100) NOT NULL
)
''')

# Insert a record
cursor.execute("INSERT INTO users (username, email) VALUES (%s, %s)",
    ("alice", "alice@example.com"))
conn.commit()
conn.close()
```

This comparison shows that while both systems support relational data management, the initial setup and connection parameters for MySQL involve additional complexities that come with the benefits of a centralized server model.

Security is another dimension in which these systems differ. SQLite's design inherently limits its exposure because the database resides as a local file, and access is managed primarily through filesystem permissions. This simplicity minimizes the surface area for attack in standalone applications. MySQL and PostgreSQL, as networked systems, require robust security mechanisms to safeguard against unauthorized access. They provide advanced features such as role-based access control, encrypted connections, and comprehensive auditing. However, proper configuration, regular updates, and continuous monitoring become essential to maintain such security, particularly in high-stakes production environments.

Scalability considerations further delineate the boundaries between SQLite and server-based databases. SQLite is typically optimized for applications with low to moderate data volumes. Its database file tends to grow linearly with data size, and performance can degrade if the file becomes excessively large or if concurrent write operations increase. In contrast, MySQL and PostgreSQL are routinely deployed in high-traffic environments where data volumes and user numbers are much larger. Their architectures allow for horizontal scaling strategies such as replication, partitioning, or clustering. PostgreSQL, with its support for advanced replication and clustering configurations, serves as a robust backbone for enterprise-level applications that demand high availability and fault tolerance.

The cost implications associated with each system are also significant. SQLite is available under the public domain, making it completely free for commercial and non-commercial use. This eliminates licensing fees and enables straightforward integration into any project, regardless of scale or budget. MySQL and PostgreSQL are open-source as well, with MySQL offering both community and enterprise editions. While the community editions are free, enterprise support and features can incur costs. PostgreSQL remains fully open-source, with a rich ecosystem of tools and extensions developed by its community, although large-scale deployments may still require investments in terms of setup, maintenance, and support.

When deciding on the appropriate database for a given project, developers must also consider the future evolution of the application. For projects that begin with limited data requirements and a small user base, the simplicity of SQLite may be advantageous. Its minimal administrative burden and ease of integration enable rapid development cycles with low overhead. As the project migrates to production with increased demand and data volume, the features and performance capabilities of MySQL or PostgreSQL may become necessary. Migration between these systems is facilitated by the fact that SQL, as a standard, is sensible across different systems, though differences in dialects and specific functionalities may require adjustments during transition.

It is worth noting that the choice between these systems often reflects the trade-off between simplicity and advanced functionality. SQLite is ideally suited for rapid prototyping, small-scale applications, offline storage, and embedded systems where deployment simplicity is paramount. MySQL and PostgreSQL, however, are better equipped for applications that demand robust multi-user support, high concurrency, extensive data analytics, and enterprise-level security features.

For developers, a thorough evaluation of application requirements will determine the optimal database system. If deployment speed, minimal resource utilization, and reduced administrative overhead are critical, SQLite presents a compelling option. However, if the project necessitates high concurrency, advanced data manipulation capabilities, and scalable performance, MySQL or PostgreSQL may offer a more suitable foundation. The decision becomes a matter of balancing immediate project needs against anticipated growth and complexity.

Both empirical performance benchmarks and practical development experience indicate that no single database system is universally superior. Instead, each system has its domain of excellence. SQLite shines in scenarios where integration and simplicity are prioritized, while MySQL and PostgreSQL dominate in environments that require advanced features, high concurrency, and scalability. Understanding these distinctions allows developers to tailor their database choices to the specific demands of their projects, ensuring that performance, reliability, and maintainability align with strategic objectives.

Careful consideration of the workload characteristics is crucial. Developers need to analyze factors such as query complexity, expected transaction volume, and data size. For instance, applications with read-heavy workloads that require compact, distributed storage solutions may benefit from SQLite's architecture. Meanwhile, data-intensive applications that benefit from advanced SQL features and optimized multi-user access find a more fitting environment in PostgreSQL or MySQL.

Ultimately, the choice among SQLite, MySQL, and PostgreSQL should stem from a holistic understanding of both the project requirements and the inherent design philosophies of these systems. By leveraging detailed comparisons and practical coding examples, developers can make informed decisions that optimize both the development process and the long-term performance of their applications.

1.6. Understanding SQLite File Structure

SQLite's file-based architecture differentiates it from other relational database management systems by encapsulating the entire database in a single cross-platform disk file. This design offers significant advantages in terms of portability, simplicity, and ease of backup, which are critical in many application scenarios. The SQLite file is not merely a container for data records but a structured format that includes a header, a series of fixed-size pages, and various internal data structures to manage tables, indexes, transactions, and metadata.

At the outset, every SQLite database file starts with a header that provides essential metadata about the database. This header includes a magic string, which is a specific sequence of bytes (commonly "SQLite format 3\0") that identifies the file as a valid SQLite database. The header also holds information regarding the page size, the file format version, and other factors that influence database operations. For instance, the page size typically defaults to 4096 bytes, though this value is configurable at the time of database creation. The use of fixed-size pages is central to SQLite's internal organization and its ability to efficiently read and write data.

Within the file, the database is organized into a series of pages, each of which serves as the basic unit of storage. These pages are used to store different types of content including table data, index data, and tree structures that form the basis for the B-tree indexing mechanism. A B-tree is a balanced tree data structure used by SQLite to store and retrieve data efficiently. The structure of these B-trees is optimized for both sequential and random access patterns, ensuring that queries can execute rapidly even on large datasets. Each page in the file has a specific role; for example, one page might be used for the database header and the first few pages could contain a master table—a special table that stores information about all the tables, indexes, triggers, and views contained within the database.

The file structure further includes several internal components designed to maintain data integrity and support ACID properties. One critical aspect is the rollback journal or, in more recent configurations, the write-ahead log (WAL) file. When a transaction is initiated, changes are first written to the rollback journal or WAL before being committed to the main database file. This mechanism ensures that in the event of a failure during a transaction, the database can revert to its previous consistent state. While the rollback journal and the WAL are separate from the primary database file, they illustrate how SQLite maintains consistency without requiring a dedicated server process.

Detailed knowledge of the SQLite file structure can be invaluable for understanding performance characteristics and potential limitations. For example, because the entire database is stored in one file, the limitations imposed by filesystem size directly affect the maximum size of an SQLite database. In practice, however, modern filesystems support large file sizes that far exceed typical application requirements. Furthermore, the single-file architecture simplifies tasks such as copying, moving, and backing up the entire database. This is particularly advantageous in scenarios where databases need to be synchronized across devices or updated in a distributed manner without the overhead of complex replication systems.

The internal page organization of an SQLite file also has a direct impact on performance. The use of fixed-size pages allows SQLite to optimize disk I/O by aligning read and write operations with underlying storage block sizes, reducing overhead and improving throughput. Moreover, because SQLite uses pages as the basic unit of data management, operations such as page caching and prefetching become highly efficient. The caching mechanism minimizes disk access by keeping frequently used pages in memory, thereby accelerating query execution. Developers and system administrators can tune the page cache size to balance memory utilization against performance needs, a flexibility that is essential for systems with varying workloads.

Inspection of an SQLite file can reveal insights into its internal structure. Tools such as `sqlite3` with the `.dump` command or specialized file viewers can be used to analyze the contents of the file, including its header information and page structures. An understanding of these internals is particularly useful when diagnosing performance issues or corruption in the database file. Advanced users may also interact directly with the file system to perform low-level diagnostics. For example, one might write a Python script to read the first 100 bytes of a SQLite file to inspect the header. An illustrative code snippet is provided below:

```
def read_sqlite_header(file_path):
    try:
        with open(file_path, 'rb') as file:
            header = file.read(100)
            print("SQLite Header (first 100 bytes):")
            print(header)
    except IOError as e:
        print("Error reading file:", e)
```

43

```
# Replace 'database.db' with the path to your SQLite database file.
read_sqlite_header('database.db')
```

This code opens a SQLite database file in binary mode and prints the first 100 bytes, providing a glimpse into the file's header. Analyzing this header can confirm the file format, reveal the configured page size, and offer other useful metadata. Such hands-on diagnostics are part of the toolkit for developers who need to ensure the soundness of their application's data management practices.

Understanding the file-based architecture also provides context for security considerations. Since the database is contained in a single file, securing it is largely a matter of filesystem security. This means that operating system-level permissions can prevent unauthorized access, and encryption can be applied to the file as a whole to secure its contents. Features like encrypted file systems or third-party encryption tools can be used to mitigate risks associated with data breaches. Developers must account for these factors when planning deployment scenarios, ensuring that databases are protected in environments ranging from local workstations to cloud-based virtual machines.

The design choices embodied in the SQLite file structure have broader implications for application development. The simplicity of having a self-contained database reduces both the development cycle and deployment complexity. Since the database exists as a single file, developers do not need to worry about configuring separate server processes, managing network connections, or handling multi-user synchronization issues that are inherent to client-server databases. This architectural simplicity enables rapid prototyping and facilitates seamless distribution of applications across various platforms, including mobile devices where storage and memory limitations demand efficient solutions.

Despite its simplicity, the file-based structure of SQLite is robust enough to support complex applications. The embedded indexing systems, transaction management via rollback journals or WAL files, and efficient page caching mechanisms combine to provide a performance that is competitive within its target use cases. Complex applications can leverage SQLite to manage data effectively without incurring the overhead typically associated with more elaborate database management systems. For instance, a mobile app that requires offline data storage can rely on SQLite to locally cache data, perform searches, and handle user transactions without needing a dedicated database server.

There are, however, considerations that need to be acknowledged. While SQLite excels in many scenarios due to its file-based nature, it is not designed to handle extreme levels of concurrency or extremely large-scale datasets. Applications that demand high write concurrency or involve massive data warehousing might find the single-file architecture to be a limiting factor. In such cases, distributed or client-server databases may offer advantages in scalability and parallel processing. Nonetheless, for a large number of use cases—particularly those involving embedded systems, mobile applications, and small to medium-sized desktop applications—the advantages of the SQLite file structure far outweigh its limitations.

The adaptability of the file-based structure is one of SQLite's most compelling features. Developers can move the database file across different operating systems, back it up, or even replicate its contents with relative ease. This portability is a cornerstone of many modern applications, particularly those that need to operate in disconnected or variable network environments. Moreover, because the file format is well-documented and stable, applications can be developed with the assurance that future versions of SQLite are likely to maintain compatibility, thereby preserving access to the stored data over long periods.

In practical terms, understanding the SQLite file structure empowers developers to optimize their application's performance and reliability. Through careful management of page sizes, caching configurations, and transaction logging, developers can tailor SQLite's behavior to match their specific operational contexts. For instance, in a memory-constrained embedded system, reducing the page size may improve performance by ensuring that active working sets are fully resident in cache. Conversely, in a desktop environment with ample memory, a larger page size might reduce the overhead of disk I/O and improve throughput.

The implications of SQLite's file-based architecture extend to engineering best practices, including backup strategies, data recovery methods, and performance tuning. Given that all critical data is encapsulated in a single file, developers must ensure that file integrity is maintained through regular backups and the use of journaling for transactional safety. Understanding how SQLite writes and commits changes to the file allows developers to design systems that are resilient to crashes and other unexpected events. This knowledge is particularly useful when implementing disaster recovery procedures or performing routine maintenance tasks.

Ultimately, the file-based architecture of SQLite offers a blend of simplicity and sophistication that caters to a diverse array of applications. Through a carefully designed file structure that encompasses metadata headers, fixed-size pages, B-tree indexes, and transaction management mechanisms, SQLite provides an efficient and portable solution for data storage. This architecture not only simplifies development but also enhances reliability and performance when properly tuned. For many developers, a deep understanding of these underlying principles is key to leveraging SQLite effectively, whether constructing lightweight mobile applications or robust desktop utilities.

Chapter 2

Setting Up Your SQLite Environment

This chapter guides you through downloading and installing SQLite across different operating systems, configuring environments, and performing basic command line operations. It also includes instructions on setting up Python and necessary libraries for SQLite integration and demonstrates using SQLite with popular Python IDEs. The chapter ensures your environment is correctly set up by providing tips to verify functionality and troubleshoot common issues.

2.1. Downloading and Installing SQLite

SQLite is a lightweight, serverless database engine that can be easily integrated into various environments. This section provides detailed instructions on how to download and install SQLite across different operating systems, including Windows, macOS, and Linux. The step-

by-step approach ensures that users correctly obtain, install, and configure SQLite to work seamlessly with Python and other applications.

The initial step involves obtaining the SQLite binaries from the official SQLite website. Users should navigate to the dedicated download
page and locate the precompiled binaries appropriate for their system.
The website typically offers compressed archive files containing the
command-line interface and dynamic libraries. It is important to verify
the integrity of these downloads by following the provided checksums
or digital signatures.

For Windows users, the process begins with downloading the ZIP
archive that contains the SQLite tools. Once the ZIP file is downloaded,
extract it using a file extraction tool such as 7-Zip or WinRAR. The extraction should result in a folder containing the executable file, usually named `sqlite3.exe`, along with associated documentation. To
facilitate ease of use, it is recommended to add the directory containing `sqlite3.exe` to the system's `PATH` environment variable. This allows the SQLite command-line tool to be executed from any Command
Prompt window without navigating to the specific folder.

A step-by-step procedure for Windows is as follows:

```
1. Open a web browser and navigate to https://www.sqlite.org/download
   .html.
2. Download the precompiled binaries for Windows (typically named "
   sqlite-tools-win32-x86-*.zip").
3. Extract the ZIP file to a directory of your choice, e.g., C:\
   SQLite.
4. Open the Control Panel and navigate to System Properties.
5. Edit the PATH environment variable to include the path to C:\
   SQLite.
6. Open a new Command Prompt window and type "sqlite3" to verify the
   installation.
```

After performing these actions, invoking the command `sqlite3` in the
Command Prompt should launch the SQLite interactive shell. By entering `.help`, users can display a list of available SQLite commands,

48

confirming that the installation was successful. If the command is not recognized, double-check that the directory has been correctly added to the system's PATH.

macOS users have several installation procedures available, with the Homebrew package manager being one of the most straightforward methods. Homebrew simplifies the process of installing and managing software packages on macOS. If Homebrew is not already installed, users should begin by installing it using the provided installation script from the Homebrew website. Once Homebrew is set up, users can install SQLite by executing a simple command in the Terminal.

The installation steps for macOS using Homebrew are:

```
1. Open Terminal.
2. Install Homebrew (if not already installed) using the following
     command:
/bin/bash -c "$(curl -fsSL https://raw.githubusercontent.com/Homebrew
     /install/HEAD/install.sh)"
3. Once Homebrew is installed, run:
     brew install sqlite
4. Verify the installation by executing:
     sqlite3 --version
```

Alternatively, users who do not wish to use Homebrew can download the source code from the SQLite website and compile it manually. This approach requires a compiler such as Xcode on macOS. While the manual compilation process may offer more customization options, it typically involves more steps and thus is less preferred by most users.

For Linux distributions, SQLite is often included in the default package repositories, and installation can usually be accomplished with the system's package manager. Users should update their package lists before proceeding with the installation using the appropriate commands for their specific distribution. For Debian-based distributions, the apt-get utility is the typical method. For Fedora or CentOS systems, dnf or yum may be used.

An example installation on a Debian-based system is provided below:

```
sudo apt-get update
sudo apt-get install sqlite3 libsqlite3-dev
```

The inclusion of the `libsqlite3-dev` package equips developers with the necessary libraries to compile programs linked against SQLite. Users should verify that SQLite is correctly installed by executing:

```
sqlite3 --version
```

In cases where the latest version of SQLite is required and the version available through the package repository is outdated, users may opt to compile SQLite from source. This process involves downloading the source code tarball from the SQLite website, extracting the archive, and running the compilation commands. An outline of the process for Linux is as follows:

```
1. Download the source tarball from https://www.sqlite.org/download.
     html.
2. Extract the tarball:
   tar xvf sqlite-autoconf-*.tar.gz
3. Change to the extracted directory:
   cd sqlite-autoconf-*
4. Configure the build environment:
   ./configure --prefix=/usr/local
5. Compile the source code:
   make
6. Install the compiled binaries:
   sudo make install
```

After installation, confirm the installation by running `sqlite3 --version` in the terminal. This verifies that the correct version is installed and that the executable is recognized in the system's `PATH`.

It is critical to address any common pitfalls during installation, such as issues with environment variables or dependency resolution. For Windows, ensure that the extraction tool does not inadvertently corrupt files, and verify that file permissions allow execution of `sqlite3.exe`. On macOS and Linux, users must ensure that their package manager or manual compilation process correctly references the system libraries. If the installation from source does not work correctly, users should inspect the output of the `./configure` script for any missing dependencies or error messages that may indicate deeper issues with the operating system's development environment.

Throughout these procedures, it is advisable to perform tests following each installation step. For instance, after setting up SQLite on Windows, starting the Command Prompt and executing the command:

```
sqlite3 test.db
```

should create a new database file named `test.db`. After entering the interactive shell, executing `.tables` will show that no tables exist in the newly created database. Exiting the shell by typing `.quit` ensures that SQLite terminates normally.

For Linux and macOS users, a similar test can be conducted in their respective terminals. Executing:

```
sqlite3 test.db
```

and then entering SQL commands for table creation, such as:

```
CREATE TABLE example(id INTEGER PRIMARY KEY, description TEXT);
.quit
```

confirms that SQLite is operational.

Installing SQLite is an essential initial step in developing database-related applications, particularly when integrating with Python. Many Python libraries, such as `sqlite3` (built into the standard library), provide a robust interface to SQLite, leveraging its lightweight architecture for rapid application development. Furthermore, configuring SQLite properly in the operating system's environment guarantees seamless communication between Python and the SQLite database. This integration is critical not only for application performance but also for ensuring consistency during development phases and automated testing.

During installation, users with additional security requirements might want to restrict file system permissions to ensure that the SQLite binaries are executable only by authorized users. This is particularly relevant in multi-user environments or on systems exposed to potential security threats. Operating system–specific guidelines for file permission adjustments should be consulted if enhanced security measures are necessary.

The installation instructions outlined above provide clarity on how to download SQLite from official sources, extract the required files in Windows, leverage Homebrew for macOS installations, and utilize package repositories or source compilation for Linux systems. Each method has its advantages and is tailored to suit the conventions and tools available on the respective platforms. Adjustments may be necessary based on the specific system configuration or the presence of network restrictions that could affect the download process.

Beyond the basic installation instructions, users are encouraged to investigate potential updates and patches to SQLite by regularly checking the official website. Maintaining an updated version mitigates risks associated with vulnerabilities and ensures access to the latest features and performance improvements. Detailed release notes provided on the SQLite website often include recommendations for upgrading and potential compatibility issues with previous versions.

The process of verifying the installation immediately after completion is integral to a successful setup. By executing specific SQLite commands, users confirm not only that the executable functions as intended but also that the environment configuration aligns with system requirements. Consistent testing throughout the installation process eliminates later issues when SQLite is integrated with more complex systems like Python IDEs.

The steps and analysis presented here aim to equip users with comprehensive knowledge to download and install SQLite efficiently across multiple platforms.

2.2. Setting Up SQLite on Windows, macOS, and Linux

Establishing a robust SQLite configuration across multiple operating systems ensures a consistent development environment and minimizes platform-specific issues. This section details the configuration of SQLite on Windows, macOS, and Linux, building upon the installation procedures discussed earlier. The focus lies on ensuring that SQLite is correctly integrated with the operating systems' environments, thereby facilitating smooth interactions with command-line interfaces, development tools, and external applications such as Python.

On Windows, configuration typically involves setting environment variables correctly and verifying that the SQLite executable is accessible system-wide. After extracting the SQLite binary, users must add the directory containing `sqlite3.exe` to the `PATH` environment variable. This is achieved through the system settings interface. By navigating to the Control Panel, selecting System Properties, and editing the environment variables, the user can specify the path where SQLite was installed. This adjustment facilitates launching SQLite from any command prompt window without the need to specify the full path.

```
# Example steps to add SQLite to the Windows PATH:
1. Open Control Panel and go to System Properties.
2. Click on "Advanced system settings" and then "Environment
    Variables".
3. Under "System Variables", find the variable named PATH.
4. Append the directory path (e.g., C:\SQLite) to the existing PATH
    variable.
5. Open a new Command Prompt window.
6. Run: sqlite3 --version
```

After setting the PATH, testing is essential. Launch the Command
Prompt and execute:

```
sqlite3 --version
```

A correctly configured environment will return the SQLite version
number, confirming that the executable is recognized. Additionally,
configuration may include customizing shortcuts or batch files to automate routine tasks such as backup operations or database initialization.

macOS users frequently utilize Homebrew to maintain consistency and
ease of updates in their environment. Installing SQLite through Homebrew ensures that the software is maintained within the broader Homebrew ecosystem, enabling simplified updates and dependency management. Once SQLite is installed using Homebrew, additional configuration may involve linking libraries for developer usage.

Users should verify that the installation path of SQLite is included in
the system's executable search paths. A common practice is to check
the following paths in the Terminal:

```
echo $PATH
```

If Homebrew is used, the binary is typically located in the
/usr/local/bin directory, which is usually part of the default PATH.
Verifying the setup involves executing:

```
sqlite3 --version
```

For integrated development environments and script execution, macOS users may need to configure additional paths in their IDE settings
to reference the correct SQLite binary. This can be accomplished by
setting the interpreter paths in the IDE's preferences.

In scenarios where Homebrew is not available or preferred, manual
configuration requires downloading the precompiled macOS binaries

or compiling SQLite from source. When compiling from source, the process entails running the `./configure` script, followed by `make` and `make install`. It is imperative to ensure that the `--prefix` option used during configuration matches the intended system installation directory, such that the binary files reside in a directory that is already part of the system's PATH.

```
# Manual compilation steps on macOS:
curl -O https://www.sqlite.org/2023/sqlite-autoconf-*.tar.gz
tar -xvf sqlite-autoconf-*.tar.gz
cd sqlite-autoconf-*
./configure --prefix=/usr/local
make
sudo make install
sqlite3 --version
```

On Linux, configuring the SQLite environment leverages the system's package manager. Most Linux distributions include SQLite in their default repositories, and using package managers like `apt`, `dnf`, or `yum` simplifies configuration and future updates. However, even after package installation, users must verify that the system paths are correctly set and that the development libraries are accessible for building applications that interact with SQLite.

For Debian-based distributions, a typical configuration involves updating the package list and installing both the SQLite binary and the development libraries:

```
sudo apt-get update
sudo apt-get install sqlite3 libsqlite3-dev
```

After installation, confirm that SQLite is present in the system's PATH by executing:

```
sqlite3 --version
```

In cases where SQLite is installed from the package manager, integration with development environments should be straightforward. However, for specialized requirements or testing of new features, compiling

55

SQLite from source allows users to specify build options. When building from source, options such as `--disable-readline` can be used to remove dependencies if a minimal environment is desired.

```
# Source compilation on Linux:
wget https://www.sqlite.org/2023/sqlite-autoconf-*.tar.gz
tar -xvf sqlite-autoconf-*.tar.gz
cd sqlite-autoconf-*
./configure --prefix=/usr/local --disable-readline
make
sudo make install
sqlite3 --version
```

Validation of the SQLite installation on Linux continues by creating a test database and running SQL commands to create tables and insert data. This operational verification helps ensure that both command-line interactions and any Python integrations behave as expected. For example, a simple testing routine in the terminal can be:

```
sqlite3 test.db
sqlite> CREATE TABLE test(id INTEGER PRIMARY KEY, name TEXT);
sqlite> .tables
sqlite> .quit
```

In addition to verifying the installation, configuring SQLite for development also involves setting up proper permissions and ensuring security integrity. On Linux systems, this can mean adjusting file ownership or group permissions, especially when SQLite databases are accessed by web servers or multi-user applications. For example, setting the correct file permissions ensures that sensitive data is not inadvertently accessible to unauthorized processes:

```
sudo chown myuser:mygroup /path/to/sqlite/db/file.db
chmod 640 /path/to/sqlite/db/file.db
```

These commands ensure that the database file is protected while remaining accessible to the application user.

Proper configuration extends to ensuring compatibility with Python integrations. The built-in `sqlite3` module in Python typically requires no additional configuration provided SQLite is installed and accessible via the system PATH. However, in certain environments, configuring dynamic library paths might be necessary. On Linux, this may involve setting the LD_LIBRARY_PATH environment variable, and on macOS, adjusting the DYLD_LIBRARY_PATH may be required. A sample configuration of LD_LIBRARY_PATH on Linux is:

```
export LD_LIBRARY_PATH=/usr/local/lib:$LD_LIBRARY_PATH
```

This command ensures that the system's dynamic linker finds the correct version of the SQLite libraries during the execution of Python scripts.

When using integrated development environments, such as PyCharm or Visual Studio Code, it is advisable to verify that the IDE's project interpreter correctly references the system Python installation that includes the necessary SQLite paths. Adjustments to environment variables in the IDE settings are sometimes required to ensure that commands such as sqlite3 --version and subsequent database operations execute without discrepancies. This level of detail in configuration reduces troubleshooting time and promotes consistency between terminal and IDE execution environments.

Furthermore, troubleshooting environment-specific issues often involves inspecting error logs generated during SQLite initialization. On Windows, misconfiguration of the PATH variable is a common issue. Users encountering errors should re-check the value of PATH and ensure that no extraneous characters have been introduced during the manual editing process. On Unix-like systems, misconfiguration of dynamic library paths is another frequently encountered problem, and setting the LD_LIBRARY_PATH (or DYLD_LIBRARY_PATH on macOS) correctly mitigates these issues.

Advanced users might also configure multi-version setups by maintaining both system-installed and custom-compiled versions of SQLite.

This is particularly relevant in development environments where testing against different versions of SQLite is necessary. In such cases, modulating the PATH variable or using symbolic links can facilitate the easy switching between versions. For example, on Linux, creating a symbolic link in a dedicated directory might allow quick version swaps:

```
sudo ln -sf /usr/local/bin/sqlite3 /usr/bin/sqlite3
```

This command forces the system to use the newly compiled version from /usr/local/bin, replacing the one originally provided by the distribution's package manager.

Lastly, ensuring that all configurations are documented is a best practice for maintaining the development environment. Keeping a record of the installation paths, environment variable changes, and any custom configurations allows for quicker resolution of issues and eases the migration process in cases such as system upgrades or transferring the configuration to a new machine.

The methodologies discussed for Windows, macOS, and Linux serve to standardize SQLite configuration across different platforms, emphasizing consistency, security, and ease of integration. By following these instructions and leveraging the provided command examples, users can effectively manage their SQLite environments, reducing the likelihood of integration errors with Python and other development tools.

2.3.   Basic Command Line Operations

The SQLite command line interface (CLI) offers a streamlined and efficient method for interacting with the database engine. Building on the previous discussions regarding installation and configuration, this section focuses exclusively on key command line operations essential for day-to-day tasks. Understanding these operations is critical, as they provide the foundation for database creation, maintenance, and troubleshooting.

At the launch of the SQLite CLI, a prompt appears that accepts either SQL commands or internal commands prefixed with a period. The internal commands, often abbreviated as dot-commands, extend beyond standard SQL functionalities by offering administrative control and ease-of-use operations. A starting point is to invoke the SQLite shell by running the command:

```
sqlite3 mydatabase.db
```

This command either opens an existing database file named mydatabase.db or creates it when it does not exist. Once in the interactive environment, the command .help can be executed to list all available commands. For example:

```
sqlite> .help
```

This displays a comprehensive list of commands, which is advantageous for new users and serves as an in-session reference.

One of the fundamental operations in the CLI is displaying the schema of the tables stored in the database. The command .schema, when executed without arguments, shows the schema for all tables. To inspect the schema of a specific table, one simply provides its name as an argument:

```
sqlite> .schema tablename
```

In practice, this is particularly useful during debugging and development, as it allows the developer to confirm the structure of the database without the need for writing custom SQL queries.

Another invaluable command for navigating the database is .tables. This command lists all tables present in the current database:

```
sqlite> .tables
```

59

The output is a succinct list, providing immediate insight into which tables have been created and are available for operations. An administrator may combine the use of .tables with .schema to verify database integrity and relationships among various entities.

Data output formatting is another aspect covered by the SQLite CLI. By default, the output format is aligned, but users might require alternate formats for better readability or for compatibility with different data processing tools. The .mode command allows switching between various output modes such as column, list, and CSV:

```
sqlite> .mode column
sqlite> SELECT * FROM tablename;
```

Customizing the output display is essential when dealing with large datasets or when preparing data for export into other applications. The CSV mode, for instance, is handy for creating exportable documents:

```
sqlite> .mode csv
sqlite> .output output.csv
sqlite> SELECT * FROM tablename;
sqlite> .output stdout
```

The above commands illustrate how data can be redirected to a file using the .output command, which is critical in data analysis workflows.

The CLI provides mechanisms for loading external SQL scripts into the environment, thereby facilitating batch processing of commands. The .read command serves this purpose, allowing a file containing SQL statements to be executed in sequence:

```
sqlite> .read filename.sql
```

This capability is particularly beneficial for setting up initial database schemas or performing complex operations that would be cumbersome to execute line-by-line interactively. By automating multi-step procedures, developers and database administrators can ensure consistency and reduce the likelihood of human error.

Debugging is another aspect where the command line operations of SQLite shine. The `.explain` command, when used before a query, provides an execution plan, which offers insights into the query planner's decision process. Although this is more advanced, it is valuable when optimizing queries:

```
sqlite> EXPLAIN QUERY PLAN SELECT * FROM tablename WHERE id = 1;
```

Understanding the execution plan can help identify inefficiencies in the way queries access the data, and it guides the user to better index design or query restructuring.

Handling transactions through the command line is seamless and intuitive. Transactions encapsulate a series of SQL commands, ensuring either complete success or rollback to preserve data consistency. Commands such as `BEGIN`, `COMMIT`, and `ROLLBACK` are available to effectively manage transactions:

```
sqlite> BEGIN;
sqlite> INSERT INTO tablename (column1, column2) VALUES ('data1', '
    data2');
sqlite> COMMIT;
```

In case of errors during any transactional operation, a rollback ensures that the partial changes do not corrupt the database state:

```
sqlite> ROLLBACK;
```

This transactional control is indispensable in maintaining the atomicity of database operations, particularly during complex data modifications.

When interacting with SQLite through the CLI, sessions must be concluded properly to avoid potential data loss or file corruption. The command `.quit` or its synonym `.exit` cleanly terminates the session:

```
sqlite> .quit
```

Proper session management includes ensuring that all transactions are committed and that any file outputs are restored to their default states. Using these commands helps maintain system stability and data integrity.

Logging and displaying detailed error messages are also integral aspects of CLI operation. When a command fails, SQLite typically provides descriptive error messages which are printed directly in the terminal. Users can leverage these messages to diagnose and resolve issues quickly. For example, attempting to create a table that already exists:

```
sqlite> CREATE TABLE sample(id INTEGER PRIMARY KEY);
sqlite> CREATE TABLE sample(id INTEGER PRIMARY KEY);
```

```
Error: table sample already exists
```

This immediate feedback underscores the importance of error checking during development and encourages iterative refinement of database commands.

In addition to interactive usage, SQLite offers capabilities for non-interactive operations. Invoking SQLite with the -batch flag can be beneficial for scripting or automation:

```
$ sqlite3 -batch mydatabase.db < myscript.sql
```

In this mode, the CLI reads commands from standard input, executes them, and then exits without further intervention. This is particularly useful in environments where database operations are part of a larger automated workflow, such as in continuous integration environments or scheduled maintenance tasks.

For advanced command line usage, developers may redirect output and error streams to capture logs or verify execution. Combining standard shell redirection with SQLite commands is achieved as follows:

```
$ sqlite3 mydatabase.db "SELECT * FROM tablename;" > output.txt 2>
    errors.txt
```

This command writes the result of the SQL query to output.txt while sending any error messages to errors.txt. Such operations are integral to developing robust scripts that can handle and log exceptions for later analysis.

A frequently overlooked aspect of command line operations is the customization of the SQLite prompt. By default, the prompt is minimal, but it may be modified using the .prompt command. This allows users to set distinct input and continuation prompts, which can help differentiate between primary input and multi-line commands:

```
sqlite> .prompt "SQL> " "   -> "
```

Custom prompts are particularly useful in educational settings or during debugging sessions, as they provide additional context during interactive use.

The CLI also handles file-based SQL import and export operations, ensuring that databases can be easily migrated or backed up. Commands like .import facilitate loading data from CSV files into a table:

```
sqlite> .mode csv
sqlite> .import data.csv tablename
```

Conversely, data can be exported into a CSV format for analysis or interoperability with other tools.

Understanding the full spectrum of these command line operations provides the user with a powerful toolkit. Each operation, from simple queries to complex batch executions and transaction control, enhances one's ability to manage SQLite databases effectively. Close attention to these operations minimizes errors during manual operations and supports the creation of scripts that automate routine tasks efficiently. Integrating such practices into daily use not only improves productivity but also reinforces best practices in database management.

The above command line operations, while straightforward, encapsulate the essence of SQLite's user-centric design.   They facilitate rapid development cycles and rigorous data integrity checks, crucial aspects for both novice developers and seasoned database administrators.   Each feature, from the environment customization to the handling of complex transactions, contributes to a comprehensive command line interface that adapts to the needs of diverse workflows.

2.4.   Installing Python and Required Libraries

Setting up Python to interact with SQLite is a critical step in building applications that leverage the durability and portability of the SQLite database engine.   Python's rich ecosystem of libraries provides robust support for SQLite operations, most notably through the `sqlite3` module, which offers a straightforward API for embedding SQLite databases within Python applications.   In this section, we provide instructions for installing Python and the necessary libraries on various operating systems, ensuring that users have a fully functional development environment for SQLite-based projects.

The process begins with installing Python itself.   Modern Python distributions are available for Windows, macOS, and Linux.   It is recommended to use the latest stable release of Python 3 to access the most recent features and security updates. After downloading the appropriate installer from the official Python website, users should ensure that the installation is configured to add Python to the system PATH. This configuration simplifies invoking the interpreter from the command line.

On Windows, the Python installer typically offers an option labeled `"Add Python 3.x to PATH"` which should be checked before proceeding with the installation. Once the installation is complete, users can confirm the installation by opening a Command Prompt and executing:

```
python --version
```

This command should display the installed Python version. Additionally, the `pip` package management tool is installed by default, which is essential for adding libraries that extend Python's functionality.

On macOS, Python can be installed using the official installer or through package managers such as Homebrew. If Homebrew is preferred, installation proceeds by running the following commands in the Terminal:

```
brew update
brew install python
```

These commands ensure that Python and its package manager, pip, are installed and available in the user's environment. Verifying the installation using:

```
python3 --version
```

confirms that the correct version is active, particularly because macOS may include an older Python version by default.

For Linux users, many distributions include Python by default. However, to install or update Python, users can rely on their distribution's package manager. For Debian-based distributions, the commands might look like:

```
sudo apt-get update
sudo apt-get install python3 python3-pip
```

Verifying the installation is accomplished by executing:

```
python3 --version
```

This command guarantees that the installation is successful and that the interpreter is available for scripting.

With Python installed, the next phase involves installing the libraries

65

necessary for SQLite integration. The primary library for SQLite operations in Python is the `sqlite3` module, which is part of Python's standard library. However, developers often require additional packages that enhance interaction with SQLite, such as `SQLAlchemy` for object-relational mapping (ORM) and ease of constructing database queries in an object-oriented manner. Installing these third-party packages is facilitated by `pip`.

To install SQLAlchemy, users should execute:

```
pip install SQLAlchemy
```

SQLAlchemy abstracts much of the SQL complexity and provides a more Pythonic query construction method. Furthermore, for applications that span multiple databases or require additional features—such as connection pooling and transaction management—it is beneficial to install libraries like `alembic` for database migrations.

```
pip install alembic
```

For instances where advanced SQLite features are needed, developers may choose to install the `pysqlite3` package, which can provide more direct access to certain SQLite functionalities not exposed by the standard library. The installation is similar to other packages:

```
pip install pysqlite3
```

Testing the integration between Python and SQLite can be completed with a simple Python script. Creating a file named `test_sqlite.py` with the following content can help validate the installation:

```python
import sqlite3

# Connect to a database (or create it if it doesn't exist)
conn = sqlite3.connect("test_database.db")
cursor = conn.cursor()

# Create a simple table
cursor.execute("CREATE TABLE IF NOT EXISTS users (id INTEGER PRIMARY
    KEY, name TEXT);")
```

```
# Insert a record into the table
cursor.execute("INSERT INTO users (name) VALUES (?);", ("Alice",))
conn.commit()

# Query the record back
cursor.execute("SELECT * FROM users;")
records = cursor.fetchall()
print("Records:", records)

# Close the connection
conn.close()
```

Running this script using

```
python test_sqlite.py
```

should print the records stored in the database, which confirms that SQLite operations are working as expected. The script creates a new SQLite database file named `test_database.db`, sets up a simple table, inserts a record, and retrieves it. This example demonstrates transaction management, command execution, and basic error handling inherent in the `sqlite3` module.

Development environments can benefit from further customization to handle dependencies and project configurations smoothly. Virtual environments in Python provide an isolated environment for managing dependencies. The `venv` module can be used to create virtual environments, which is especially useful when projects rely on different library versions. To create and activate a virtual environment, the following commands can be executed:

```
python -m venv venv
source venv/bin/activate    # On Windows, use: venv\Scripts\activate
```

Once activated, `pip` installs and upgrades occur only within the virtual environment. Installing required libraries such as SQLAlchemy, `alembic`, and others should be done in this isolated context. Virtual environments also simplify dependency tracking, which becomes vital in larger projects or in teams where consistent development environments are required.

Another consideration involves the integration of SQLite into graphical and integrated development environments (IDEs) such as PyCharm or Visual Studio Code. In these IDEs, configuring the interpreter to use the correct Python installation or virtual environment ensures that all installed libraries, including those for SQLite, are recognized by the project. In PyCharm, for example, navigate to the project settings, select the interpreter, and ensure that it points to the Python executable of the desired virtual environment. This step is essential to prevent errors related to missing packages during development and debugging sessions.

Furthermore, ensuring that the system PATH and environment variables are configured correctly plays a crucial role. On Linux and macOS, if SQLite libraries are installed in non-standard locations due to manual compilations, the LD_LIBRARY_PATH (or DYLD_LIBRARY_PATH for macOS) may need to be updated so that the dynamic linker can locate the appropriate libraries during Python execution. An example configuration is:

```
export LD_LIBRARY_PATH=/usr/local/lib:$LD_LIBRARY_PATH
```

This command can be added to the shell's startup file (e.g., .bashrc or .zshrc) to persist through sessions.

When building applications with SQLite and Python, proper error handling and logging are important practices to implement. Utilizing try-except blocks around database operations can prevent unexpected crashes and provide informative error messages. An extended version of the earlier script with error handling might look like:

```
import sqlite3
import sys

def initialize_database(db_name):
```

```
    try:
        conn = sqlite3.connect(db_name)
        return conn
    except sqlite3.Error as err:
        sys.exit("Database connection failed: {}".format(err))

def create_table(conn):
    try:
        cursor = conn.cursor()
        cursor.execute("CREATE TABLE IF NOT EXISTS users (id INTEGER
    PRIMARY KEY, name TEXT);")
        conn.commit()
    except sqlite3.Error as err:
        print("Error creating table: {}".format(err))
        conn.rollback()

def insert_user(conn, name):
    try:
        cursor = conn.cursor()
        cursor.execute("INSERT INTO users (name) VALUES (?);", (name
    ,))
        conn.commit()
    except sqlite3.Error as err:
        print("Error inserting data: {}".format(err))
        conn.rollback()

def main():
    db_name = "robust_database.db"
    conn = initialize_database(db_name)
    create_table(conn)
    insert_user(conn, "Bob")
    cursor = conn.cursor()
    cursor.execute("SELECT * FROM users;")
    print("Users in database:", cursor.fetchall())
    conn.close()

if __name__ == "__main__":
    main()
```

This example demonstrates the incorporation of robust error handling practices, ensuring that any issues during database operations are communicated clearly and that the database state remains consistent by performing rollbacks when needed.

Integrating Python and SQLite does not end with the mere installation

69

of the required software. Developers must also be mindful of version compatibility issues, particularly when working in heterogeneous environments. Ensuring that the Python interpreter's version, SQLite version, and any additional third-party packages are compatible is essential. This compatibility check often involves reviewing the release documentation for each component and testing the application in a staging environment before deploying to production.

This section has outlined the process of installing Python and its required libraries with an emphasis on ensuring that developers have the necessary tools to interact effectively with SQLite. From obtaining the latest Python version on various operating systems and setting up virtual environments to installing critical libraries such as SQLAlchemy and incorporating robust error handling practices, the guide has presented a comprehensive roadmap for establishing a productive and reliable development environment.

2.5. Using SQLite with Python IDEs

Integrating SQLite within popular Python Integrated Development Environments (IDEs) streamlines both development and database management tasks. Leveraging the features of IDEs such as PyCharm and Visual Studio Code enhances productivity by providing built-in tools for code editing, debugging, version control, and even direct database interactions. This section explores practical approaches to integrating SQLite with these IDEs, offering detailed configuration instructions, coding examples, and techniques to troubleshoot common issues encountered during development.

Within PyCharm, the integration of SQLite is facilitated by its robust database tools. PyCharm Professional Edition provides a dedicated Database tool window that supports connecting to local databases, including SQLite. To integrate SQLite in PyCharm, users should begin by creating or opening a project with the desired Python interpreter. It is important that the interpreter is correctly configured to include the standard `sqlite3` module, available by default in Python's standard library. Within PyCharm, navigate to the Database tool window, usually located on the right side of the interface. The user has the option to add a new data source by clicking the + icon and selecting SQLite from the list of available drivers.

After selecting SQLite as the data source, specify the path to the SQLite database file. For instance, if a database file named `mydatabase.db` exists in the project directory, inputting the full path ensures that PyCharm recognizes the database correctly. PyCharm automatically detects the database structure and populates the schema browser with tables, views, and indexes. This integration enables users to perform direct SQL query execution, review table data, and even modify the schema interactively within the IDE. The ability to run queries without switching to an external command line improves development efficiency and supports rapid prototyping.

In addition to connecting to an existing database, PyCharm facilitates the creation of new SQLite databases. Using the Database tool window, users can execute a command to initialize a new database file, and immediately follow up by creating tables and inserting data. A typical workflow in PyCharm might involve writing SQL commands directly in the integrated query console. For example, to create a new table, one might enter:

```
CREATE TABLE IF NOT EXISTS users (
    id INTEGER PRIMARY KEY,
    name TEXT,
    email TEXT
);
```

Executing this command within the query console allows instant verification of the database schema. Furthermore, PyCharm supports advanced features such as schema diff and version control integrations

71

for SQL scripts, which are beneficial in collaborative development environments.

For developers who primarily use Visual Studio Code (VS Code), the process of integrating SQLite also emphasizes flexibility and extensibility. VS Code, being a lightweight yet powerful text editor, can be augmented with extensions that provide SQLite support. One of the most popular extensions is the SQLite Viewer, which allows users to open, query, and manage SQLite databases directly from the editor. Installation of such an extension is typically accomplished through the built-in Extensions marketplace. Users should search for and install an extension like SQLite or SQLite Viewer.

Once the appropriate extension is installed, VS Code can be configured to open SQLite database files with a graphical interface for browsing tables, running queries, and displaying results. This enables a workflow where developers can write Python code in one tab and toggle to a side panel or separate window to inspect the database schema and query results. For instance, after establishing the database connection using Python code, a developer may update the database and then immediately verify the changes within VS Code by reloading the view provided by the extension.

A typical Python script used alongside VS Code to interact with SQLite might include the following:

```
import sqlite3

def setup_database():
    # Connect and create a new database or open an existing one
    connection = sqlite3.connect('project_database.db')
    cursor = connection.cursor()
    # Create a table if it does not exist
    cursor.execute('''
        CREATE TABLE IF NOT EXISTS products (
            id INTEGER PRIMARY KEY,
            name TEXT,
            price REAL
        );
```

```
    ''')
    connection.commit()
    return connection

def add_product(connection, name, price):
    cursor = connection.cursor()
    cursor.execute('INSERT INTO products (name, price) VALUES (?, ?)
    ', (name, price))
    connection.commit()

def query_products(connection):
    cursor = connection.cursor()
    cursor.execute('SELECT * FROM products')
    return cursor.fetchall()

if __name__ == '__main__':
    db_connection = setup_database()
    add_product(db_connection, 'Widget', 19.99)
    products = query_products(db_connection)
    print("Current Products:", products)
    db_connection.close()
```

This script illustrates common database operations, including creating tables, inserting records, and querying data. When using VS Code, a developer can open the integrated terminal to execute the script, and then use the SQLite extension to inspect the updated database state. Rapid feedback from both the code execution and the database viewer helps streamline the development process.

Another significant aspect of integrating SQLite with Python IDEs is debugging. Both PyCharm and VS Code provide comprehensive debugging environments that can be utilized to step through Python code interacting with SQLite. Setting breakpoints in the code, especially around database operations, allows developers to inspect variables, verify connection status, and evaluate SQL statements before they are committed to the database. Debugging with PyCharm involves using its full-featured debugger that supports step execution and variable inspection, while VS Code offers similar capabilities through its Debugger for Python extension. In practice, a developer may pause the execution after a database connection has been established and examine

73

the state of the connection object to ensure that it is not None and that the database file is correctly referenced.

Both IDEs also offer the facility to execute parts of the code interactively. In PyCharm, the Python Console can be used as an interactive shell to test individual SQLite commands. Similarly, VS Code's interactive window or Jupyter Notebook integration enables users to evaluate code snippets and immediately view the outputs. For developers switching between writing application code and executing ad-hoc queries, such interactive features greatly enhance the workflow.

Version control integration within these IDEs further augments SQLite-related development. Maintaining SQL scripts and migration files in version control systems such as Git ensures that changes to the database schema are tracked and reversible. Both PyCharm and VS Code provide robust Git integrations, making it convenient to commit changes, review commit histories, and resolve merge conflicts in SQL files. This is particularly helpful when multiple developers collaborate on the same project, as database schema changes can be handled with the same rigor as code changes.

Moreover, configuring the environment within the IDE to handle environment variables and interpreter settings is essential for consistency across development, staging, and production environments. In PyCharm, users can set environment variables through run/debug configuration dialogs, ensuring that the proper database paths and configurations are used during execution. VS Code allows similar configurations by modifying the launch.json file within the workspace settings. These configurations are critical when the project relies on dynamic paths or when different environments (such as development and production) require separate SQLite databases.

Additional plugins and tools available for these IDEs may support advanced features such as SQL auto-completion, syntax highlighting, and even query plan analysis, which further facilitate efficient development. Indeed, integration with such analytical tools can help developers optimize queries and database performance, ensuring that the application remains responsive even as data volume grows.

The process of combining Python code with a direct interface to SQLite within these IDEs also opens pathways for educational and research activities. Developers new to SQLite can experiment with database operations and immediately observe the effects of their queries, thereby accelerating the learning process. The interactive nature of these environments bridges the gap between theory and practical application, making complex database interactions more approachable.

By leveraging the integrated tools and features provided by PyCharm and VS Code, developers benefit from a unified environment where editing, testing, debugging, and database management occur seamlessly. This established workflow minimizes context switching between external tools and maximizes productivity by utilizing a single platform for all aspects of development. Through careful configuration and the use of dedicated extensions, working with SQLite within these popular Python IDEs becomes both efficient and intuitive, supporting a wide range of project requirements from simple prototypes to large-scale applications.

Combining descriptive tool features, configuration details, and practical coding examples provides a comprehensive overview of how to effectively integrate SQLite with popular Python IDEs. The approach outlined here helps ensure that developers not only have access to robust database management tools but also establish a workflow that supports rapid development and thorough testing.

2.6.   Verifying the Setup

After completing the installation and configuration of SQLite and Python, it is essential to verify that the environment operates as expected. This section outlines methods and procedures to test the functionality of SQLite and its integration with Python by running basic SQLite commands, both in the command line interface and through Python scripts. Verifying the setup through these tests is a critical step to ensure that the development environment is correctly configured and that there are no latent issues which could affect future development.

A primary verification method involves using the SQLite command line interface to execute fundamental operations. This direct approach confirms that the SQLite executable is located correctly in the system's PATH and that the database engine responds to queries. To begin, open the terminal or command prompt and run the command:

```
sqlite3 --version
```

A proper installation should return the installed version of SQLite. If the version number is displayed, it confirms that the executable is correctly placed and accessible system-wide. Conversely, an error message would indicate a misconfiguration of the PATH or an incomplete installation, prompting further troubleshooting.

Once the version is confirmed, the next step is to create a new SQLite database. This procedure tests both file creation and basic database operations. In the terminal, type:

```
sqlite3 verify_setup.db
```

This call either opens an existing file named `verify_setup.db` or creates a new database file if one does not exist. Within the SQLite shell, run the following commands to create a simple table and to insert sam-

76

ple data:

```
sqlite> CREATE TABLE IF NOT EXISTS test_table (
   id INTEGER PRIMARY KEY,
   info TEXT
);
sqlite> INSERT INTO test_table (info) VALUES ('Test data');
sqlite> SELECT * FROM test_table;
```

The response to the SELECT command should list the table's contents, confirming that the database engine is processing SQL statements correctly. Use the .tables and .schema commands to further verify that the structure has been created as intended:

```
sqlite> .tables
sqlite> .schema test_table
```

These outputs demonstrate that the commands execute without error and that the database schema reflects the expected design.

In addition to interactive testing through the command line, verifying the setup through Python scripts is an important aspect, especially because Python is the intended interface for further application development with SQLite. A minimal Python script can be employed to test the built-in sqlite3 module. Consider the following example, which performs similar operations as those executed in the SQLite CLI:

```python
import sqlite3

def verify_database():
    # Establish connection to the SQLite database.
    connection = sqlite3.connect("verify_setup.db")
    cursor = connection.cursor()

    # Create a test table.
    cursor.execute("""
        CREATE TABLE IF NOT EXISTS test_table (
            id INTEGER PRIMARY KEY,
            info TEXT
        );
    """)

    # Insert test data.
```

```
    cursor.execute("INSERT INTO test_table (info) VALUES (?);", ("
     Data verified",))
    connection.commit()

    # Retrieve and print data.
    cursor.execute("SELECT * FROM test_table;")
    records = cursor.fetchall()
    print("Retrieved records:", records)

    # Clean up by closing the connection.
    connection.close()

if __name__ == "__main__":
    verify_database()
```

Running this Python script using:

```
python verify_setup.py
```

will display the data retrieved from the test_table. The output, printed to the terminal, should reflect the inserted data; for instance, a typical output might be:

```
Retrieved records: [(1, 'Data verified')]
```

This result confirms that the Python interpreter successfully interacts with SQLite, verifying that the sqlite3 module is properly integrated and that the database operations are functioning.

The verification process should extend to testing error handling and transaction capabilities. Running scenarios that involve both valid and erroneous operations helps identify potential issues that might not be evident during a straightforward execution. A script with robust error handling may look like this:

```
import sqlite3
import sys

def perform_transaction():
    try:
        connection = sqlite3.connect("verify_setup.db")
        cursor = connection.cursor()
```

```
    # Begin a transaction.
    cursor.execute("BEGIN;")

    # Attempt to insert a record.
    cursor.execute("INSERT INTO test_table (info) VALUES (?);",
("Transaction test",))

    # Introduce an error to force rollback.
    cursor.execute("INSERT INTO non_existing_table (data) VALUES
('error');")

    # Commit the transaction if no error occurs.
    connection.commit()
except sqlite3.Error as error:
    print("Transaction failed:", error)
    connection.rollback()
finally:
    connection.close()

if __name__ == "__main__":
    perform_transaction()
```

In this script, a deliberate error is introduced by attempting to insert data into a nonexistent table. The exception is caught, and a rollback is performed. This demonstrates that error handling is operational and that the environment can manage transactional integrity. If the error message is printed and the transaction is rolled back without affecting the actual database integrity, the setup is verified as robust.

Verifying the setup also involves ensuring that any added libraries, such as SQLAlchemy or other third-party extensions for SQLite, are correctly installed and that they interact seamlessly with the database. For example, a brief test using SQLAlchemy might involve creating an engine and performing a simple query. The following code demonstrates this:

```
from sqlalchemy import create_engine, text

def test_sqlalchemy():
    engine = create_engine("sqlite:///verify_setup.db")
    with engine.connect() as connection:
        result = connection.execute(text("SELECT name FROM
    sqlite_master WHERE type='table';"))
```

79

```
        tables = result.fetchall()
        print("Tables available:", tables)

if __name__ == "__main__":
    test_sqlalchemy()
```

Running this script confirms that SQLAlchemy can establish a connection to the SQLite database and list the available tables. A correct output, such as:

```
Tables available: [('test_table',)]
```

indicates that SQLAlchemy is functioning as intended, further verifying that the overall environment is properly configured.

Verifying the setup is not only about executing commands, but also about checking configurations that impact performance and security. It is advisable to inspect the file permissions of the SQLite database, ensuring that they allow for safe read and write operations. In Unix-like systems, one might run:

```
ls -l verify_setup.db
```

This command outputs the file permissions and ownership settings. Correct permissions ensure that the database file is not inadvertently exposed to unauthorized users, particularly in a multi-user environment or when the database resides on a networked file system.

A further aspect of verifying the setup involves ensuring that environment variables used during configuration persist correctly across sessions. If the SQLite installation required adjusting dynamic library paths—using variables like LD_LIBRARY_PATH on Linux or DYLD_LIBRARY_PATH on macOS—it is beneficial to re-open the terminal or restart the session and re-check the configuration. For instance:

```
echo $LD_LIBRARY_PATH
```

The output should include the path to where the SQLite libraries are installed. If the verification script in Python still encounters issues after this check, it could indicate an inconsistency in the system environment or an error in how the environment variables were set, prompting further review.

For integrated development environments, verifying the setup may also involve examining the project settings in the IDE. In PyCharm, for example, reviewing the Python interpreter settings under project configuration ensures that the correct environment is used, including the proper installation of SQLite and the associated libraries. The built-in terminal in PyCharm can be used to execute the same command-line tests discussed previously. Similarly, in VS Code, a user can open an integrated terminal and run the verification scripts, ensuring consistency between the development environment and external testing conditions.

Beyond testing individual commands, a comprehensive verification should include a workflow run that simulates the typical operations developers expect to perform. This may involve a combination of Python scripts that build a database, execute a series of transactions, and finally export data to a file. For exporting data, the following example demonstrates how to redirect output to a CSV file:

```python
import sqlite3
import csv

def export_to_csv(db_name, csv_file):
    connection = sqlite3.connect(db_name)
    cursor = connection.cursor()
    cursor.execute("SELECT * FROM test_table;")
    rows = cursor.fetchall()

    with open(csv_file, 'w', newline='') as file:
        writer = csv.writer(file)
        writer.writerow([i[0] for i in cursor.description])
        writer.writerows(rows)

    connection.close()
```

81

```
    print("Data exported to", csv_file)

if __name__ == "__main__":
    export_to_csv("verify_setup.db", "exported_data.csv")
```

When executed, this script confirms that the database not only stores data correctly but can also interface with other file formats—a critical capability for data migration and reporting.

Ensuring the overall environment is properly configured involves a series of verification steps that cover command line operations, Python integration, error handling, performance checks, and security measures. Each of these components contributes to a fully operational development setup that minimizes surprises during later stages of development. Validating the setup using the techniques outlined here proves invaluable and fosters confidence that subsequent application development using SQLite and Python will proceed smoothly.

Chapter 3

Basic SQL Operations with SQLite

This chapter introduces fundamental SQL operations using SQLite, such as creating databases and tables, inserting data, and executing SELECT queries for data retrieval. It covers updating and deleting records, using WHERE clauses for filtering, and sorting and limiting query results. These foundational SQL techniques are essential for effective database management and manipulation within the SQLite environment.

3.1. Creating Databases and Tables

Creating and managing databases and tables is a fundamental aspect of working with SQLite. This section focuses on understanding the internal structure of SQLite databases and the SQL statements employed to create these structures. SQLite databases are file-based and self-contained, which simplifies both the development and deployment processes. In SQLite, a database is represented by a single file, and within this file, tables are used to store structured data.

The creation of a database in SQLite is implicitly performed when a connection to a file that does not exist is established. This behavior differs from other database management systems that require an explicit command to create the database. When using SQLite, one simply opens a connection to a filename, and if the file does not exist, SQLite creates it automatically. For example, using the `sqlite3` command-line interface or a Python script, one may connect to a new database file without prior setup. The following Python snippet demonstrates this process:

```
import sqlite3

# Establish a connection to a new or existing SQLite database file
connection = sqlite3.connect('example.db')
cursor = connection.cursor()
```

Once the database file exists, the next step is to define the structure of the data containers, known as tables. Tables in SQLite are defined using the SQL `CREATE TABLE` statement. When creating a table, it is important to specify the name of the table along with a detailed description of each column. Each column definition typically includes the column name, its data type, and various constraints such as `PRIMARY KEY`, `NOT NULL`, or `UNIQUE`. Careful planning of these specifications enhances data integrity and enforces the rules required by the application logic.

A typical creation of a table might look as follows:

```
CREATE TABLE IF NOT EXISTS employees (
    id INTEGER PRIMARY KEY,
    name TEXT NOT NULL,
    department TEXT,
    hire_date DATE
);
```

This SQL command creates a table named employees with four

84

columns. The `id` column is an integer designated as the primary key, ensuring the uniqueness of each record. The `name` column is a text field marked as `NOT NULL`, thereby requiring that every record include a valid name. The other fields—`department` and `hire_date`—are optional, allowing records to be inserted without mandatory values for these columns. The use of `IF NOT EXISTS` ensures that the command does not result in an error if the table already exists.

SQLite supports a variety of data types, but it employs a dynamic type system. This means that while column definitions suggest certain data types, SQLite does not enforce strict data type checking as other SQL databases might. Nevertheless, adhering to intended data types is beneficial for consistency and clarity when designing a database schema. Standard data types encountered in SQLite include `INTEGER`, `TEXT`, `BLOB`, `REAL`, and `NUMERIC`. Understanding how these types operate is essential when planning complex database applications.

Complex table structures sometimes require relationships between tables. Though SQLite does not enforce foreign key constraints by default, it allows their definition to ensure referential integrity. When referencing another table, the column intended as a foreign key should match the primary key of the parent table, and the constraint can be activated using a PRAGMA statement. The SQL statement for defining a foreign key might appear as follows:

```
CREATE TABLE IF NOT EXISTS orders (
    order_id INTEGER PRIMARY KEY,
    customer_id INTEGER,
    order_date DATE,
    FOREIGN KEY(customer_id) REFERENCES customers(customer_id)
);
```

After defining tables and their respective relationships, certain operational details must be considered. First, it is essential to execute the `CREATE TABLE` statements within a transactional context. Transactions ensure that either all operations succeed, or, in the case of an error,

85

the system reverts to the previous consistent state. This mechanism prevents partial updates that can result in data inconsistencies. In the Python example provided earlier, the commit() function is used to finalize database changes:

```
# Creating the table within a transaction
cursor.execute("""
CREATE TABLE IF NOT EXISTS employees (
    id INTEGER PRIMARY KEY,
    name TEXT NOT NULL,
    department TEXT,
    hire_date DATE
);
""")
# Commit changes to the database
connection.commit()
connection.close()
```

Another important aspect is the use of constraints when creating tables. Constraints such as PRIMARY KEY, NOT NULL, UNIQUE, and CHECK play a vital role in ensuring that the data adheres to defined business rules. For example, the CHECK constraint allows the specification of conditions which must be met for the data to be valid. Consider the following table definition that includes a CHECK constraint on a salary column:

```
CREATE TABLE IF NOT EXISTS employees (
    id INTEGER PRIMARY KEY,
    name TEXT NOT NULL,
    salary REAL CHECK(salary > 0),
    department TEXT
);
```

By incorporating such constraints, the database enforces restrictions automatically. This minimizes potential errors during data insertion and reduces the need for additional validations in application code.

SQLite also provides support for defining default values for columns. Default values are applied when a record is inserted without explicitly providing a value for a given column. The DEFAULT keyword can be used in the table creation SQL statement. For example, establishing a default creation timestamp for a record is often beneficial:

```
CREATE TABLE IF NOT EXISTS customers (
    customer_id INTEGER PRIMARY KEY,
    first_name TEXT NOT NULL,
    last_name TEXT NOT NULL,
    email TEXT UNIQUE,
    created_at TIMESTAMP DEFAULT CURRENT_TIMESTAMP
);
```

This command initializes the `created_at` field to the current timestamp at the moment of insertion, ensuring that each record is automatically stamped with its creation time.

Managing database schemas also involves careful consideration of naming conventions and data modeling best practices. Consistent naming conventions improve the readability and maintainability of the database schema. Typical naming conventions include using lowercase letters and underscores to separate words. Furthermore, relational databases are designed around the concept of normalization, which involves organizing tables efficiently to reduce redundancy and dependency. While normalization is a broader topic, designing tables with clearly defined roles and relationships reinforces the reliability and scalability of the database.

When designing tables, it is prudent to plan for potential future modifications. This planning might include anticipating common queries and indexing columns that are frequently used in search conditions. Explicit index creation is performed using the `CREATE INDEX` statement, which optimizes lookup speed for large datasets. For instance, to improve query performance on the `name` column of the `employees` table, an index can be introduced as follows:

```
CREATE INDEX idx_employees_name ON employees(name);
```

Employing indexes judiciously is important as they accelerate data retrieval but also incur a cost during data insertion and update operations. Therefore, indexes should be designed based on the specific query patterns anticipated in an application.

Data integrity extends beyond individual table definitions to the overall design of the database. SQLite supports triggers, which are procedures that automatically execute in response to certain events on a table, such as the insertion, update, or deletion of records. Triggers ensure that specific business rules are upheld automatically. An example of a trigger might involve ensuring that modifications to employee salaries are recorded in a separate audit table:

```
CREATE TRIGGER salary_update_trigger
AFTER UPDATE OF salary ON employees
BEGIN
    INSERT INTO salary_audit(employee_id, old_salary, new_salary,
    update_time)
    VALUES (old.id, old.salary, new.salary, CURRENT_TIMESTAMP);
END;
```

Triggers like this provide an automated solution for tracking changes without requiring explicit insertion of audit records in application code. Such mechanisms contribute to a robust and self-regulating database design.

Investing time in the creation of a well-structured database and table schema significantly simplifies subsequent operations, such as data insertion, querying, updating, and deletion. The careful definition of columns, constraints, and relationships lays the foundation for an efficient database system. This approach minimizes errors and improves the reliability of data manipulation processes carried out in later sections.

Effective use of SQL statements in SQLite requires an understanding of both the syntax and the strategic purposes of each command. The practices introduced here form the basis upon which advanced techniques are built. Solid comprehension of these core operations is essential for maintaining data consistency and supporting the diverse needs of modern applications.

The strategies discussed here integrate seamlessly with prior topics, enhancing the overall understanding of SQLite management. Each SQL command and design decision contributes to creating a stable, maintainable, and scalable database environment.

3.2. Inserting Data into Tables

Inserting data into tables is a crucial process for populating a database with records that can later be manipulated and queried. This section explores techniques for adding records via SQL INSERT operations, building on the fundamental understanding of database and table creation. Given the dynamic nature of relational databases, it is necessary to understand not only the syntax of the INSERT statement but also how to manage various data insertion scenarios, including batch inserts, conflict resolution, and the use of parameterized queries for enhanced security.

The basic SQL INSERT operation is straightforward. The general form of an INSERT statement is as follows:

```
INSERT INTO table_name (column1, column2, column3, ...)
VALUES (value1, value2, value3, ...);
```

This syntax specifies the target table and a corresponding list of columns that will be filled with the provided values. For example, consider inserting a record into an employees table defined earlier. The SQL statement may appear as:

```
INSERT INTO employees (name, department, hire_date)
VALUES ('Alice Johnson', 'Engineering', '2023-09-15');
```

When columns are omitted, SQLite implicitly assumes that default values exist or that NULL values can be recorded if permitted. Explicitly

89

listing the target columns is a recommended practice to prevent unintended errors, particularly when table definitions evolve over time.

In practice, data insertion is frequently automated via application code. For instance, the Python sqlite3 module integrates seamlessly with SQL operations using parameterized queries to prevent SQL injection vulnerabilities. The following Python snippet demonstrates a secure method for inserting a record:

```
import sqlite3

connection = sqlite3.connect('example.db')
cursor = connection.cursor()

# Parameterized query to ensure secure data insertion
insert_query = """
INSERT INTO employees (name, department, hire_date)
VALUES (?, ?, ?);
"""
data = ('Bob Smith', 'Marketing', '2023-08-20')
cursor.execute(insert_query, data)

connection.commit()
connection.close()
```

Parameterized queries use placeholders (denoted by ? in SQLite) where the data values are bound at runtime. This approach not only protects against SQL injection but also improves readability and maintainability of the code.

Batch insertion is another common scenario encountered when multiple records must be inserted concurrently. Batch operations enhance performance by reducing the overhead of multiple transaction commits. In SQLite, the executemany() method enables batch processing via Python, as illustrated in the following example:

```
import sqlite3

connection = sqlite3.connect('example.db')
cursor = connection.cursor()

# Prepare multiple records for insertion
```

```
batch_data = [
    ('Charles Green', 'Sales', '2023-07-11'),
    ('Diana Prince', 'Research', '2023-06-15'),
    ('Eleanor Rigby', 'Development', '2023-05-10')
]

# Perform batch insertion
cursor.executemany("""
INSERT INTO employees (name, department, hire_date)
VALUES (?, ?, ?);
""", batch_data)

connection.commit()
connection.close()
```

In addition to batch processing, SQLite offers advanced options for handling conflicts during insertion. By default, if an INSERT operation results in a conflict, such as attempting to insert a duplicate value in a column declared as UNIQUE, SQLite will abort the operation. However, conflict resolution strategies can be specified using clauses such as OR IGNORE or OR REPLACE. For example, to insert data while ignoring duplicates on a unique column, the statement might use:

```
INSERT OR IGNORE INTO employees (id, name, department, hire_date)
VALUES (1, 'Alice Johnson', 'Engineering', '2023-09-15');
```

Alternatively, if the design of the database allows for updates upon conflicts, the OR REPLACE clause can be used. This clause instructs SQLite to delete the existing record that conflicts with the new record, then insert the new data. The syntax is similar to:

```
INSERT OR REPLACE INTO employees (id, name, department, hire_date)
VALUES (1, 'Alice Johnson', 'Engineering', '2023-09-15');
```

These conflict resolution strategies are particularly useful in environments with high volumes of data entry where duplicate data may arise or where updates need to be efficiently managed.

Transactions serve as an essential mechanism to ensure the integrity and consistency of database operations. If multiple INSERT operations are intended to be performed as a single unit, wrapping these operations in a transaction guarantees that either all of them succeed or none. For example, using Python, one can begin a transaction, execute several INSERT commands, and then commit the transaction as follows:

```
import sqlite3

connection = sqlite3.connect('example.db')
cursor = connection.cursor()

try:
    # Begin transaction
    cursor.execute("BEGIN TRANSACTION;")
    cursor.execute("INSERT INTO employees (name, department,
     hire_date) VALUES (?, ?, ?);", ('Frank Ocean', 'Music',
     '2023-04-25'))
    cursor.execute("INSERT INTO employees (name, department,
     hire_date) VALUES (?, ?, ?);", ('Grace Hopper', 'Research',
     '2023-03-17'))
    # Commit transaction if all inserts are successful
    connection.commit()
except sqlite3.Error as e:
    # Rollback transaction in case of error
    connection.rollback()
finally:
    connection.close()
```

This approach enforces a level of atomicity in the execution of the database operations, ensuring that incomplete or corrupted data states are not committed.

Beyond simple value insertion, SQLite permits the insertion of data derived from subqueries. This process enables the population of one table with data selected and possibly transformed from another. Consider the scenario where data from a temporary table needs to be inserted into a permanent table. The SQL statement might look as follows:

```
INSERT INTO permanent_table (column1, column2)
SELECT column1, column2
FROM temporary_table
WHERE condition;
```

This method is particularly potent when migrating data or when data transformations are required before final storage. The utilization of subqueries makes it possible to leverage the full power of the SQL language during the data insertion process.

Inserting data also has a significant impact on performance, especially when handling large datasets. It is advisable to disable journaling or synchronous settings temporarily during bulk inserts to enhance performance, provided that data loss is not a critical concern. Developers must measure the performance trade-offs and possibly re-enable these settings once bulk insertions are complete to ensure long-term durability and security.

Moreover, the quality of inserted data impacts the overall consistency and quality of the database. Strict adherence to column data types, constraints, and integrity rules plays a significant role in maintaining high-quality data. Employing routines such as data validation before executing INSERT statements can mitigate issues arising from malformed or unexpected input.

For developers requiring greater flexibility during the insertion process, SQLite functions can be used to manipulate data on the fly. For instance, the date() and datetime() functions allow dynamic insertion of temporal data. An example that uses the current date during an insert can be formatted as:

```
INSERT INTO events (event_name, event_date)
VALUES ('Launch Event', date('now'));
```

This dynamic evaluation ensures that each record reflects the accurate timestamp, without the need for manual intervention by the application layer.

When inserting data, one should also consider the implications of triggers and default values defined during table creation. Triggers, for example, may automatically execute additional SQL commands in response to an insert operation to enforce business rules or maintain audit logs. Similarly, default values will be applied when a column value is not explicitly provided, ensuring that records remain complete even in the absence of certain data elements.

Optimizing insertion performance can be further achieved by organizing the database schema to facilitate rapid data writing. Partitioning large tables or creating specialized temporary tables for bulk operations can significantly reduce insertion times. These strategies are particularly beneficial in applications with high write throughput or in systems where rapid data ingestion is a priority.

Attention to proper error handling is critical. Errors during insertion can be caused by constraint violations, data type mismatches, or unintended logical errors in the application code. Ensuring that such errors are caught and appropriately handled will prevent the introduction of inconsistent data into the system. Logging insertion errors and maintaining robust exception handling routines are recommended practices for production environments.

Techniques for inserting data into SQLite tables extend to scenarios where data transformation is required. For example, when importing data from external sources in CSV or JSON formats, the data may require transformation before it is inserted into a relational schema. In such cases, middleware layers in application code process and clean the data, with the transformed output then inserted using the standard SQL INSERT mechanism.

High-frequency insertion operations benefit from the use of parameterized queries and transactions. Combining these techniques ensures that data is inserted safely and efficiently, minimizing the risks of SQL injection, data corruption, and performance bottlenecks. Enhanced performance during insertion operations leads to more responsive applications and reduces the overall latency of data-driven processes.

94

The discussed techniques for data insertion form an integral part of the broader workflow in SQLite database operations. Mastery of these methods provides a foundation for effective data manipulation, integration with application logic, and the development of robust database systems. Each method and strategy introduced here builds upon the principles of sound database design, ensuring that the insertion process is efficient, secure, and maintainable.

3.3. Querying Data with SELECT

Querying data is fundamental in working with relational databases. The SQL SELECT statement in SQLite is the principal command for retrieving data stored in tables, and its versatility makes it suitable for both simple and complex queries. This section builds upon previously discussed topics such as table creation and data insertion, guiding the reader through the various techniques for querying data, managing result sets, and leveraging SQLite's functions to perform specialized data retrieval.

At its simplest, the SELECT statement allows for the retrieval of all rows and columns from a table. The basic syntax is as follows:

```
SELECT * FROM table_name;
```

This command returns every column for every row in the specified table. However, practical applications often necessitate retrieving a specific subset of columns. For example, to retrieve only the name and department columns from an employees table, the query becomes:

```
SELECT name, department FROM employees;
```

Selecting explicit columns not only refines the output but can also enhance performance especially when handling large tables.

SQLite supports the inclusion of expressions and function calls within

95

the SELECT statement.   Functions such as COUNT(), AVG(), MIN(), MAX(), and SUM() are used for aggregation and statistical analysis. For instance, the total number of employees can be determined by:

```
SELECT COUNT(*) AS total_employees FROM employees;
```

The use of the alias AS total_employees makes the result more descriptive. Aliases are particularly useful when dealing with complex expressions or subqueries because they clarify the purpose of the output.

Filtering is a central aspect of querying data. The WHERE clause is appended to the SELECT statement to specify conditions that rows must meet in order to be included in the result set. A typical example is filtering employees by department:

```
SELECT name, hire_date FROM employees
WHERE department = 'Engineering';
```

Multiple conditions can be combined using logical operators such as AND, OR, and NOT. For instance, to retrieve employees from the Engineering or Research departments who were hired after a specific date, one might use:

```
SELECT name, department, hire_date FROM employees
WHERE (department = 'Engineering' OR department = 'Research')
   AND hire_date > '2023-01-01';
```

The manipulation of result sets is another critical area. Sorting the output is achieved through the ORDER BY clause. By specifying one or more columns and the sorting order (ASC for ascending and DESC for descending), the data can be organized in a meaningful way. For instance, listing employees by hire date in descending order might be achieved with:

```
SELECT name, hire_date FROM employees
ORDER BY hire_date DESC;
```

For large datasets, it is often necessary to limit the number of rows

96

returned. The LIMIT clause restricts the number of rows in the output, and the optional OFFSET clause specifies the starting point. This is particularly useful for paginating query results:

```
SELECT name, department FROM employees
ORDER BY name ASC
LIMIT 10 OFFSET 20;
```

This query retrieves 10 rows starting from the 21st row after ordering the results by name.

In scenarios where data is spread across multiple tables, SQLite supports JOIN operations. Joins are used to combine rows from two or more tables based on related columns. The most common type is the INNER JOIN, which returns rows when there is a match in both tables. Consider two tables, employees and departments. To retrieve the employee names along with their department names, one might use:

```
SELECT e.name, d.department_name
FROM employees e
INNER JOIN departments d ON e.department = d.department_id;
```

This query utilizes table aliases (e and d) for brevity and clarity, and it demonstrates the typical pattern of joining related data.

SQLite also supports several outer join types, including LEFT JOIN and RIGHT JOIN (although the latter is not directly supported in SQLite, the same effect can be achieved by reversing the order of the tables in a LEFT JOIN). A LEFT JOIN will return all rows from the left table and matched rows from the right table, filling in with NULL if no match exists. The syntax appears as:

```
SELECT e.name, d.department_name
FROM employees e
LEFT JOIN departments d ON e.department = d.department_id;
```

Subqueries provide another level of sophistication in querying. A subquery is a query nested within another query, and it can be used in the FROM, WHERE, or SELECT clauses. This is useful for filtering based on aggregate values. For example, to retrieve employees hired after the average hire date of all employees, the query can be structured as follows:

```
SELECT name, hire_date FROM employees
WHERE hire_date > (SELECT AVG(hire_date) FROM employees);
```

Subqueries allow complex filtering and can compact many query operations into a single statement. They enhance the expressiveness of the SQL language and allow users to perform nested calculations.

Using SQLite's built-in functions further extends the querying capabilities. Functions such as date(), time(), and datetime() enable time-based calculations and formatting directly within the query. For example, to display the recruitment month for each employee, one might write:

```
SELECT name, strftime('%m', hire_date) AS hire_month FROM employees;
```

This query extracts the month from the hire_date using the strftime function and assigns it a user-friendly alias.

Complex queries often involve aggregation across groups of rows. The GROUP BY clause is used in combination with aggregate functions to summarize data. For instance, if one wishes to determine the number of employees in each department, the query is formulated as:

```
SELECT department, COUNT(*) AS num_employees
FROM employees
GROUP BY department;
```

When combined with the HAVING clause, the output can be further refined to include only groups meeting specific criteria. For example, to display only departments with more than two employees, the query becomes:

```
SELECT department, COUNT(*) AS num_employees
FROM employees
GROUP BY department
HAVING COUNT(*) > 2;
```

Integrating these techniques in application code is facilitated by parameterized queries with languages such as Python. Using a combination of SELECT statements, data can be retrieved and processed effectively. A Python code snippet for executing a query and processing its results might appear as:

```
import sqlite3

connection = sqlite3.connect('example.db')
cursor = connection.cursor()

# Retrieve employee names and departments
cursor.execute("""
SELECT name, department FROM employees
WHERE hire_date > '2023-01-01'
ORDER BY hire_date;
""")

# Process results
rows = cursor.fetchall()
for row in rows:
    print("Name:", row[0], "Department:", row[1])

connection.close()
```

Running the above snippet produces an output similar to the following:

```
Name: Alice Johnson Department: Engineering
Name: Bob Smith Department: Marketing
...
```

This example demonstrates how the retrieved data can be iterated over and utilized within an application. Handling result sets programmatically bridges the gap between the static database environment and dynamic application requirements.

For more advanced queries, the integration of window functions can be beneficial. Although SQLite's support for window functions is relatively recent, these functions facilitate operations such as ranking, run-

99

ning totals, and moving averages within result sets. An example of using a window function to rank employees by hire date is:

```
SELECT name, hire_date,
       RANK() OVER (ORDER BY hire_date) AS hire_rank
FROM employees;
```

The inclusion of window functions like RANK() provides an analytical layer to SQL queries, allowing queries to return additional context without requiring complex subqueries or additional processing.

Understanding data retrieval using the SELECT statement also necessitates an appreciation for query performance. The efficiency of SELECT queries can be influenced by several factors, including the use of indexes, the complexity of the WHERE clause, and the volume of data processed. Ensuring that columns frequently used in filtering or joining are indexed can substantially accelerate query execution. Analyzing query performance using SQLite's EXPLAIN command is a recommended practice that provides insight into how the query optimizer processes a given statement.

Each technique and query customization option discussed here serves to enhance SQLite's data retrieval capabilities. The practices introduced in this section allow for comprehensive data interrogation from simple lookups to complex analytical queries. Collaborative application of these techniques results in expressive, efficient, and maintainable data access operations, forming the backbone of robust database-centric applications.

3.4. Updating Existing Records

Modifying existing records within a database is an essential operation that facilitates the maintenance of data accuracy and relevance over time. The SQL UPDATE statement in SQLite is the tool that enables de-

100

velopers to modify one or more columns of existing rows within a table. Building on the concepts of table creation, data insertion, and querying discussed in previous sections, this section focuses on the syntax, methodologies, and best practices for updating data effectively.

The basic syntax for the UPDATE statement is as follows:

```
UPDATE table_name
SET column1 = value1, column2 = value2, ...
WHERE condition;
```

This command specifies the table to be updated, the new values for one or more columns, and the condition that identifies the rows to be modified. The WHERE clause is pivotal, as it ensures that only the intended rows are affected. Without a WHERE clause, the update operation would affect every record in the table, potentially leading to undesired data modifications.

To illustrate, consider an employees table previously created with columns such as name, department, and hire_date. To update the department for a specific employee, the query may be written as:

```
UPDATE employees
SET department = 'Human Resources'
WHERE name = 'Alice Johnson';
```

This command modifies the department of the employee with the name Alice Johnson to Human Resources. It is important to note that the condition in the WHERE clause must uniquely identify the target row(s) to avoid unintentional updates across multiple records.

In practical applications, update operations are typically executed from an application layer using programming languages like Python. The integration of parameterized queries not only enhances security by mitigating SQL injection risks but also increases flexibility. A Python example using the sqlite3 module is provided below:

```
import sqlite3
```

```
connection = sqlite3.connect('example.db')
cursor = connection.cursor()

update_query = """
UPDATE employees
SET department = ?
WHERE name = ?;
"""
data = ('Human Resources', 'Alice Johnson')
cursor.execute(update_query, data)

connection.commit()
connection.close()
```

The use of placeholders (?) in the query helps separate the data from the SQL code, ensuring that the values are correctly escaped and treated as parameters rather than executable code.

Batch updates, where multiple records require changes based on similar conditions, are another common scenario. Updating many records in a single SQL command is efficient compared to executing numerous individual updates. For instance, if an organization is restructuring departments, an update could be structured as follows:

```
UPDATE employees
SET department = 'Marketing'
WHERE department = 'Sales';
```

This command modifies every row where the current department is Sales, reassigning those employees to Marketing. Batch updates underscore the importance of using precise conditions in the WHERE clause; improper conditions might inadvertently modify unintended rows.

When working with updates, it is also common to utilize expressions and arithmetic operations to transform data dynamically. Consider a scenario where an annual salary increment is required for employees in a particular department. Assuming the employees table contains a salary column, an update query might use an arithmetic expression

102

as follows:

```
UPDATE employees
SET salary = salary * 1.05
WHERE department = 'Development';
```

This command increases the salary for every employee in the Development department by 5%. Arithmetic operations directly within the UPDATE statement allow for smooth, iterative transformations of numerical data without the need for external processing.

Another advanced technique involves updating records based on data from other tables. Although SQLite does not support traditional join syntax within an UPDATE statement, similar results can be achieved using subqueries. For instance, to update records in one table based on the values in another, consider the following example where a new bonus column in employees is to be updated with corresponding data from a bonuses table:

```
UPDATE employees
SET bonus = (
    SELECT bonus_amount
    FROM bonuses
    WHERE bonuses.employee_id = employees.id
)
WHERE EXISTS (
    SELECT 1
    FROM bonuses
    WHERE bonuses.employee_id = employees.id
);
```

In this example, the subquery retrieves the bonus amount for each employee based on a matching record in the bonuses table. The WHERE EXISTS clause ensures that the update is applied only to those employees who have an associated bonus record. This approach elegantly combines data from multiple tables within a single update operation.

Error handling and transaction management are critical when performing update operations. As with data insertion, grouping multiple updates within a single transaction ensures that all changes are committed only if every operation is successful. If an error occurs during one of the update operations, a transaction rollback maintains data integrity. An example using Python demonstrates this strategy:

```python
import sqlite3

connection = sqlite3.connect('example.db')
cursor = connection.cursor()

try:
    cursor.execute("BEGIN TRANSACTION;")
    cursor.execute("""
        UPDATE employees
        SET salary = salary * 1.03
        WHERE department = 'Marketing';
    """)
    cursor.execute("""
        UPDATE employees
        SET department = 'Sales'
        WHERE department = 'Retail';
    """)
    connection.commit()
except sqlite3.Error as error:
    connection.rollback()
    print("Error occurred:", error)
finally:
    connection.close()
```

This transactional approach ensures that if any part of the update sequence fails, no partial updates are retained. Such practices are fundamental in maintaining consistent and reliable database states, especially in systems where data integrity is paramount.

It is also essential to consider the performance implications of update operations. Large tables or frequent update operations might lead to performance degradation if not managed properly. Indexes on the WHERE clause columns can speed up row selection, while keeping transactions concise minimizes locking and improves concurrency. Additionally, analyzing query performance using SQLite's EXPLAIN or EXPLAIN QUERY PLAN commands can provide valuable insights into how updates are executed and where optimizations are possible.

Another important aspect is ensuring that update operations respect business logic and data integrity constraints. Constraints defined at the time of table creation, such as NOT NULL, CHECK, and foreign key relationships, automatically govern the data being updated. However, certain business rules might require additional validation before an update is executed. In such cases, application-level logic or database triggers can be employed to enforce complex rules. For example, a trigger can prevent an update that would result in an invalid state:

```
CREATE TRIGGER validate_salary_update
BEFORE UPDATE OF salary ON employees
FOR EACH ROW
WHEN NEW.salary <= 0
BEGIN
    SELECT RAISE(ABORT, 'Salary must be positive');
END;
```

This trigger prevents updates that set an employee's salary to a non-positive value, thus enforcing a business rule at the database level. Leveraging constraints and triggers together with UPDATE statements ensures robust data validation throughout the application lifecycle.

In scenarios where the update conditions involve a range of values or require complex logic, developers can combine multiple conditions with logical operators to fine-tune the impacted dataset. For instance, a query to update the status of employees based on multiple criteria might look like:

```
UPDATE employees
SET status = 'Senior'
WHERE years_of_experience > 10
  AND department = 'Engineering';
```

This statement effectively promotes eligible employees to a new status based on measurable criteria. Incorporating multiple conditions provides granular control over data modifications and supports sophisticated business requirements.

Developers must also be aware that updates may trigger cascading effects in relational databases. When tables have relationships defined through foreign keys, updating a key value in one table might necessitate corresponding changes in related tables. SQLite supports cascading updates using the ON UPDATE CASCADE clause during table creation. Although updates primarily target non-key columns, in scenarios where key updates are justified, understanding cascading behaviors is crucial to avoiding inconsistent data. For example, a table definition that enables cascading updates is structured as:

```
CREATE TABLE orders (
    order_id INTEGER PRIMARY KEY,
    customer_id INTEGER,
    order_date DATE,
    FOREIGN KEY(customer_id)
        REFERENCES customers(customer_id)
        ON UPDATE CASCADE
);
```

When the customer_id in the customers table is updated, the cascading effect automatically propagates the change to the orders table. Awareness of such behavior helps in planning updates that span multiple interconnected tables.

The evolution of database applications often requires data modifications that are both frequent and complex, making the efficient use of the UPDATE statement a cornerstone of database management. Each update operation must be carefully crafted to target the correct rows, ensure data integrity, and perform efficiently. From simple adjustments of textual data to complex operations involving subqueries and arithmetic expressions, effective updating techniques are integral to sustaining an accurate and performant database environment.

By integrating comprehensive error handling, transaction management, and performance optimization strategies, developers can confidently modify data while preserving the reliability of their database systems. The methodologies detailed in this section lay a strong foundation for advanced data manipulation, reinforcing the principles of sound database design and effective application development.

3.5. Deleting Data from Tables

Deleting records is a fundamental operation in managing a database, ensuring that data remains current and relevant. The SQL DELETE statement in SQLite is the primary mechanism to remove one or more rows from a table. Building on previously discussed topics such as creating databases, inserting data, and updating records, this section provides an in-depth examination of techniques for deleting data, including syntax details, practical examples, and important considerations related to data integrity and performance.

The basic structure of a DELETE operation in SQLite is straightforward. The most common syntax is as follows:

```
DELETE FROM table_name
WHERE condition;
```

The clause WHERE condition is critical; it specifies which rows in the table are subject to deletion. Omitting the WHERE clause results in the removal of every record from the table. For instance, a statement that deletes all records from the employees table would be written as:

```
DELETE FROM employees;
```

In most cases, such a command is not desirable unless the intention is to clear a table completely, such as during a maintenance operation or when reinitializing a database. Therefore, careful crafting of the condition is required to avoid unintended data loss.

One of the most common scenarios is deleting a single record. For example, consider a situation where a specific employee, identified by a unique identifier, must be removed from the employees table. The SQL

107

command for this operation might be:

```
DELETE FROM employees
WHERE id = 10;
```

Here, the condition ensures that only the row with id = 10 is removed, leaving all other records intact. This approach demonstrates the importance of using unique identifiers, such as primary keys, to target specific rows.

In practical applications, deletion operations are often executed through application code. The Python sqlite3 module, for example, facilitates robust interactions with the database, using parameterized queries to safely delete records. A typical Python example might appear as follows:

```
import sqlite3

connection = sqlite3.connect('example.db')
cursor = connection.cursor()

delete_query = """
DELETE FROM employees
WHERE id = ?;
"""
# Delete the employee with id 10
cursor.execute(delete_query, (10,))

connection.commit()
connection.close()
```

Using parameterized queries, represented by the placeholder ?, helps prevent SQL injection and maintains clarity in the code base. In scenarios where multiple records must be deleted based on a shared attribute, such as removing all entries for a discontinued department, the WHERE clause can include multiple conditions. For example:

```
DELETE FROM employees
WHERE department = 'Sales';
```

This statement removes all records from the employees table where

108

the department is listed as Sales. Such bulk deletions should be approached with caution, ensuring that the condition accurately reflects the intended dataset to be removed.

Transaction management is an integral part of deleting records, particularly when multiple related deletion operations must occur as a single atomic action. Performing deletion operations within a transaction ensures that the database remains in a consistent state even if an error occurs during the process. Consider the following Python snippet that demonstrates executing multiple deletions atomically:

```
import sqlite3

connection = sqlite3.connect('example.db')
cursor = connection.cursor()

try:
    cursor.execute("BEGIN TRANSACTION;")
    # Remove employees with a specific condition
    cursor.execute("""
    DELETE FROM employees
    WHERE department = 'Temporary';
    """)
    # Remove records from another table related to cleanup operations
    cursor.execute("""
    DELETE FROM attendance
    WHERE date < '2022-01-01';
    """)
    connection.commit()
except sqlite3.Error as error:
    connection.rollback()
    print("An error occurred:", error)
finally:
    connection.close()
```

In this example, multiple DELETE statements are included within a transaction. If any part of the process fails, the entire transaction is rolled back, preserving the integrity of the database. This is particularly important in environments where relationships between tables might be affected by deletions.

Foreign key constraints are another critical consideration when deleting data. In relational databases, tables often have dependencies enforced through foreign key relationships. SQLite supports foreign key constraints with optional cascading deletes. When a parent record is deleted, a cascading delete will automatically remove corresponding child records if the foreign key was defined with the ON DELETE CASCADE clause. For instance, consider a database where each order is linked to a customer. The table definition might include:

```
CREATE TABLE customers (
    customer_id INTEGER PRIMARY KEY,
    name TEXT NOT NULL
);

CREATE TABLE orders (
    order_id INTEGER PRIMARY KEY,
    customer_id INTEGER,
    order_date DATE,
    FOREIGN KEY(customer_id)
        REFERENCES customers(customer_id)
        ON DELETE CASCADE
);
```

With this setup, deleting a customer record automatically results in the deletion of all associated orders. This behavior simplifies the management of related datasets, but it also requires careful planning to avoid accidental loss of dependent data.

The possibility of unintended deletions also underscores the importance of performing backups or using the ROLLBACK feature during development and testing. In production environments, it is advisable to confirm deletion operations by executing a SELECT statement using the same WHERE clause conditions prior to running the DELETE command. This precautionary step ensures that the targeted records are accurately identified. For example:

```
SELECT * FROM employees
WHERE department = 'obsolete';
```

By verifying the result of the selection, developers can confirm that the

110

subsequent deletion will affect only the intended rows.

Another sophisticated use of the DELETE statement involves subqueries. Subqueries can refine the selection criteria based on information from related tables or more complex conditions. For example, one might delete records from the employees table for those employees who have not logged any activity in a related activity_log table:

```
DELETE FROM employees
WHERE id IN (
    SELECT id FROM employees
    EXCEPT
    SELECT DISTINCT employee_id FROM activity_log
);
```

In this example, the inner query identifies employees that have logged activity by using a subquery on the activity_log table. The EXCEPT operator then isolates the records that do not appear in the log, and the outer DELETE statement removes these inactive records. Such complex queries enable refined control over database cleanup tasks.

Deleting data from tables also has implications for performance. Large-scale deletions can generate significant overhead, particularly if the database must write to disk extensively or update many indexes. In some cases, it may be beneficial to temporarily disable non-critical indexes during bulk deletions and then rebuild them after the operation has completed. However, such optimizations must be balanced against the potential risk of data inconsistency during the downtime of index functionality. Monitoring performance using SQLite's EXPLAIN and EXPLAIN QUERY PLAN can yield insights into optimization opportunities.

It is important to note that delete operations are not reversible without backups unless the deleted data is recovered from a journal or log. Therefore, ensuring that deletion commands are executed with verified conditions and within controlled transactions is vital for maintaining data safety. Integrating application-level logging or even immediate post-deletion audits can help track changes and provide a safety net should accidental deletions occur.

In some cases, instead of permanently deleting data, a logical deletion approach might be employed. This strategy involves marking a record as inactive or deleted, typically by setting a flag column within the record instead of removing it. Although the data remains physically in the database, it is excluded from standard query results. An example of logical deletion might look like:

```
UPDATE employees
SET is_active = 0
WHERE id = 10;
```

Using this method, the record remains part of the table, which supports potential future recovery or auditing, while application logic filters out records where is_active is set to 0. Logical deletions are particularly valuable in systems where historical data retention is required, or where legal compliance necessitates data archiving.

Each deletion strategy—be it physical deletion using the DELETE statement or logical deletion using an update mechanism—must be selected based on the specific needs of the application and the operational requirements of the business. Factors such as data volume, performance constraints, and the need for historical auditing play significant roles in determining the optimal approach.

Thorough testing in a controlled environment is advised before deploying deletion commands in live applications. Test databases should mirror production environments closely so that the impact of deletions and related cascading behaviors can be accurately assessed and mitigated. Proper error handling, often encapsulated within transactions as demonstrated earlier, is essential for maintaining database consistency, particularly when deletions span multiple related tables.

The ability to remove records efficiently and safely is a key component

112

in the lifecycle management of databases. The techniques explored in this section, from basic deletions to complex subqueries and cascading behaviors, provide developers with the necessary tools to maintain data integrity over time. Employing best practices, such as confirming conditions with preliminary SELECT queries and using transaction control, further ensures that deletions are executed accurately and without unintended consequences.

The methodologies discussed herein serve to empower developers to manage the evolution of their database content robustly. Through targeted deletion techniques, developers are able to remove outdated or erroneous data and optimize the performance of their applications, thereby supporting the overall health and scalability of their systems.

3.6. Using WHERE Clauses

Filtering data is a vital component of SQL as it allows developers to precisely target the records they wish to retrieve, update, or delete. The WHERE clause in SQL serves as the gatekeeper for query results, enabling the specification of conditions that filter rows based on column values. This section examines how to leverage the WHERE clause in SQLite, detailing the syntax, various operators, and strategies to construct robust and effective filtering criteria.

The basic syntax of the WHERE clause is straightforward. It is appended to a SQL statement such as SELECT, UPDATE, or DELETE to restrict the scope of the operation to only those rows that fulfill a specified condition. The general form is as follows:

```
SELECT column1, column2, ...
FROM table_name
WHERE condition;
```

Conditions can involve simple comparisons such as equality, inequality, greater than, or less than, among others. For example, to retrieve all records from an `employees` table in which the department is 'Engineering', one can use:

```
SELECT *
FROM employees
WHERE department = 'Engineering';
```

Equality is but one of the many tests available. The `WHERE` clause supports a variety of comparison operators including =, <> (or != in some SQL dialects), >, >=, <, and <=. These operators enable filtering numeric, text, and date values. For example, to select employees who were hired after January 1, 2022, the query would be:

```
SELECT name, hire_date
FROM employees
WHERE hire_date > '2022-01-01';
```

Logical operators provide additional flexibility by allowing the combination of multiple conditions. The operators `AND`, `OR`, and `NOT` can be used to build complex expressions. Consider a scenario where one needs to retrieve employees in the 'Engineering' department who were hired after January 1, 2022. The `WHERE` clause would combine two conditions using `AND` as shown below:

```
SELECT name, department, hire_date
FROM employees
WHERE department = 'Engineering'
  AND hire_date > '2022-01-01';
```

When multiple conditions are combined using logical operators, the order of evaluation can be controlled by parentheses. This is particularly useful in cases where a mix of `AND` and `OR` operators are present. For instance, to retrieve employees who work in either the 'Engineering' or 'Research' departments and were hired after a specific date, one may construct a query as follows:

```
SELECT name, department, hire_date
FROM employees
WHERE (department = 'Engineering' OR department = 'Research')
```

```
AND hire_date > '2022-01-01';
```

SQLite also provides pattern matching capabilities through the use of the `LIKE` operator. This operator allows developers to filter textual data using wildcard characters. The % symbol matches any sequence of characters, while the underscore (_) matches a single character. As an example, to find employees whose names begin with the letter 'A', the query would be:

```
SELECT name
FROM employees
WHERE name LIKE 'A%';
```

Pattern matching not only improves data retrieval when exact matches are uncertain, but it also enables user-driven searches where full string matches may not be known in advance. In addition to `LIKE`, SQLite supports the `GLOB` operator for simple pattern matching using Unix file globbing syntax. For example, to find names that conform to a specific pattern, one can use:

```
SELECT name
FROM employees
WHERE name GLOB 'A[a-z]*';
```

Filtering based on a range of values is achieved using the `BETWEEN` operator. This operator makes it easier to specify conditions that must fall within a particular range. To retrieve employees with salaries between 50000 and 100000, one might execute:

```
SELECT name, salary
FROM employees
WHERE salary BETWEEN 50000 AND 100000;
```

For cases where the value of a column might be one among several possibilities, the `IN` operator simplifies the syntax. Rather than constructing multiple `OR` conditions, the `IN` operator allows the developer to specify a list of acceptable values. For example:

```
SELECT name, department
```

```
FROM employees
WHERE department IN ('Engineering', 'Research', 'Development');
```

Handling NULL values in SQL requires special attention since NULL represents the absence of data and does not behave like other values in comparisons. The keywords IS NULL and IS NOT NULL are used instead of standard comparison operators to determine if a column contains a NULL value. For instance, to find all employees who do not have an assigned department, the query can be written as:

```
SELECT name
FROM employees
WHERE department IS NULL;
```

In many applications, developers need to filter based on computed values, and SQLite allows the incorporation of expressions within the WHERE clause. This means arithmetic or function-based conditions can be evaluated on the fly. For example, to select records where the computed value of a discount on sales exceeds a threshold, one might have:

```
SELECT product_name, price, discount
FROM products
WHERE price * discount > 50;
```

Combining subqueries with the WHERE clause further heightens the power of SQL filtering. A subquery embedded within a WHERE clause can dynamically determine the set of rows based on criteria in another table. For instance, consider filtering employees based on their presence in another table that logs performance metrics:

```
SELECT name, department
FROM employees
WHERE id IN (
    SELECT employee_id
    FROM performance_reviews
    WHERE score > 80
);
```

In this case, only employees who have a corresponding entry in the performance_reviews table with a score greater than 80 will appear in the results. Such nested queries are particularly useful when filtering criteria rely on the relationships between tables.

The intricacies of the WHERE clause extend to its interplay with other SQL commands. For example, when updating records, the same filtering principles apply. An UPDATE statement may incorporate a WHERE clause to modify only a subset of rows. Consider the following update operation intended to increase the salary by 10% for employees in the 'Sales' department:

```
UPDATE employees
SET salary = salary * 1.10
WHERE department = 'Sales';
```

Similarly, the DELETE statement uses the WHERE clause to accurately target rows for removal. This consistent use of the clause across various SQL commands ensures that operations are applied only to authorized records, protecting the integrity of the dataset.

Performance considerations are also central when using the WHERE clause. The use of indexes on columns frequently referenced in conditions can drastically improve query performance. For instance, if the department column is often used to filter records, creating an index on that column can lead to faster data retrieval:

```
CREATE INDEX idx_department ON employees(department);
```

Understanding how the query planner utilizes indexes in conjunction with the WHERE clause can provide valuable insights into potential performance bottlenecks. The EXPLAIN QUERY PLAN command can be invoked prior to executing a query to observe how SQLite intends to process the statement. For example:

```
EXPLAIN QUERY PLAN
SELECT name, hire_date
FROM employees
WHERE department = 'Engineering'
  AND hire_date > '2022-01-01';
```

The output from this command helps in tuning the query by revealing whether indexes are used or if a full table scan might occur. Optimizing WHERE clause conditions to use indexed columns is a key aspect of developing scalable database applications.

Another critical technique when constructing WHERE clauses is the careful ordering of conditions. In many SQL engines, the evaluation of the WHERE clause follows a left-to-right sequence, and prioritizing conditions that are more selective can lead to early elimination of rows. This is especially crucial in large datasets where performance improvements can be significant. Testing various conditions and analyzing query plans helps determine the most effective order of operations.

In complex applications, dynamic query building is common, where the filtering criteria may vary based on user input or application state. In such scenarios, it is paramount to ensure that all clauses are constructed securely. The use of parameterized queries is recommended since it not only clarifies the distinction between SQL code and data values but also mitigates SQL injection risks. Parameterized examples in Python demonstrate this practice clearly:

```
import sqlite3

connection = sqlite3.connect('example.db')
cursor = connection.cursor()

query = """
SELECT name, department, hire_date
FROM employees
WHERE department = ? AND hire_date > ?;
"""
parameters = ('Engineering', '2022-01-01')
cursor.execute(query, parameters)

for row in cursor.fetchall():
    print("Name: ", row[0], "Department: ", row[1], "Hire Date: ",
    row[2])
```

```
connection.close()
```

This example illustrates how parameters can be passed to filter conditions safely and efficiently, ensuring that only the intended dataset is processed by the query.

Overall, the WHERE clause is indispensable for delineating exactly which rows in a table should participate in a query operation. Its versatility in supporting simple comparisons, pattern matching with operators such as LIKE and GLOB, range checks using BETWEEN, and list evaluations using IN allows the developer to craft precise and effective filters. Moreover, the ability to nest subqueries within the WHERE clause and combine multiple conditions using logical operators further empowers advanced data retrieval, update, and deletion functionalities.

Employing best practices, such as confirming filter criteria through preliminary SELECT queries before executing updates or deletions, using indexes efficiently, and carefully structuring complex logical expressions with parentheses, ensures that database operations perform reliably and efficiently. This comprehensive approach to filtering not only enhances data integrity but also contributes to the overall performance and scalability of SQLite-based applications.

3.7. Sorting and Limiting Query Results

Sorting and limiting query results are pivotal to the effective presentation and management of data in SQLite. The ORDER BY clause facilitates the organization of data in a specified sequence while the LIMIT and optionally OFFSET clauses restrict the number of rows returned. These tools are fundamental when dealing with large datasets, enabling developers to display data in a manageable form and optimize the performance of applications.

119

The ORDER BY clause is used to arrange the result set in either ascending or descending order. By default, the order is ascending; however, specifying DESC (descending) alters the sort. A typical ORDER BY clause is structured as follows:

```
SELECT column1, column2
FROM table_name
ORDER BY column1 ASC, column2 DESC;
```

This statement sorts the results first by column1 in ascending order. For rows where column1 is identical, column2 is sorted in descending order. Sorting by multiple columns is particularly useful when the dataset has hierarchical relationships or when additional clarification is needed after an initial primary sort.

For instance, consider a scenario with an employees table where the dataset is to be ordered by the department and then by the hire date. The SQL query may be formulated as:

```
SELECT name, department, hire_date
FROM employees
ORDER BY department ASC, hire_date DESC;
```

This query first organizes the employees alphabetically by department and, within each department, orders them by the most recent hire date. Such ordering is beneficial when presenting data in an interface where users expect grouped and sequentially ordered information.

Sorting is not merely an aesthetic or organizational tool; it can influence query performance. When the database has indexes on columns used in the ORDER BY clause, SQLite can perform the sort operation more efficiently by leveraging these indexes. Developers should monitor performance by using diagnostic tools such as the EXPLAIN QUERY PLAN command to verify whether an index is being employed in the sorting process.

Beyond sorting, controlling the volume of returned data is critical when dealing with extensive tables. The LIMIT clause allows developers to specify the maximum number of rows to return. For example, to retrieve only the first 10 rows of a query result, the following SQL can be used:

```
SELECT name, department, hire_date
FROM employees
ORDER BY hire_date DESC
LIMIT 10;
```

This query selects the 10 most recently hired employees, as determined by sorting the hire_date in descending order. Such a limitation is particularly useful in scenarios like paginated displays where only a subset of data is shown on a given page.

The OFFSET clause complements LIMIT by specifying a row number from which the returned results should commence. This clause is frequently employed in pagination. For example, retrieving rows 11 to 20 can be achieved by setting an offset of 10 and a limit of 10:

```
SELECT name, department, hire_date
FROM employees
ORDER BY hire_date DESC
LIMIT 10 OFFSET 10;
```

This approach supports applications where users can navigate through pages of results, ensuring that each page displays a fixed number of rows. The combination of LIMIT and OFFSET thus empowers developers to construct efficient paginated data retrieval systems.

Practical scenarios often require dynamic query construction where the sort order and row limits can change based on user preferences or application context. For example, an interactive reporting tool might allow a user to choose which column to sort by and how many records to display per page. In such cases, parameterized queries are recommended to secure and dynamically adjust the SQL statements. A Python example demonstrates this dynamic behavior:

```
import sqlite3
```

```
def fetch_employees(sort_column, sort_order, limit, offset):
    connection = sqlite3.connect('example.db')
    cursor = connection.cursor()

    # Construct query using parameters to prevent SQL injection
    query = f"""
SELECT name, department, hire_date
FROM employees
ORDER BY {sort_column} {sort_order}
LIMIT ? OFFSET ?;
"""
    cursor.execute(query, (limit, offset))
    results = cursor.fetchall()

    connection.close()
    return results

# Example usage: sort by hire_date descending, return 10 rows
    starting from the 11th row
employees = fetch_employees("hire_date", "DESC", 10, 10)
for emp in employees:
    print(emp)
```

In this example, dynamic interpolation of column names and sort order is demonstrated carefully. Caution should be exercised to validate such inputs if they form part of the SQL string, especially when user-provided values are involved. Using parameterized queries for the LIMIT and OFFSET values prevents common injection vulnerabilities.

For complex queries involving joins, grouping, or filtering, ordering and limiting results continue to play a fundamental role. When combining multiple operations, the ORDER BY clause should appear after filtering and grouping. Consider a query that retrieves the number of employees in each department, orders the departments by employee count in descending order, and limits the output to the top five departments:

```
SELECT department, COUNT(*) AS num_employees
FROM employees
GROUP BY department
ORDER BY num_employees DESC
LIMIT 5;
```

This query introduces aggregation through GROUP BY and then sorts the aggregated results based on the total count per department. The final output, restricted to five rows, succinctly informs managerial decisions regarding departmental size and resource allocation.

Sometimes it is helpful to review the interplay between sorting, limiting, and the underlying data structures. For instance, if the table contains multiple ordering attributes or if the developer requires a secondary ordering criterion to break ties, additional fields in the ORDER BY clause can resolve ambiguities. An extended example might look like the following:

```
SELECT name, department, salary, hire_date
FROM employees
ORDER BY department ASC, salary DESC, hire_date ASC
LIMIT 15;
```

In this query, the data is primarily sorted by department, then within each department, employees with higher salaries appear first, and finally, among employees with equal salary, the one hired earlier is prioritized. This multi-dimensional ordering supports nuanced data perspectives, particularly in analytical applications.

Another advanced use case involves integration with window functions to produce ranked results. While window functions extend beyond simple sorting, they enable refined control over ordered sets. For example, ranking employees within each department based on salary can be implemented as follows:

```
SELECT name, department, salary,
       RANK() OVER (PARTITION BY department ORDER BY salary DESC) AS
    rank
FROM employees;
```

While this query does not inherently limit rows, combining it with an outer query that implements LIMIT can focus on top-ranking segments within each partition. Such constructions often appear in advanced reporting and dashboards that require ranking and limiting simultaneously.

In addition to application-level constructs, sorting and limiting are critical for efficient data migration or export tasks. When exporting large datasets, it is often necessary to process data incrementally rather than in one monolithic query. Splitting the data retrieval into manageable chunks using the LIMIT and OFFSET clauses not only prevents memory overuse but also improves network transfer efficiency when handling remote databases.

It is also important to consider the impact of sorting and limiting on query performance. Sorting operations can become resource-intensive, especially if they necessitate a full scan and sort of large datasets. Ensuring that sorting columns are indexed, as noted with the earlier examples, can accelerate these operations. In some cases, evaluating the query performance with and without the ORDER BY clause may be necessary to understand the cost of sorting relative to the application requirements.

The techniques discussed in this section are directly applicable to both read-intensive analytical applications and transactional systems where user responsiveness is paramount. Sorting not only orders the data for better visual comprehension but also acts as a precursor step for join and aggregation operations. Similarly, limiting the result set ensures that applications remain responsive and memory efficient when navigating potentially extensive datasets.

Combining these approaches—ordering the data meaningfully and subsequently limiting it to a manageable size—offers practical benefits. Developers can provide users with paginated and easily navigable data while ensuring that both the application and the database engine operate optimally. As queries evolve to handle more complex scenarios, the principles of sorting and limiting remain constant: they are tools to structure output effectively and drive performance improvements.

Through considered application of `ORDER BY`, `LIMIT`, and `OFFSET`, SQLite users can derive meaningful insights from their data and build applications that scale. Each coding example and conceptual explanation provided here reinforces the value of these SQL constructs in managing result sets. Mastery of these operations paves the way for advanced database querying techniques, ensuring that developers can cater to varied requirements with precision and efficiency.

Chapter 4

Advanced SQL Features in SQLite

This chapter delves into advanced SQL capabilities in SQLite, exploring joins, subqueries, and index usage for optimized performance. It covers triggers, transaction handling, and view implementation for managing complex queries. Additionally, it addresses aggregate functions for data summarization and date and time functions for temporal data management, equipping readers with enhanced skills for sophisticated database operations.

4.1. Understanding Joins and Subqueries

Joins are an essential mechanism for combining data from two or more tables based on related columns, thereby enabling complex queries that filter, transform, and aggregate large datasets. In SQLite, join operations are widely used to retrieve related information spread across

normalized tables. Understanding the proper application and optimization of joins significantly improves the clarity and performance
of SQL queries. The typical join types in SQLite include the inner join,
left outer join, and cross join. While some relational databases provide
additional join types such as right outer join or full outer join, SQLite
primarily supports inner and left joins along with natural join variants.

An inner join returns records that have matching values in both tables.
For example, consider two tables: employees and departments. The
query below retrieves the names of employees along with their department names only if the employee is assigned to a valid department identifier. The SQL command can be illustrated as follows:

```
SELECT e.name, d.department_name
FROM employees e
INNER JOIN departments d
ON e.department_id = d.id;
```

The above query operates by filtering records in which
e.department_id equals d.id.   This type of join ensures that
only employees with an associated department are returned.   In
instances where tables are designed with partial information, the left
outer join is employed. A left outer join returns all records from the
left table (in this instance, employees) and the corresponding records
from the right table if they exist; otherwise, it substitutes NULL values
for columns from the right table. An example is given below:

```
SELECT e.name, d.department_name
FROM employees e
LEFT OUTER JOIN departments d
ON e.department_id = d.id;
```

In this query, every record from employees is included even if the join
condition does not find an associated department in departments. It
is an effective technique for retrieving all employee data even in the
presence of incomplete relationships.

Another join variant, the cross join, produces the Cartesian product of

128

the rows from two tables. The cross join brings together every row from the first table with every row from the second table, which might be useful under certain controlled circumstances. For instance, a cross join might be applied when one needs to evaluate all possible combinations of two datasets:

```
SELECT e.name, d.department_name
FROM employees e
CROSS JOIN departments d;
```

The utility of cross joins lies in generating comprehensive pairings, but caution must be exercised since it can lead to performance issues when dealing with large tables.

Subqueries, also known as nested queries, are instrumental in enhancing data retrieval, especially when a nested result set is needed to filter or compute values used by the outer query. They can be used in various SQL clauses including the WHERE, FROM, and SELECT clauses. One common application is filtering records based on aggregated data computed in a subquery. Consider a scenario where one needs to extract employees whose salaries exceed the departmental average. The following SQL query demonstrates this pattern:

```
SELECT name, salary, department_id
FROM employees
WHERE salary > (
    SELECT AVG(salary)
    FROM employees
    WHERE department_id = employees.department_id
);
```

The subquery here calculates the average salary for the respective department of each employee. Since dependent values from the outer query are referenced inside the subquery, this is an example of a correlated subquery, which is executed once for each row considered in the outer query. Correlated subqueries provide a dynamic filtering mechanism but may impact performance if applied on large datasets; consequently, cautious index planning and query optimization practices are recommended.

Subqueries are equally effective when used within the FROM clause, acting as derived tables. A derived table allows the encapsulation of complex query logic, which can then be reused by the outer query. For example, if we wish to first compute the total sales per department and subsequently filter departments based on sales figures, a derived table is suitable:

```
SELECT department_id, total_sales
FROM (
    SELECT department_id, SUM(sales) AS total_sales
    FROM sales_transactions
    GROUP BY department_id
) AS dept_sales
WHERE total_sales > 100000;
```

This query first aggregates sales data by department, then immediately filters to include only those departments where total sales exceed $100,000. Derived tables enhance readability and modularize query logic, allowing for easier debugging and maintenance.

In addition to filtering, subqueries may serve in the SELECT clause to compute dynamic expressions based on related table data. For instance, consider a requirement to display each employee's name and the count of projects they are assigned to. Instead of performing a join with a grouping, a subquery in the selection list can encapsulate the count logic efficiently:

```
SELECT
    name,
    (SELECT COUNT(*)
     FROM projects p
     WHERE p.employee_id = e.id) AS project_count
FROM employees e;
```

This approach simplifies the query by avoiding additional grouping logic in the outer query and directly embeds subquery results as part of the projection.

Proper use of joins and subqueries can lead to more maintainable code. Joins facilitate the combination of data when relationships are well-known, while subqueries offer the flexibility to compute and filter based on intermediate results. However, the performance impact of subqueries, especially correlated ones, should be monitored. Good practices include evaluating query execution plans and ensuring that proper indexes are in place on columns used for joins and within conditions referenced by subqueries. SQLite's query planner can often optimize natural join queries, yet manual adjustments may be necessary if the performance bottlenecks arise.

Index design plays a critical role in the efficient execution of both join and subquery operations. Updating indexes on columns that are frequently used in join conditions or in the where clauses of subqueries will substantially reduce query execution time. Combining the correct join type with carefully planned subqueries ensures that the database system returns accurate data faster without incurring unnecessary resource overhead. Structured query formulations using clear conditions and proper formatting also improve the readability and debugging of SQL scripts.

Furthermore, the readability of SQL code influences maintainability across a team environment. Aligning join conditions directly next to the involved table references and clearly aligning subqueries with their relative outer query conditions contributes to overall understanding. In more complex scenarios, designers could restructure SQL logic by simplifying subqueries into common table expressions (CTEs) if the SQLite version in use supports these, in order to enhance clarity and manageability while enabling reusability of code segments.

SQLite's flexibility with join and subquery use illustrates the power of the SQL language in solving multifaceted data retrieval problems. Although simple scenarios might involve straightforward joins and subqueries, real-world applications often require nested multiple layers of data aggregation and relationship handling. Developers are encouraged to experiment with various structures and study the query execution output using SQLite performance monitoring tools to choose the most effective approach for their specific application needs.

The analysis and testing of different query formulations can be observed with the help of SQLite's EXPLAIN QUERY PLAN statement. This command offers insight into how our database engine processes join and subquery instructions. For instance, evaluating a query with nested subqueries might be as simple as:

```
EXPLAIN QUERY PLAN
SELECT e.name, e.salary
FROM employees e
WHERE e.salary > (
    SELECT AVG(salary)
    FROM employees
    WHERE department_id = e.department_id
);
```

The output provided by this command elucidates the execution path chosen by SQLite, thereby suggesting opportunities for optimization. Such results can be output as seen in the following sample output:

```
SCAN TABLE employees AS e
CORRELATED SUBQUERY 1
  SEARCH TABLE employees USING INDEX idx_salary ON (department_id=?)
```

The detailed output illustrates how SQLite processes the outer query alongside the correlated subquery. Identifying steps like table scans and index usage signals to the developer areas where further optimization is possible, whether by modifying indexes or simplifying query structure.

Combining these insights establishes a robust understanding of how to retrieve data using joins and subqueries. Efficient discrimination between join types based on relationship cardinality and query purpose, along with optimized subquery usage, results in more efficient data retrieval and manipulation. Such precision in SQL constructs fosters better-managed code and improved performance across applications handling vast amounts of relational data.

The expertise in joins and subqueries directly contributes to the overall strategy of designing resilient and high-performance database queries. Leveraging SQL's intrinsic capabilities aids in constructing queries that not only satisfy business requirements but are also scalable, maintainable, and aligned with rigorous computational principles.

4.2. Working with Indexes

Indexes are critical for optimizing query performance in SQLite, serving as auxiliary data structures that improve the efficiency of data retrieval. An index in SQLite is typically implemented as a B-tree, allowing for fast lookup, insertion, and deletion operations. In this context, correctly applying indexes can reduce query times drastically, particularly in large datasets where scanning entire tables would be computationally expensive. Traditional queries that join multiple tables or work with complex conditions benefit significantly when indexes are applied to key columns.

The process of creating an index on a table is straightforward in SQLite. A common command used for this purpose is shown below:

```
CREATE INDEX idx_employees_department
ON employees(department_id);
```

This command creates an index named `idx_employees_department` on the `department_id` column in the `employees` table. When queries filter or join using this column, SQLite can use the index to quickly locate the matching rows. This capability is particularly beneficial for join operations where the underlying table is large and without an index the database engine would otherwise perform a full table scan.

133

The utility of indexes is not limited to single columns. Composite indexes, which include more than one column, can further enhance query performance when multiple conditions are applied simultaneously. For instance, consider a scenario where queries frequently filter on both department_id and hire_date in the employees table. In such cases, a composite index can be established as follows:

```
CREATE INDEX idx_employees_dept_hiredate
ON employees(department_id, hire_date);
```

A composite index is particularly effective when the first column, here department_id, has high selectivity and is used in many queries. The order in which columns are indexed is significant; the index can efficiently satisfy queries that filter on the leading column(s).

While indexes enhance data retrieval speed, they also introduce trade-offs in terms of write performance and storage requirements. Updating or inserting records in tables with multiple indexes requires the indexes to be updated correspondingly, which might slow down these operations. Therefore, a balanced approach is needed, applying indexes judiciously on columns that are frequently queried. The design of indexes should take into consideration the read to write ratio, as well as the overall schema design.

Uniqueness is another aspect that can be enforced by an index. When data integrity constraints require that column values be unique, a unique index ensures that no duplicate entries are inserted. The following command creates a unique index on the email column in the employees table:

```
CREATE UNIQUE INDEX idx_employees_email
ON employees(email);
```

With this unique index in place, any attempt to insert duplicate email addresses will result in a constraint violation error. This mechanism is similar to defining a primary key but allows for uniqueness enforcement on non-primary key fields as well.

SQLite also supports the creation of partial indexes, which are indexes built on a subset of rows that satisfy a conditional expression. Partial indexes, when supported, are useful for optimizing queries that frequently operate on filtered datasets. For example, if queries often target active employees, a partial index can be defined to include only those records:

```
CREATE INDEX idx_active_employees
ON employees(department_id)
WHERE status = 'active';
```

This index only includes rows where the status column is equal to 'active', reducing its size and potentially improving query performance when the condition is met.

In execution, indexes are used by SQLite's query planner to determine the most efficient way to retrieve data. A well-optimized query plan reduces the number of rows scanned during query execution. For instance, a query that requests employee details based on a specific department_id leverages an index to limit the scanned rows significantly:

```
SELECT name, hire_date
FROM employees
WHERE department_id = 3;
```

Without the index on department_id, SQLite would perform a full scan of the employees table. By using the index, the database engine finds the relevant rows by traversing the B-tree structure, providing a performance improvement that scales with table size.

Furthermore, choosing which columns to index requires an understanding of the underlying data distribution and query patterns. Columns that are frequently used in WHERE clauses, join conditions, or ORDER BY clauses are prime candidates for indexing. Analyzing

135

query performance through tools such as EXPLAIN QUERY PLAN provides insights into how indexes are utilized during execution. For example, the following command outlines the usage plan for a specific query:

```
EXPLAIN QUERY PLAN
SELECT name, email
FROM employees
WHERE department_id = 2;
```

A sample output may look like:

```
SCAN TABLE employees USING INDEX idx_employees_department (department_id=?)
```

This output confirms that the index on department_id is actively used in optimizing the query by reducing the search space.

In more complex queries, especially those involving joins between multiple tables, indexing on foreign keys can significantly reduce response times. Given a scenario where an employees table is joined with a departments table using a foreign key, an index on the foreign key in the employees table facilitates rapid matching of records. Consider the following query:

```
SELECT e.name, d.department_name
FROM employees e
INNER JOIN departments d
ON e.department_id = d.id;
```

Here, having indexes on employees.department_id and departments.id assists SQLite in quickly correlating the rows. Indexes significantly reduce the scanning time, especially if the join involves a large number of records. The decision on which table to index should account for table sizes and the frequency of query conditions.

Analyzing index fragmentation is also essential for maintaining overall database performance. As tables grow and undergo frequent up-

136

dates and deletions, the physical structure of indexes may become suboptimal. SQLite handles fragmentation implicitly, but understanding this concept is critical when migrating or performing maintenance on the database. Rebuilding indexes occasionally or performing a VACUUM operation can help consolidate space and optimize performance in such scenarios.

It is equally important to recognize when an index might not be beneficial. For example, if a table has a small number of rows or if a column has low selectivity (i.e., many rows have the same value), the overhead of maintaining an index might outweigh its performance benefits. In cases of low selectivity, SQLite may bypass the index altogether. Therefore, continuous monitoring of query performance and periodic review of the indexing strategy are recommended.

A critical aspect of index management in SQLite is understanding that the database engine optimizes query execution based on the available indexes and data distribution. Adjustments to indexing strategy should be based on empirical evidence gathered from query profiling. Developers working on performance tuning often update or remove indexes to fine-tune performance. When applying such modifications, it is advisable to use a test environment to evaluate the impact on query performance before applying them to production databases.

Indexes are also beneficial in scenarios involving range queries, where conditions such as BETWEEN or inequality operators are used. Consider a query that retrieves all employees hired between two specific dates:

```
SELECT name, hire_date
FROM employees
WHERE hire_date BETWEEN '2020-01-01' AND '2021-01-01';
```

An index on the hire_date column allows SQLite to perform an efficient range scan, reducing the need to inspect every row in the table. As data expands over time, such optimizations become increasingly significant.

Designing an effective indexing strategy requires evaluating the cost-benefit ratio for each index. The benefits gained in query performance must be balanced against the overhead incurred during data modifications. Maintaining indexes may impose additional storage requirements and could slow down write operations. Consequently, indexes should be designed with an awareness of the typical workload, ensuring that they support frequent data access patterns without severely impacting update performance.

The insights on index creation and utilization interconnect with previously discussed SQL features such as joins and subqueries. When these feature-rich queries are executed, the presence of well-constructed indexes ensures that the database engine can quickly filter and join data, even in complex query plans. By strategically placing indexes on the most queried columns and periodically reassessing their effectiveness, developers can achieve significant performance improvements, necessary for building scalable and efficient SQLite applications.

This approach to indexing in SQLite reflects a principled balance between theoretical benefits and practical considerations in database design. The effective use of indexes underpins the performance of advanced SQL operations and reinforces the importance of a measured approach to database optimization.

4.3. Using SQLite Triggers

Triggers in SQLite provide a mechanism to automatically execute predefined SQL code in response to certain events affecting the database. These events typically include INSERT, UPDATE, and DELETE operations. Triggers are particularly useful in enforcing business rules, maintaining audit trails, and propagating changes across related tables. By embedding complex logic into triggers, one can ensure data integrity and consistency without rewriting the application logic.

Triggers in SQLite are defined relative to a single table and are activated either before or after the execution of the triggering event. The two primary types of triggers are BEFORE triggers and AFTER triggers. BEFORE triggers run the specified SQL code prior to the event execution, allowing for changes to be made or validations to be performed that may influence the operation. In contrast, AFTER triggers execute following the successful completion of the triggering event, ensuring that any auxiliary actions, such as logging or updating an audit table, are applied only after the original transactional change.

SQLite also supports INSTEAD OF triggers, which are particularly used in conjunction with views. These triggers allow developers to substitute trigger logic in place of standard operations on a view, effectively transforming the view into an updatable virtual table. This flexibility is especially beneficial when dealing with complex business logic that cannot be readily expressed in a standard view configuration.

A common use case for triggers is maintaining an audit log. Consider a scenario where an audit table records all changes made to a primary table. Creating an AFTER INSERT trigger on that primary table automatically captures all new insertions and writes the corresponding details into an audit table. This capability ensures that critical changes are recorded without the need for manual logging in application code.

```
CREATE TABLE employee_audit (
    audit_id INTEGER PRIMARY KEY,
    employee_id INTEGER,
    action TEXT,
    action_time DATETIME DEFAULT CURRENT_TIMESTAMP
);

CREATE TRIGGER trg_employee_insert_audit
AFTER INSERT ON employees
BEGIN
    INSERT INTO employee_audit (employee_id, action)
    VALUES (NEW.id, 'INSERT');
END;
```

In the example above, the trigger `trg_employee_insert_audit` is designed to monitor the `employees` table for new insertions. The keyword `NEW` provides access to the new row being inserted, and the trigger inserts a corresponding record into the `employee_audit` table. This ensures that every modification is traceable in an automated manner, reinforcing the integrity of the change history.

Triggers can also be used to enforce business logic by validating or modifying data before it is committed. A `BEFORE UPDATE` trigger, for example, can be used to verify that updates meet certain criteria. Suppose there is a business rule that prohibits salary reductions for employees, or requires a particular validation check on data before updating a record. A trigger can intercept the update operation to enforce this constraint.

```
CREATE TRIGGER trg_employee_update_salary
BEFORE UPDATE OF salary ON employees
BEGIN
    SELECT CASE
        WHEN NEW.salary < OLD.salary THEN
            RAISE(ABORT, 'Salary reduction is not permitted')
    END;
END;
```

This trigger, `trg_employee_update_salary`, examines any update operation affecting the `salary` column. The use of `OLD` and `NEW` pseudotables enables the trigger to compare the existing salary with the new proposed salary. By issuing a `RAISE(ABORT,…)` statement, the trigger cancels the update if the new salary is lower than the old one, thus enforcing a business rule that protects employee salaries from decrease.

Triggers can also be employed to perform more complex data synchronization between tables. Consider a scenario where the deletion of a record in a parent table necessitates a corresponding deletion in a child table to maintain referential integrity. Although SQLite supports foreign key constraints, there are cases where custom logic is required to perform supplementary actions beyond standard cascading deletes. In such circumstances, a BEFORE DELETE trigger can be used on the parent table to proactively remove dependent data or update related records.

```
CREATE TRIGGER trg_employee_delete_cleanup
BEFORE DELETE ON employees
BEGIN
    DELETE FROM employee_projects
    WHERE employee_id = OLD.id;
END;
```

In this snippet, the trigger trg_employee_delete_cleanup is activated before a record is deleted from the employees table. It ensures that all associated records in the employee_projects table are also removed, maintaining consistency across related datasets. The automatic cleanup action simplifies the application logic and minimizes the risk of orphaned data.

Triggers offer the potential to modify data during insertions or updates. This functionality is commonly utilized to calculate and store derived values. For instance, one might create a trigger that automatically updates a timestamp column each time a record is modified. This eliminates the need for the application layer to manage such updates and guarantees that the timestamp is updated accurately in all scenarios.

```
CREATE TRIGGER trg_employee_update_timestamp
AFTER UPDATE ON employees
BEGIN
    UPDATE employees
    SET last_modified = CURRENT_TIMESTAMP
    WHERE id = NEW.id;
END;
```

In this example, the trigger trg_employee_update_timestamp updates the last_modified column to the current timestamp after any update on the employees table. Although this trigger resubmits an update on the same record, it demonstrates how triggers can automate repetitive tasks, ensuring that data remains current without explicit intervention.

There are considerations and caveats associated with using triggers in

SQLite. Because triggers execute as part of the transaction that invoked them, their failure or delay can impact the overall transaction performance. Developers should design trigger logic to be as efficient as possible, avoiding complex operations that may lead to long execution times or blocking of transactions. Additionally, debugging triggers can be challenging because the errors they generate are sometimes less descriptive than those produced by application-level code. It is therefore advisable to keep trigger logic simple and maintain comprehensive logging mechanisms.

Another important aspect is the order of execution when multiple triggers are defined on the same table. SQLite supports multiple triggers per event, but the order in which they fire is not guaranteed unless explicitly managed. This scenario necessitates careful design to ensure that interdependent triggers do not interfere with each other. Testing and simulation of real-world use cases are essential steps in verifying that triggers perform as intended.

Security concerns also arise when relying on triggers. Since triggers can modify data automatically, they potentially introduce vulnerabilities if not properly controlled. It is critical to thoroughly review the logic within triggers to prevent unintended data modifications or the circumvention of business rules. Secure design practices include limiting the privileges of users who can create or modify triggers and applying rigorous testing to validate their behavior.

The interplay between triggers and indexes further emphasizes the importance of designing a comprehensive database architecture. When triggers are used to enforce constraints or perform cascading actions, the performance of these operations may benefit from well-placed indexes on the affected columns. For example, an index on the foreign key columns involved in a deletion trigger can facilitate rapid access to the dependent records that require cleanup. This synergy between triggers and indexes contributes to overall query and transaction efficiency.

Advanced applications of triggers include the use of INSTEAD OF triggers, which effectively convert non-updatable views into updatable entities. An INSTEAD OF trigger intercepts the standard operation on a view and replaces it with custom logic that maps the operation onto underlying base tables. This approach is useful when creating complex data representations that require the simplicity of views while retaining the ability to modify data.

```
CREATE VIEW view_employee_details AS
SELECT e.id, e.name, d.department_name
FROM employees e
JOIN departments d ON e.department_id = d.id;

CREATE TRIGGER trg_view_employee_update
INSTEAD OF UPDATE ON view_employee_details
BEGIN
    UPDATE employees
    SET name = NEW.name,
        department_id = (
            SELECT id FROM departments
            WHERE department_name = NEW.department_name
        )
    WHERE id = OLD.id;
END;
```

The trigger trg_view_employee_update demonstrates how an INSTEAD OF trigger can facilitate updates through a view by translating the update operation into commands on the underlying tables. This encapsulation of update logic within the trigger simplifies the interface presented to the application while ensuring that complex underlying relationships are maintained correctly.

Triggers, when utilized judiciously, offer significant benefits in terms of automation, data integrity, and abstraction. Proper implementation of triggers requires a clear understanding of the order and timing of execution, the proper use of NEW and OLD references, and awareness of performance implications. Testing trigger behavior in controlled environments is essential to ensure that they not only meet functional requirements but also exhibit acceptable performance under production loads.

The integration of triggers with other SQL features such as joins, subqueries, and indexes illustrates the holistic approach required in designing robust database applications. By leveraging triggers to enforce business rules, automate data logging, or synchronize related tables, developers can create systems that are both efficient and reliable. Continuous assessment of trigger performance and security, combined with best practices in schema design and query optimization, forms the cornerstone of effective trigger utilization in SQLite.

4.4. Handling Transactions

Transaction management is a critical aspect of database systems, ensuring that operations either complete fully or leave the database in its prior consistent state. In SQLite, transactions provide a mechanism to group multiple SQL statements into a single unit of work such that either all modifications are applied, or none are. This atomicity guarantees that intermediate states do not affect data integrity, thereby safeguarding against corruption when errors occur or when multi-step operations execute concurrently.

The primary commands used to manage transactions in SQLite are BEGIN, COMMIT, and ROLLBACK. The BEGIN command marks the start of a transaction, while COMMIT confirms the execution of all operations, permanently saving changes. In contrast, ROLLBACK aborts the transaction, reverting the database to its state before the transaction commenced. These commands ensure that each transaction adheres to the ACID (Atomicity, Consistency, Isolation, Durability) properties.

A simple transaction sequence in SQLite is demonstrated by the follow-

144

ing example:

```
BEGIN TRANSACTION;
INSERT INTO employees (name, department_id, salary)
VALUES ('Alice Smith', 2, 75000);
UPDATE departments SET employee_count = employee_count + 1
WHERE id = 2;
COMMIT;
```

In this example, both the INSERT and UPDATE statements are encapsulated within a transaction. If both statements execute successfully, the COMMIT command finalizes the changes. Should an error arise at any point during these operations, executing a ROLLBACK ensures that none of the changes are applied, thereby preserving data integrity.

Transactions become especially useful in multi-step operations that depend on each other. For instance, in banking applications, transferring funds between accounts involves debiting one account and crediting another. A failure in any step would necessitate not only reverting the successful operation but also preventing inconsistent account balances that could result from a partial update. Consider the following SQL snippet for a fund transfer:

```
BEGIN TRANSACTION;

UPDATE accounts
SET balance = balance - 100
WHERE account_id = 1;

UPDATE accounts
SET balance = balance + 100
WHERE account_id = 2;

COMMIT;
```

In this scenario, if an error occurs during the debit or credit operation, a ROLLBACK is required to ensure that neither account reflects an inaccurate balance. Implementing such logic in application code involves detecting errors and executing the appropriate rollback command within the transaction block.

145

SQLite supports various modes of transactions, such as IMMEDIATE, EXCLUSIVE, and the default DEFERRED mode. The DEFERRED mode does not acquire locks until the first read or write operation occurs within the transaction. This mode offers flexibility but may be susceptible to race conditions in high-concurrency environments. The IMMEDIATE mode explicitly acquires a reserved lock during the transaction initiation, preventing other transactions from modifying the database until the transaction concludes. Meanwhile, the EXCLUSIVE mode secures an exclusive lock, blocking all other operations until the transaction is finished. Choosing the appropriate mode depends on the application's concurrency requirements and the criticality of maintaining strict isolation.

Error handling within transactions is a significant concern. Transactions should be designed to anticipate potential failures, such as constraint violations or system errors. In automated scripts or application routines, it is common to structure transaction management with exception handling that monitors for errors and issues a ROLLBACK when necessary. The following pseudocode illustrates how such handling might be approached in an application:

```
BEGIN TRANSACTION;
-- Execute series of SQL commands
IF error_occurs THEN
    ROLLBACK;
ELSE
    COMMIT;
END IF;
```

This logic ensures that any anomalous execution is handled gracefully, preventing partial updates that could jeopardize data consistency. Although SQLite does not support structured exception handling within its SQL language, application-level code written in languages like Python or C can incorporate exception handling constructs around SQL execution statements.

In Python, transaction management is often handled using the `sqlite3` module. The module provides a context manager that automatically commits a transaction if the block executes successfully or rolls back if an exception is raised. An illustrative code example is presented below:

```
import sqlite3

connection = sqlite3.connect('company.db')
try:
    with connection:
        connection.execute(
            "INSERT INTO employees (name, department_id, salary)
        VALUES (?, ?, ?)",
                ('Bob Johnson', 3, 68000)
        )
        connection.execute(
            "UPDATE departments SET employee_count = employee_count +
        1 WHERE id = ?",
                (3,)
        )
except sqlite3.DatabaseError as error:
    print("An error occurred:", error)
finally:
    connection.close()
```

In this Python snippet, the context manager provided by `with connection:` ensures that transactions are managed automatically. If an exception occurs, the context manager commits a rollback, and if not, the transaction is committed. This automation greatly simplifies the handling of transactions in Python applications.

Transaction isolation is another critical concept. SQLite defaults to the `SERIALIZABLE` isolation level, which prevents other transactions from seeing intermediate states until the transaction is completed. This level of isolation is essential for preventing phenomena such as dirty reads and non-repeatable reads in concurrent environments. However, developers might need to design specific strategies when interfacing with external systems or when scalability demands a trade-off between strict isolation and performance.

The durability aspect of transactions guarantees that once a transaction is committed, its effects persist even in the event of a system crash. SQLite achieves durability by writing to a log file and employing a rollback journal to maintain the integrity of ongoing transactions. In the event of a system failure, SQLite uses these files to restore the state of the database accurately. Modern file systems and hardware improvements generally minimize the likelihood of such failures, but understanding these mechanisms is vital for designing resilient systems.

For scenarios where long-running transactions are necessary, developers must be cautious to avoid locking issues or performance bottlenecks. Long transactions can hold locks that prevent concurrent reads or writes, thereby affecting the overall system responsiveness. Breaking complex operations into smaller, well-defined transactions can alleviate these issues. Additionally, designing applications to reduce transaction duration aligns with best practices for concurrent database operations.

Moreover, the interplay between transactions and other advanced database features, such as triggers and indexes, underscores the importance of viewing a database system holistically. For instance, triggers that execute as part of a transaction inherit the transaction's properties. If an error occurs in the trigger execution, the entire transaction will be rolled back. This behavior enforces a consistent operational model, whereby automated business rules implemented through triggers do not compromise the transactional integrity of data modifications.

Performance considerations must also be taken into account when managing transactions. Although transactions enhance the reliability and integrity of data, they can also introduce overhead. Batch processing and consolidation of multiple modifications into a single transaction can help in optimizing performance, as repeated transactions might not be as efficient as processing several operations together. In environments with high transaction throughput, balancing the load and minimizing lock contention become paramount.

Database maintenance tasks, such as bulk data imports or schema migrations, benefit significantly from careful transaction management. Performing these tasks outside of transaction blocks may lead to partial updates and inconsistent states if errors occur. Encapsulating such tasks within a transaction ensures that either all modifications are applied or the database remains unchanged. An example of a bulk operation within a transaction is as follows:

```
BEGIN TRANSACTION;
-- Bulk insert operations
INSERT INTO employees (name, department_id, salary) VALUES ('Carol
    White', 1, 82000);
INSERT INTO employees (name, department_id, salary) VALUES ('David
    Green', 1, 79000);
-- More operations can be added here
COMMIT;
```

This encapsulation provides a safety net so that any error during the bulk import will negate any partial changes, thereby preserving the database's overall consistency.

Advanced users might leverage savepoints, a feature that allows for more granular control within a transaction. Savepoints enable subtransactions by marking specific points in the transaction that can be rolled back independently of the entire transaction. This functionality can be useful when part of a larger transaction requires error correction without discarding all prior successful operations. An example utilizing savepoints in SQLite is shown below:

```
BEGIN TRANSACTION;

-- Operation 1
INSERT INTO orders (customer_id, order_total) VALUES (101, 500);
SAVEPOINT sp_order;

-- Operation 2, which might fail
UPDATE inventory SET quantity = quantity - 5 WHERE product_id = 20;

-- Conditional logic or error check here
```

```
-- In case of failure for Operation 2
ROLLBACK TO sp_order;

-- Continue with additional operations if needed
COMMIT;
```

The use of SAVEPOINT and ROLLBACK TO empowers developers to man-age partial rollbacks and finely control their transaction workflows. This granularity is particularly beneficial during complex operations where some steps can tolerate failure while others cannot.

Transaction management in SQLite is designed to maintain the in-tegrity and consistency of data under diverse operational scenarios, from routine updates to high-stake financial transfers. The ability to effectively group commands and handle errors through COMMIT and ROLLBACK ensures that developers can rely on the database to return to a known good state in the event of any failure. Continuous testing and performance profiling are recommended to fine-tune transaction han-dling and ensure that database operations adhere to both functional requirements and performance benchmarks.

4.5. Utilizing Views for Complex Queries

Views in SQLite allow developers to encapsulate complex queries within a virtual table, simplifying the process of data retrieval without duplicating data. A view is essentially a stored query that can be treated as a table in subsequent SQL statements. This abstraction enhances readability and maintainability by isolating intricate SQL logic while promoting code reusability and modular design. Views are particularly effective when queries involve multiple joins, subqueries, or aggregation computations that are reused across different parts of an application.

The creation of a view in SQLite is achieved using the CREATE VIEW statement. For instance, consider a scenario where information from several tables such as employees, departments, and projects must be combined to present a consolidated snapshot of employee details along with their departmental and project information. Instead of embedding this complex join logic in every query, one can define a view that encapsulates the relationships and derived data:

```
CREATE VIEW view_employee_details AS
SELECT
    e.id,
    e.name,
    e.salary,
    d.department_name,
    p.project_count
FROM
    employees e
JOIN
    departments d ON e.department_id = d.id
LEFT JOIN
    (SELECT employee_id, COUNT(*) AS project_count
    FROM projects
    GROUP BY employee_id) p ON e.id = p.employee_id;
```

In this example, the view view_employee_details aggregates data from three sources. The inner query within the left join calculates the number of projects per employee, while the main query combines employee details with their corresponding department names. By consolidating these operations into a view, subsequent queries can be simplified. Instead of rewriting the entire join query, a simple SELECT statement from the view suffices.

Utilizing views can also provide an abstraction layer for sensitive or complex data structures. By enabling the filtering of columns and rows, views can serve as a security mechanism to restrict direct access to underlying base tables. For example, if only non-sensitive employee details should be exposed to certain users, a view can be designed to include only the necessary columns:

```
CREATE VIEW view_public_employee AS
SELECT
```

151

```
    name,
    department_id,
    hire_date
FROM
    employees;
```

This view omits sensitive fields such as salary or personal identifiers, thereby enforcing access control through SQL. In scenarios where business rules necessitate dynamic data transformation, views allow for the presentation of computed columns such as formatted dates or derived metrics, contributing to clearer reporting interfaces.

Regarding performance considerations, views in SQLite do not store data physically unless they are materialized, which SQLite does not support natively. Instead, views are computed on demand, meaning that their performance depends on the efficiency of the underlying query. Although views enhance code modularity, it is essential to design the underlying query to be efficient, utilizing indexes and optimized joins where applicable. In the earlier examples, the use of indexes on employees.department_id or projects.employee_id would ensure that the view executes efficiently, especially when the dataset is large.

Expanding on the use of views, consider the requirement to aggregate data in a reporting scenario where monthly sales figures need to be summarized by region. Instead of repeatedly writing the aggregation query, a view can encapsulate the logic to compute totals and averages:

```
CREATE VIEW view_monthly_sales AS
SELECT
    region,
    strftime('%Y-%m', sale_date) AS month,
    SUM(sale_amount) AS total_sales,
    AVG(sale_amount) AS average_sales
FROM
    sales
GROUP BY
    region, month;
```

With this view, any query that requires monthly sales summaries can directly reference `view_monthly_sales`. This not only reduces code redundancy but also minimizes errors that may result from inconsistent aggregation mechanisms across different queries. Furthermore, if the aggregation logic needs to be adjusted, for example, by incorporating additional filters or metrics, the view definition can be updated in one place, ensuring consistency across all dependent queries.

A further benefit of views is the simplification of complex subqueries. When a query involves several nested subqueries, debugging and optimization can become challenging. Encapsulating the nested logic in a view enables developers to treat the subquery as a reusable table, easily integrating it with additional conditions. For example, consider a case where data from an audit log is combined with current records to generate a historical view of employee salary changes. Rather than embedding the subqueries directly into the main query, a view can represent the historical computation:

```
CREATE VIEW view_salary_history AS
SELECT
    e.id,
    e.name,
    a.old_salary,
    a.new_salary,
    a.change_date
FROM
    employees e
JOIN
    salary_audit a ON e.id = a.employee_id;
```

This view neatly encapsulates the history of salary changes for employees, allowing for subsequent queries to focus on reporting or further analysis without the complexity of joining multiple audit and current data sources every time.

Another advantage provided by views is abstraction from complex business rules. In environments where the structure of the database may change, views can remain consistent while the underlying tables evolve.

153

This layer of abstraction protects application code from being affected by schema changes. For instance, if a new requirement emerges to split the employees table into multiple tables for different employee categories, a view can merge these splits into a single unified interface. As long as the view is updated accordingly, the end users and application queries experience a seamless transition.

Views also facilitate the implementation of logical data models wherein physical storage is distributed among several tables. A logical view can present a unified picture of the data without exposing the physical data layout. This is particularly useful when dealing with normalized databases where data is segmented to eliminate redundancy. The view combines related pieces of information into one composite dataset, offering a simplified interface for client applications. Consolidation of related information through views contributes to easier debugging and maintenance by centralizing changes in view definitions rather than altering multiple application queries.

Despite the benefits, developers should exercise caution when using views. Since views are evaluated every time they are accessed, complex views can lead to performance bottlenecks if not carefully constructed. As with all queries, appropriate indexing and query planning are necessary. The EXPLAIN QUERY PLAN statement can be employed to investigate the underlying execution plan of a view and to identify performance issues. Testing the performance impact of views, especially when they involve multiple joins and aggregation functions, is crucial to ensure that they do not become a hindrance in high-traffic environments.

Another potential consideration with views is the handling of updates. Although views simplify read operations, modifying data through views can be challenging due to limitations on the types of views that are updatable. SQLite supports INSTEAD OF triggers on views to enable updates on non-materialized views. Such triggers can translate

insert, update, or delete operations on the view into corresponding
operations on the base tables. For example, to update a view that
combines employee details from several tables, an INSTEAD OF trigger
can be defined:

```
CREATE TRIGGER trg_view_employee_update
INSTEAD OF UPDATE ON view_employee_details
BEGIN
    UPDATE employees
    SET name = NEW.name,
        salary = NEW.salary
    WHERE id = OLD.id;

    UPDATE departments
    SET department_name = NEW.department_name
    WHERE id = (SELECT department_id FROM employees WHERE id = OLD.id
    );
END;
```

This trigger intercepts update operations on view_employee_details
and translates them into the necessary modifications on the underlying
tables. Though enabling views to be updatable can add complexity, it
increases the flexibility of using views in applications that require both
read and write operations.

Overall, the strategic use of views in complex queries aids in managing
large codebases, allows for centralized modification of logic, and significantly enhances data security through the abstraction of sensitive data.
The balance between view abstraction and direct table access should
be considered based on the application requirements, the complexity
of query logic, and the performance characteristics of the workload.

Designing effective views often involves an iterative approach. Developers should begin by identifying recurring query patterns and then
refactor these patterns into view definitions. Reusable views not only
reduce the risk of errors but also promote a more organized, modular
approach to data retrieval. Constant review and refactoring of view
definitions as business requirements evolve will ensure that views con-

tinue to serve their intended purpose in simplifying the interactions with complex underlying data.

Developers are encouraged to leverage views as a means of promoting code clarity and reducing technical debt. With views, changes in business logic or data structure can be managed centrally through view maintenance, rather than being propagated across multiple application queries. This strategy aligns well with the broader principles of database normalization and modular programming, contributing to robust, scalable database applications.

The utilization of views for complex queries exemplifies a powerful tool in the SQLite developer's toolkit. Careful construction of views, combined with sound performance practices and secure design, can lead to significant improvements in both the maintainability and efficiency of database systems.

4.6. Implementing Aggregate Functions

Aggregate functions are essential tools in SQL that enable the summarization of extensive datasets into concise, meaningful results. In SQLite, functions such as COUNT, SUM, and AVG compile numerical and statistical summaries from multiple rows into a single representative value. These functions underpin a wide range of analytical queries, facilitating the transformation of detailed transactional data into usable metrics for reporting and decision-making.

The COUNT function is primarily used to determine the number of rows that satisfy given conditions or, when combined with a specified column, to count the number of non-null values. For instance, counting the number of employees in a particular department can be performed with a query like:

```
SELECT COUNT(*) AS total_employees
```

```
FROM employees
WHERE department_id = 3;
```

This query returns the total number of records in the `employees` table where `department_id` equals 3. When applied to a specific column, such as counting employees with a non-null email address, the function is invoked as:

```
SELECT COUNT(email) AS employees_with_email
FROM employees;
```

The `SUM` function aggregates numeric values by computing their total. This is particularly useful in financial calculations, inventory management, or any scenario where cumulative totals provide insights into operational performance. For example, calculating the total sales for a particular product category can be accomplished with:

```
SELECT SUM(sale_amount) AS total_sales
FROM sales
WHERE product_category = 'Electronics';
```

This statement sums all the values in the `sale_amount` column for records that meet the condition specified in the `WHERE` clause. When dealing with datasets containing multiple groups, the aggregation is typically combined with the `GROUP BY` clause. An illustrative example is grouping total sales by region:

```
SELECT region, SUM(sale_amount) AS regional_sales
FROM sales
GROUP BY region;
```

The `AVG` function calculates the arithmetic mean of numeric values. Average computations are common in performance analysis, resource utilization studies, and quality control. An example query that calculates the average salary of employees within each department demonstrates the combined use of aggregate functions with grouping:

```
SELECT department_id, AVG(salary) AS average_salary
FROM employees
```

```
GROUP BY department_id;
```

This query computes the average salary for every distinct department_id present in the employees table.

It is important to distinguish between aggregate functions and regular functions. While regular functions operate on individual rows, aggregate functions compute values over a set of rows. Their effectiveness is enhanced when used in conjunction with the GROUP BY clause, which partitions the dataset into subgroups for independent analysis. In cases where aggregation across the entire dataset is required, omitting GROUP BY results in a single set of results summarizing the entire dataset.

Another element to consider is the use of the HAVING clause, which serves as a filter for groups created by the GROUP BY clause. Unlike the WHERE clause that filters individual rows before the aggregation, the HAVING clause filters groups after they have been aggregated. For example, to list departments with an average salary exceeding a certain threshold, the query might be written as:

```
SELECT department_id, AVG(salary) AS average_salary
FROM employees
GROUP BY department_id
HAVING AVG(salary) > 50000;
```

This query ensures that only those groups where the calculated average salary is above 50,000 are returned. Utilization of HAVING enhances query precision by allowing conditions to be imposed on aggregated data.

In analyzing execution plans for aggregate queries, it is advisable to employ the EXPLAIN QUERY PLAN command. This reveals how SQLite's query planner optimizes queries involving aggregates, thereby enabling refinement of indexing strategies. For instance, given a query aggregating sales data by region, an examination of the query plan can

158

highlight whether an index on the `region` column would be beneficial. An example command is:

```
EXPLAIN QUERY PLAN
SELECT region, SUM(sale_amount) AS regional_sales
FROM sales
GROUP BY region;
```

The output, which may display steps such as a full table scan or index usage, assists in identifying performance bottlenecks. Adjustments to indexing based on these insights can make aggregate queries more efficient, particularly as the underlying tables expand in size.

Aggregate functions are frequently incorporated into views, offering a layer of abstraction that simplifies complex reporting queries. By encapsulating an aggregate query within a view, subsequent queries can reference the summarized data directly. For example, creating a view for monthly sales offers a modular approach:

```
CREATE VIEW view_monthly_sales AS
SELECT strftime('%Y-%m', sale_date) AS month,
       SUM(sale_amount) AS total_sales,
       AVG(sale_amount) AS average_sales,
       COUNT(*) AS sale_count
FROM sales
GROUP BY month;
```

Such a view aggregates sales data on a monthly basis, presenting totals, averages, and counts. Subsequent queries that need to analyze monthly sales patterns can simply select from `view_monthly_sales`, ensuring uniformity and ease of maintenance across the application code.

In instances where aggregate functions are nested within subqueries, careful structuring is required to prevent ambiguity and ensure optimal performance. For example, integrating an aggregate function into a subquery to compare individual records against aggregate statistics from the entire dataset can be achieved as follows:

```
SELECT employee_id, salary
```

```
FROM employees
WHERE salary > (
    SELECT AVG(salary)
    FROM employees
);
```

This query selects employees whose salary exceeds the average salary computed from the entire employees table. The subquery calculates the overall average, which is then used in a conditional expression in the outer query. Combining subqueries with aggregates can extend the analytical capabilities of SQL, although attention must be paid to the potential performance implications of correlated subqueries.

In practice, aggregate functions are also vital when generating statistical metrics such as variance, standard deviation, and percentiles. Although SQLite does not provide direct built-in functions for all these statistical measures, user-defined functions or additional calculations in the application layer can employ aggregates to compute these metrics. For example, to compute variance using aggregate expressions, one approach might be to first calculate the average and then derive the sum of squared differences. Such calculations rely heavily on the basic aggregate functions discussed.

Throughout implementations, the optimization of aggregate queries remains a critical consideration. Large datasets may yield significant performance delays if aggregate functions operate on unindexed columns or incomplete query plans. Regular review of the database schema, refinement of GROUP BY conditions, and strategic use of indexes on grouping columns are necessary to maintain efficiency. Utilizing the query planner to understand the paths taken during execution can provide insights into potential improvements.

Employing aggregate functions in operational databases requires attention to data integrity and consistency. When data volumes are high, parallel processing may be warranted, and the design of transactions should ensure that aggregate results remain accurate, even in concurrent access scenarios. The interplay between aggregate functions and transaction management further emphasizes the importance of a well-structured schema and sound query design. Adaptive strategies, including the temporary storage of intermediate results or the use of materialized views in other systems, can bolster performance in scenarios that involve heavy aggregation.

The utilization of aggregate functions in SQLite provides a robust framework for data summarization. Through the careful formulation of queries, appropriate use of GROUP BY and HAVING clauses, and integration with views and subqueries, developers can derive precise and efficient summaries from complex datasets. The consistent use of aggregates in both transactional and reporting contexts underscores their central role in maintaining clarity and precision within database operations.

4.7. Working with Date and Time Functions

SQLite provides a rich set of built-in functions for working with date and time values, enabling developers to manage, convert, and manipulate temporal data effectively. These functions are essential for applications that record events, perform scheduling, generate time-based reports, or require any form of historical or future data analysis. SQLite does not enforce a specific date and time data type; instead, it relies on well-known text representations to store temporal data. The focus is primarily on flexibility and simplicity, allowing dates and times to be stored and manipulated as text in the ISO-8601 format, as Julian days, or as Unix Time stamps.

The primary functions available for date and time manipulation in SQLite include date(), time(), datetime(), julianday(), and strftime(). Each function serves a specific purpose while offering

161

modifiable parameters to adjust the resulting value. These functions can be used standalone or combined with arithmetic modifiers that add or subtract days, months, or years from a given date.

For example, the date() function extracts the date component from a given time value. The expression date('now') returns the current date in the format YYYY-MM-DD. A basic query leveraging this function might look as follows:

```
SELECT date('now') AS current_date;
```

This query retrieves the current system date. Modifiers can be appended to specify an alternative date. For instance, adding '+1 day' computes tomorrow's date:

```
SELECT date('now', '+1 day') AS tomorrow_date;
```

The time() function focuses on extracting the time component. It returns the current time from a given input, facilitating time-only calculations. A simple usage is illustrated by:

```
SELECT time('now') AS current_time;
```

The datetime() function returns a combined date and time value in the standard ISO-8601 format, YYYY-MM-DD HH:MM:SS. It is particularly useful when a complete timestamp is required. For example, the following query retrieves the current date and time:

```
SELECT datetime('now') AS current_timestamp;
```

Using arithmetic modifiers with datetime() enables complex scheduling or deadline computation. For instance, adding an interval of three hours to the current time is achieved as:

```
SELECT datetime('now', '+3 hours') AS time_plus_three;
```

Beyond these functions, the julianday() function computes the Julian day number, which represents the continuous count of days since

162

a defined starting point, usually January 1, 4713 BC. This function is useful when calculating intervals between two dates. For example, subtracting Julian day values can reveal the number of days between events:

```
SELECT julianday('2023-10-15') - julianday('2023-10-01') AS
    day_difference;
```

Another powerful function is strftime(), which offers advanced formatting capabilities for date and time values. By specifying a format string, strftime() can return customized output that follows user-defined patterns. A typical format specifier is '%Y-%m-%d', which formats a date in standard notation. For instance:

```
SELECT strftime('%Y-%m-%d', 'now') AS formatted_date;
```

In addition to standard formatting, strftime() accepts numerous format specifiers such as '%H', '%M', and '%S' to retrieve specific time components. Such precision allows developers to build queries that generate diverse reports, like extracting the hour from a timestamp to analyze peak activity times.

Temporal arithmetic in SQLite is accomplished through the use of modifiers. Common modifiers include '+N days', '+N months', and '+N years', which enable the addition or subtraction of time intervals. For example, to compute a date one month in the future, the query is structured as:

```
SELECT date('now', '+1 month') AS next_month_date;
```

Similarly, subtracting two weeks from the current date involves the modifier '-14 days':

```
SELECT date('now', '-14 days') AS two_weeks_ago;
```

These modifiers can be combined in a single query to perform more complex calculations. For instance, if an application needs to determine the date three months and ten days in the future, it can use:

163

```
SELECT date('now', '+3 months', '+10 days') AS future_date;
```

Working with local versus universal (UTC) time is another critical consideration in many applications. SQLite provides the `'localtime'` modifier to adjust a UTC timestamp to the system's local time zone. This is particularly useful in logging or scheduling functionalities where local time context is essential. For example:

```
SELECT datetime('now', 'localtime') AS local_timestamp;
```

Conversely, storing dates in UTC and converting to local time only when necessary is a common best practice that prevents inconsistencies in distributed systems. SQLite supports this pattern through its optional modifiers.

Date and time functions are also extensively used in filtering and grouping data. Consider a scenario where a table records user logins with a timestamp, and the analyst requires reports on daily activity. A query that groups login events by date could be written as:

```
SELECT date(login_time) AS login_date, COUNT(*) AS total_logins
FROM user_logins
GROUP BY login_date;
```

This query extracts the date component from the `login_time` column, groups the results by date, and counts the number of logins per day. Such grouping is invaluable for generating daily, weekly, or monthly metrics.

Another application involves filtering records based on time intervals. For instance, identifying all records logged within the past seven days can be achieved by comparing date values after applying date modifiers:

```
SELECT *
FROM user_logins
WHERE login_time >= datetime('now', '-7 days');
```

164

This query retrieves all login events from the last week, ensuring that analytical tasks such as monitoring active users or detecting anomalies can be performed efficiently.

Advanced usage of these functions might integrate the computed time differences with other aggregate operations. An example is computing the average time difference between consecutive logins, which can involve a subquery that calculates individual differences using the julianday() function:

```
SELECT AVG(diff) AS average_days_between_logins
FROM (
    SELECT julianday(login_time) - julianday(
        LAG(login_time) OVER (ORDER BY login_time)
    ) AS diff
    FROM user_logins
    WHERE login_time IS NOT NULL
);
```

This query makes use of a window function LAG() to compute the difference between successive logins, then calculates the average difference across all records. Such advanced constructs combine the power of date and time functions with modern SQL features, enabling granular analysis of temporal patterns.

Storing temporal data in SQLite necessitates confidence in the underlying date and time handling functions. Since SQLite accepts dates and times in various formats—ISO-8601 strings, Julian day numbers, or Unix Time—consistent usage of functions like datetime() and strftime() is encouraged to maintain clarity and reduce errors in date manipulation. Converting between these representations when needed allows developers to perform mathematical operations on temporal data while still presenting human-readable formats where appropriate.

Furthermore, understanding the inherent limitations of these functions is crucial. While SQLite provides robust support for date and time

165

operations, it performs arithmetic on textual representations rather than specialized date types. This design choice emphasizes simplicity and portability but requires careful attention when constructing complex queries. For example, ensuring proper indexing of the textual date fields can significantly improve performance when filtering or grouping by date.

Employing these date and time functions in practical applications, developers can automate processes such as generating periodic reports, scheduling application events, and managing historical data. Consistent use of these functions fosters uniformity across queries and simplifies the transition if storage strategies evolve over time. Given the importance of temporal data in most modern applications, leveraging SQLite's comprehensive support for date and time manipulation is a strategic advantage for developers seeking precise, readable, and efficient SQL code.

The capabilities of these functions extend further when integrating business logic that depends on time calculations. Whether determining expiration dates, calculating renewal periods, or managing time-sensitive discounts, SQLite's date and time functions offer the tools necessary for these operations. Ultimately, the practical application of these functions aligns well with the general principles of database design, including the use of indexes, transaction management, and view construction, by providing a reliable foundation for handling dynamic, time-based data reliably and efficiently.

Chapter 5

Integrating SQLite with Python

This chapter outlines the integration of SQLite with Python, detailing how to connect to databases and execute SQL commands within scripts. It includes methods for fetching and displaying query results, handling exceptions, and using context managers for resource management. Techniques for executing parameterized queries and employing SQLite with Pandas for data analysis are also discussed, enhancing Python's capability in database manipulation.

5.1. Connecting to SQLite from Python

Establishing a connection to an SQLite database in Python is a straightforward task made possible by Python's built-in `sqlite3` module, which provides a lightweight disk-based database that doesn't require a separate server process. This module is included as part of the Python standard library, ensuring that no additional installations are necessary. The process of connecting to an SQLite database is essential for any application that requires persistent data storage, rapid prototyping, or a small footprint without the overhead of larger database management systems.

The connection process begins with importing the sqlite3 module. Once imported, a connection object is created using the connect() method, which can take a database filename as its argument. If the specified database file does not exist, SQLite will create it automatically. In this manner, the connection serves the dual purpose of either opening an existing database or initializing a new one. The following code snippet demonstrates this fundamental procedure:

```
import sqlite3

# Establish connection to a new or existing SQLite database file
database_file = "example.db"
connection = sqlite3.connect(database_file)

# Optionally, retrieve a cursor object to execute SQL commands
cursor = connection.cursor()
```

This code creates a file called example.db in the current working directory if it does not already exist. The creation of the connection object is critical because it serves as the gateway through which all subsequent interactions with the database occur. In practical applications, it is advisable to encapsulate this connection process within a function or a context manager to ensure that the connection is properly closed after operations conclude.

The sqlite3.connect() method also accepts additional parameters that enhance the flexibility and functionality of the database interactions. One frequently used parameter is timeout, which sets the duration in seconds that the connection will wait for the database lock to be released if the database is locked by another process. The following example illustrates how to specify a timeout value:

```
connection = sqlite3.connect(database_file, timeout=10)
```

Specifying a timeout is particularly useful in multi-threaded or multi-process environments where concurrent database access may lead to temporary locks. Additionally, the detect_types parameter can be employed to enable extended type detection, which can be useful when storing and retrieving complex data types such as dates and times. This is achieved by setting detect_types=sqlite3.PARSE_DECLTYPES during the connection, enabling the database to correctly interpret declared column types.

```
connection = sqlite3.connect(database_file, detect_types=sqlite3.
    PARSE_DECLTYPES)
```

For scenarios where the database does not require persistence beyond the runtime of the application, an in-memory database can be established by passing the special name ":memory:" as the database file. This method is particularly advantageous for testing purposes, rapid prototyping, or when the overhead of disk I/O should be minimized.

```
connection = sqlite3.connect(":memory:")
```

The reliability and efficiency of SQLite connections are augmented by the inherent transaction management that SQLite employs. When a connection is established, it automatically handles transactions so that every SQL command is executed in a transaction by default. It is important to commit these transactions explicitly using the connection's commit() method, ensuring that all changes are written to the database. Although a commit is implicit during the closing of a connection, manual commits are considered best practice when multiple changes are applied in a sequence, as this helps maintain data integrity. For instance, after executing several SQL commands, one may commit the changes using the following code:

```
# Execute a series of SQL commands
cursor.execute("CREATE TABLE IF NOT EXISTS Users (id INTEGER PRIMARY
```

169

```
    KEY, name TEXT)")
cursor.execute("INSERT INTO Users (name) VALUES ('Alice')")
cursor.execute("INSERT INTO Users (name) VALUES ('Bob')")

# Commit the transaction to persist changes
connection.commit()
```

When developing robust applications, proper handling of errors during the connection process is essential. The sqlite3 module raises specific exceptions that provide detailed diagnostic information. For example, failure to locate a file or lack of write permissions can trigger an sqlite3.OperationalError. By leveraging Python's try-except construct, developers can gracefully handle such exceptions, thereby ensuring that the application can provide clear error messages or undertake remedial actions when necessary. Consider the following approach to error management while establishing a database connection:

```
try:
    connection = sqlite3.connect(database_file)
except sqlite3.OperationalError as error:
    print("OperationalError occurred: ", error)
except Exception as error:
    print("An unexpected error occurred: ", error)
```

In addition to error handling, an important consideration is the use of context managers for managing the database connection lifecycle. Python's with statement provides a concise way of ensuring that the connection is properly closed after completion of tasks, even in the event of an error. A context manager automatically calls the __enter__ and __exit__ methods, which facilitates resource management. An example of using a context manager with SQLite is as follows:

```
with sqlite3.connect(database_file) as connection:
    cursor = connection.cursor()
    # Execute SQL commands within the context
    cursor.execute("CREATE TABLE Sample (id INTEGER, value TEXT)")
    cursor.execute("INSERT INTO Sample (id, value) VALUES (1, 'Test')
    ")
    # No explicit commit is necessary if using the 'with' context, as
      it commits automatically
```

In this code snippet, the connection object automatically commits the transaction upon successful completion of the block and calls `rollback()` if an exception is encountered, provided that `isolation_level` is not set to None. This feature is particularly useful in scenarios where ensuring the consistent state of the database is critical.

Performance considerations also come into play when connecting to an SQLite database. The `sqlite3` module provides methods to fine-tune performance via pragmas, which are special SQLite commands used to modify operational settings of the database connection. For example, executing a pragma command to enable write-ahead logging (WAL) can improve concurrency and performance of the database. The following example demonstrates how to set a pragma via the connection:

```
cursor = connection.cursor()
cursor.execute("PRAGMA journal_mode=WAL;")
```

Write-ahead logging is particularly important in environments where concurrent read and write operations occur frequently. In addition, adjusting cache size and synchronous settings through pragmas can yield better performance in environments with heavy I/O operations. These adjustments, however, must be made with caution since they might affect the balance between performance and data integrity under specific circumstances.

It is essential to appreciate the design philosophy behind SQLite and its integration with Python. SQLite is designed to be embedded within the application, offering a robust and self-contained solution for most lightweight database needs. Its file-based nature implies that the database is portable and can be easily backed up or transferred across systems. This portability, combined with Python's intuitive syntax and extensive standard library, creates a versatile environment for building data-intensive applications with minimal overhead.

171

When establishing a connection, one must consider key factors such as concurrency, disk I/O considerations, and proper transaction management—all of which influence the durability and performance of the application. The built-in capabilities of the `sqlite3` module allow developers to handle these concerns with minimal additional complexity. By following best practices for connection management and incorporating error handling and resource management techniques, developers can create stable and efficient data-driven applications that scale effectively even under varying operational conditions.

The integration of SQLite with Python is further enhanced by the seamless transition between using a persistent database file and an in-memory database. This flexibility allows developers to tailor their environment to the specific needs of development, testing, or production deployments without needing significant changes in codebase structure. The ability to swiftly switch between databases can expedite the development cycle, facilitate automated testing protocols, and aid in performance tuning.

A sound understanding of the connection process lays the groundwork for advanced database operations, such as executing SQL commands, handling query results, and managing complex transactions. The simplicity of the connection process provided by SQLite in Python means that developers can focus on higher-level tasks without needing to manage low-level database operations manually. Emphasizing clear, concise, and effective database connection practices not only fosters robust software design but also minimizes potential errors during database interactions.

By mastering the procedure for connecting to an SQLite database using Python's `sqlite3` module, one lays the foundation for interacting with the database in a consistent and efficient manner. This foundational skill underpins subsequent operations such as command execution, data manipulation, query processing, and advanced database functionalities that are essential for developing comprehensive data-driven applications.

5.2. Executing SQL Commands in Python

After establishing a connection to an SQLite database, the next essential step is executing SQL commands from Python scripts. The `sqlite3` module provides several methods to execute SQL statements, each designed to handle different types of operations and command batches. Central to this operation is the cursor object, which acts as the primary interface to perform SQL queries and to retrieve results.

The cursor object is created directly from a connection instance. Once instantiated, it enables the execution of SQL commands by invoking its `execute()` method. For individual SQL commands such as creating tables, inserting data, updating records, or deleting entries, `execute()` is sufficient. A typical workflow begins with forming the SQL statement as a string and then passing that string to `execute()` for execution. The following example demonstrates creating a table and inserting a record:

```
import sqlite3

connection = sqlite3.connect("example.db")
cursor = connection.cursor()

# Creating a new table in the database
create_table_command = """
CREATE TABLE IF NOT EXISTS Employees (
    id INTEGER PRIMARY KEY,
    name TEXT NOT NULL,
    department TEXT,
    salary REAL
);
"""
cursor.execute(create_table_command)
```

```
# Inserting a single record into the table
insert_command = "INSERT INTO Employees (name, department, salary)
    VALUES ('John Doe', 'Engineering', 75000)"
cursor.execute(insert_command)

connection.commit()
connection.close()
```

In the code above, a multi-line SQL string is employed to create the Employees table. Such multi-line strings, often enclosed in triple quotes, enhance readability and are particularly useful when handling complex SQL syntax. The use of IF NOT EXISTS in the table creation command demonstrates a safe pattern to avoid errors if the table already exists.

For inserting multiple records or performing batch operations, the executemany() method is highly effective. This method accepts a SQL command and an iterable of parameters, executing the command once for each parameter set. This mechanism not only simplifies the process of inserting multiple rows but also optimizes performance by reducing the number of individual calls to the database engine. The following example illustrates how to use executemany():

```
records = [
    ('Alice Johnson', 'HR', 62000),
    ('Bob Smith', 'Finance', 58000),
    ('Charlie Lee', 'Engineering', 80000)
]

insert_command_batch = "INSERT INTO Employees (name, department,
    salary) VALUES (?, ?, ?)"
cursor.executemany(insert_command_batch, records)
connection.commit()
```

The placeholder question marks (?) in the SQL command denote parameterized query markers. This approach is essential for preventing SQL injection attacks, as it separates SQL code from data values. When the command is executed, the sqlite3 engine safely binds the provided values to their respective placeholders.

174

In more complex scenarios, especially when multiple statements need to be executed consecutively, the `executescript()` method provides an efficient solution. This method accepts a string containing multiple SQL statements separated by semicolons and executes them as a single operation. Such scripts are useful for initializing a database schema or executing a series of commands that establish a broader execution context. Consider the following example:

```
script = """
DROP TABLE IF EXISTS Departments;

CREATE TABLE Departments (
    id INTEGER PRIMARY KEY,
    name TEXT NOT NULL
);

INSERT INTO Departments (name) VALUES ('Human Resources');
INSERT INTO Departments (name) VALUES ('Finance');
INSERT INTO Departments (name) VALUES ('Engineering');
"""

cursor.executescript(script)
connection.commit()
```

Using `executescript()` simplifies the execution flow when multiple SQL commands must be run sequentially. Unlike `execute()` or `executemany()`, `executescript()` does not support parameter substitution; therefore, care must be taken to properly sanitize the input if dynamic content is required.

The execution of SQL commands is not limited solely to data manipulation. It is also critical for performing administrative tasks such as setting pragmas, which modify the operational parameters of the SQLite engine. For example, enabling foreign key constraints in SQLite is not automatic and requires explicit activation using a pragma command. This can be done immediately after establishing the connection, as shown below:

```
cursor.execute("PRAGMA foreign_keys = ON;")
```

Pragmas serve as a control mechanism that affects the behavior of the SQLite database. They can adjust configurations related to journaling modes, synchronous settings, cache sizes, and other operational aspects. Understanding how to execute such commands is important for tuning the database's performance and ensuring data integrity during intricate operations.

It is important to consider error detection and handling during the execution of SQL commands. The `sqlite3` module raises exceptions such as `sqlite3.OperationalError` or `sqlite3.IntegrityError` when SQL-related errors occur. Integrating error handling within the execution workflow supports robust application development. A typical error-handling approach wraps the execution commands within a try-except block to catch any exceptions that may be thrown during execution:

```
try:
    cursor.execute("INSERT INTO Employees (name, department, salary)
    VALUES (?, ?, ?)", ('David Green', 'Marketing', 54000))
    connection.commit()
except sqlite3.Error as error:
    print("Failed to execute SQL command:", error)
    connection.rollback()
```

In this code, an exception triggered during the execution of the insert statement calls for a rollback to revert any changes made within the current transaction. Rolling back ensures that the database remains in a consistent state if an error is encountered. This level of error management is critical, especially in applications performing multiple interdependent operations.

Another significant aspect of executing SQL commands from Python is the flexibility offered by parameterized queries. Integrating parameters directly into SQL commands is a best practice as it not only enhances security by preventing SQL injection, but it also simplifies the process of updating query values dynamically. By employing placeholders and passing the corresponding parameters as a tuple, developers can design SQL commands whose behavior is contingent on runtime values:

```
def insert_employee(cursor, name, department, salary):
    query = "INSERT INTO Employees (name, department, salary) VALUES
    (?, ?, ?)"
    cursor.execute(query, (name, department, salary))

insert_employee(cursor, 'Ellen Parker', 'Operations', 67000)
connection.commit()
```

The encapsulation of such operations within a dedicated function such as insert_employee promotes code reusability and improves overall readability. Parameterized queries are especially critical when user-input data is involved, as they mitigate the risk of malicious SQL code being executed.

When retrieving data from the database, executing a SELECT statement is performed in much the same way as data manipulation commands. However, after executing a SELECT query, the cursor can be used to fetch data. Methods such as fetchone(), fetchmany(), and fetchall() provide a comprehensive set of options for retrieving query results:

```
# Execute a query to retrieve all employees with salary above a
    threshold
query = "SELECT * FROM Employees WHERE salary > ?"
cursor.execute(query, (60000, ))
results = cursor.fetchall()

for record in results:
    print(record)
```

In the example above, the cursor is used to retrieve all rows that meet a specific criterion. The fetchall() method returns all matching records as a list of tuples, each representing a row in the database. If the volume of data is large, fetchmany() or fetchone() may be more appropriate to limit memory usage and allow for iterative processing.

Executing SQL commands within Python scripts is further enhanced by the ability to combine multiple operations within a single transaction. Transactions ensure that a set of operations either complete entirely or not at all, preserving the integrity of the data. By default, SQLite runs each command in a transaction, but explicit control over transactions is achieved using `commit()` and `rollback()` commands. Grouping several SQL operations into a transaction block can be performed as shown in the following code snippet:

```
try:
    cursor.execute("UPDATE Employees SET salary = salary * 1.1 WHERE
    department = ?", ('Engineering', ))
    cursor.execute("DELETE FROM Employees WHERE name = ?", ('Bob
    Smith', ))
    connection.commit()
except sqlite3.Error as error:
    connection.rollback()
    print("Transaction failed:", error)
```

This code illustrates how multiple SQL commands can be executed as part of a single transaction. If any command fails, the `rollback()` method reverts all changes made during that transaction, thereby securing the database against partial updates.

A further point of consideration when executing SQL commands is the possibility of adopting an optimized pattern for managing multiple similar operations. When a large number of similar commands must be executed, the performance benefit of using `executemany()` cannot be overstated. This method executes a precompiled SQL command repeatedly for each parameter sequence in the provided iterable. Its usage not only simplifies the code but also leverages internal optimizations to manage database I/O efficiently.

The integration of SQL command execution into Python scripts is expanded by the possibility of generating dynamic SQL. While dynamically generated SQL commands can provide powerful functionality when the query structure is not static, they must be managed with rigorous input sanitization to prevent any inadvertent security vulnerabilities. A combination of Python's string formatting and parameterized queries often yields a flexible yet secure method for dynamic query construction.

Advanced applications may also require the use of conditional and iterative SQL command execution. In these cases, Python's inherent control structures can be used to iterate over datasets and execute specific SQL commands based on runtime conditions. This paradigm is particularly useful when processing large volumes of data or when performing maintenance tasks that conditionally update or delete records.

The methods discussed for executing SQL commands directly from Python scripts illustrate the versatility and efficiency provided by the `sqlite3` module. By leveraging the capabilities of the cursor object and the various execution methods, developers are equipped to handle a wide variety of database operations. Whether performing single command executions, batch processing via `executemany()`, or executing multi-statement scripts with `executescript()`, Python's built-in libraries provide a robust framework for interacting with SQLite databases.

The systematic approach to executing SQL commands described above encourages developers to write clean, maintainable, and secure database access code. By integrating error handling, transaction management, and parameterized queries into the execution process, the development of data-driven applications is significantly streamlined. The seamless execution of SQL commands directly from Python scripts thus serves as a critical component in realizing complex and efficient application designs.

5.3. Fetching and Displaying Query Results

After executing SQL commands to retrieve data from the database, the next key step is to process and present the results. Python's `sqlite3` module provides several methods for fetching query results, allowing developers to access the output in various formats. These methods include `fetchone()`, `fetchmany()`, and `fetchall()`. Each of these methods serves different purposes by providing varying levels of granularity and control over the data retrieval process.

The `fetchone()` method retrieves the next available row from the result set as a tuple. This method is especially useful when only a single record is of interest or when processing results one at a time. Consider the scenario where a query returns several rows but the application processes each record sequentially. The following code demonstrates how to use `fetchone()` effectively:

```
import sqlite3

connection = sqlite3.connect("example.db")
cursor = connection.cursor()

# Execute a query that may return multiple rows
cursor.execute("SELECT id, name, department, salary FROM Employees")
record = cursor.fetchone()

while record is not None:
    print("ID:", record[0], "Name:", record[1], "Department:", record
    [2], "Salary:", record[3])
    record = cursor.fetchone()

connection.close()
```

In the above example, the loop continues until `fetchone()` returns None, indicating no further records are available. This technique is efficient when handling large datasets since it processes one record at a time, reducing memory overhead.

For situations where it is necessary to fetch a specific number of rows at once, the `fetchmany()` method provides flexibility by retrieving a defined number of records. This is particularly useful in paginated displays or systems where rendering the entire result set simultaneously may not be optimal. By passing an integer value to `fetchmany()`, developers can control the batch size of the records. The following example illustrates the usage of `fetchmany()`:

```
connection = sqlite3.connect("example.db")
cursor = connection.cursor()

cursor.execute("SELECT id, name, department, salary FROM Employees")

# Specify the batch size for each fetch
batch_size = 2
batch = cursor.fetchmany(batch_size)

while batch:
    for record in batch:
        print("ID:", record[0], "Name:", record[1], "Department:",
        record[2], "Salary:", record[3])
    batch = cursor.fetchmany(batch_size)

connection.close()
```

This method allows the developer to control memory usage effectively, especially when working with large result sets. By processing records in smaller groups, the application can maintain performance while still providing a user-friendly display of information.

The `fetchall()` method retrieves all rows from the query result at once, returning them as a list of tuples. This approach is advantageous when the entire dataset is needed for further processing or when the total number of records is known to be relatively small. The following example demonstrates how `fetchall()` can be used:

```
connection = sqlite3.connect("example.db")
cursor = connection.cursor()

cursor.execute("SELECT id, name, department, salary FROM Employees")
results = cursor.fetchall()

for record in results:
```

```
    print("ID:", record[0], "Name:", record[1], "Department:", record
        [2], "Salary:", record[3])

connection.close()
```

While `fetchall()` simplifies the code by retrieving all records at once, it is important to consider that this method may lead to high memory consumption if the query returns an extensive number of rows. Therefore, it is best applied when the result set size is manageable.

Once data is fetched, the next aspect to consider is presentation. A readable format is critical when the retrieved data is intended for direct observation by users or for debugging purposes. The simplest method to display data is by printing each tuple in a structured format. Concatenating strings with the tuple elements is one common technique to align output columns. An example using formatted string literals (f-strings) in Python is provided below:

```
connection = sqlite3.connect("example.db")
cursor = connection.cursor()

cursor.execute("SELECT id, name, department, salary FROM Employees")
results = cursor.fetchall()

print("{:<5} {:<20} {:<15} {:<10}".format("ID", "Name", "Department",
        "Salary"))
print("-" * 55)

for record in results:
    print("{:<5} {:<20} {:<15} {:<10.2f}".format(record[0], record
        [1], record[2], record[3]))

connection.close()
```

This code leverages Python's string formatting capabilities to align the data into columns. The use of {:<5}, {:<20}, and similar format specifiers allocates fixed widths to each field, thereby ensuring that the displayed output is neatly arranged. Such formatting methods are particularly useful when exporting results to a console or when generating text-based reports.

In cases where graphical data representation or enhanced user interface elements are desired, additional libraries such as Pandas or PrettyTable may be utilized. However, focusing on built-in capabilities allows for a deeper understanding of the underlying mechanisms. For example, Pandas can convert the list of tuples into a DataFrame, which then provides built-in functions for pretty-printing tables, as illustrated below:

```
import pandas as pd
import sqlite3

connection = sqlite3.connect("example.db")
cursor = connection.cursor()
cursor.execute("SELECT id, name, department, salary FROM Employees")
results = cursor.fetchall()
connection.close()

# Create a DataFrame from the results
df = pd.DataFrame(results, columns=["ID", "Name", "Department", "
    Salary"])
print(df)
```

When using Pandas for data display, almost automatic formatting and alignment of columns is achieved, which greatly benefits the readability of the output. While Pandas is not strictly a built-in library, its use is widespread in Python data operations, and its inclusion here serves to demonstrate the diversity of techniques available for presenting query results.

Another important aspect involves handling empty result sets gracefully. Applications should check whether the result set contains data before attempting to display it. Adding an if-condition can mitigate errors arising from processing empty lists. The following example demonstrates a simple check:

```
connection = sqlite3.connect("example.db")
cursor = connection.cursor()
cursor.execute("SELECT id, name, department, salary FROM Employees
    WHERE salary > ?", (100000,))
results = cursor.fetchall()
```

```
if not results:
    print("No records found matching the criteria.")
else:
    print("{:<5} {:<20} {:<15} {:<10}".format("ID", "Name", "
    Department", "Salary"))
    print("-" * 55)
    for record in results:
        print("{:<5} {:<20} {:<15} {:<10.2f}".format(record[0],
        record[1], record[2], record[3]))

connection.close()
```

In this scenario, a message is printed if the query does not yield any results. This practice enhances the user experience by explicitly indicating the absence of data rather than presenting an empty output.

Error handling remains vital even during the fetching and display of query results. The same try-except constructs applied during SQL command execution can be used to catch and manage fetching errors. For instance, if a query is malformed or if an unexpected data type is encountered during formatting, an error can be captured to prevent the application from terminating abruptly. An approach that integrates error handling is demonstrated below:

```
try:
    connection = sqlite3.connect("example.db")
    cursor = connection.cursor()
    cursor.execute("SELECT id, name, department, salary FROM
    Employees")
    results = cursor.fetchall()

    if results:
        print("{:<5} {:<20} {:<15} {:<10}".format("ID", "Name", "
        Department", "Salary"))
        print("-" * 55)
        for record in results:
            print("{:<5} {:<20} {:<15} {:<10.2f}".format(record[0],
            record[1], record[2], record[3]))
    else:
        print("No records found.")

except sqlite3.Error as error:
    print("An error occurred:", error)
finally:
```

184

```
connection.close()
```

This example encapsulates the fetching logic within a try block, ensuring that any SQL errors are caught and managed. The finally block guarantees that the database connection is closed, maintaining good resource management practices even in error situations.

Displaying query results in a readable format may also entail additional formatting for specific data types, such as dates, floating-point numbers, or binary data. Custom formatting functions can be written to convert raw data values retrieved from the database into a human-readable string format. For example, if a query retrieves timestamps stored in a numerical format, converting these into formatted date strings can be achieved using Python's datetime module:

```
import datetime

cursor.execute("SELECT id, name, join_date FROM Employees")
results = cursor.fetchall()

print("{:<5} {:<20} {:<20}".format("ID", "Name", "Join Date"))
print("-" * 50)
for record in results:
    join_date = datetime.datetime.fromtimestamp(record[2]).strftime
    ("%Y-%m-%d")
    print("{:<5} {:<20} {:<20}".format(record[0], record[1],
    join_date))
```

By converting and formatting data as it is fetched, the final output becomes more accessible for users who might otherwise be confronted with raw numerical data. This additional layer of post-processing emphasizes the importance of considering data types and their display requirements when presenting query results.

The comprehensive understanding of fetching query results and displaying them in a readable format forms an essential component of database-driven application development. The methods provided by the sqlite3 module facilitate tailored data access that complements

both iterative and bulk processing approaches. By leveraging techniques such as batch fetching with `fetchmany()` and comprehensive
retrieval with `fetchall()`, developers are empowered to process large
data sets efficiently. Simultaneously, thoughtful formatting using
Python's built-in string methods enhances the legibility of output, providing users with clear and organized data presentations.

This approach not only fosters maintainable code but also ensures that
applications can scale from simple command-line tools to more complex graphical user interfaces where data presentation is paramount.
The techniques described underscore the level of control that Python
provides over database operations—from execution to final display—
ensuring that data is both accessible and actionable within diverse application frameworks.

5.4. Handling Exceptions and Errors

When interacting with SQLite databases in Python, robust error and exception management is crucial for building reliable applications. The
`sqlite3` module raises a variety of exceptions that can be caught and
handled to ensure that database operations are executed safely. By
understanding the exception hierarchy and employing best practices
for exception handling, developers can maintain data integrity and deliver clear diagnostic messages that contribute to easier debugging and
maintenance of the codebase.

The `sqlite3` module defines a base exception, `sqlite3.Error`,
from which several more specific exception classes are derived.
These specific exceptions include `sqlite3.OperationalError`,
`sqlite3.IntegrityError`,   `sqlite3.ProgrammingError`,   and
`sqlite3.InterfaceError`.   Each of these exceptions addresses
distinct types of errors. For instance, `OperationalError` may
be raised when the database file is inaccessible or when the SQL

186

command violates operational constraints, while `IntegrityError` is triggered by a violation of database integrity constraints, such as inserting duplicate values into a column that requires unique entries.

A central component of handling exceptions in database interactions is the use of Python's try-except construct. This construct allows developers to wrap database operations such as connection establishment, query execution, and result fetching, ensuring that any potential error is captured and handled appropriately. The following example demonstrates the structured approach to managing exceptions during a database connection and query execution:

```python
import sqlite3

try:
    connection = sqlite3.connect("example.db")
    cursor = connection.cursor()
    cursor.execute("CREATE TABLE IF NOT EXISTS Employees (id INTEGER
     PRIMARY KEY, name TEXT, department TEXT, salary REAL)")
    connection.commit()
except sqlite3.IntegrityError as ie:
    print("Integrity error encountered:", ie)
    connection.rollback()
except sqlite3.OperationalError as oe:
    print("Operational error encountered:", oe)
except sqlite3.Error as e:
    print("General SQLite error:", e)
    connection.rollback()
finally:
    if connection:
        connection.close()
```

In this code snippet, the database operations are enclosed within a try block. If an `IntegrityError` occurs—perhaps due to inserting duplicate entries—the developer is informed of the issue by printing the error message, and the transaction is rolled back to maintain the consistency of the database. The use of multiple except clauses permits tailored responses depending on the type of error encountered. A generic catch with `sqlite3.Error` ensures that any other exceptions not specifically captured are still handled gracefully.

Using rollbacks is a vital practice in managing errors. SQLite automatically encapsulates each transaction, meaning that failure during a multi-step operation should not leave the database in an inconsistent state. By explicitly rolling back the transaction in the event of an error, the code prevents partial transactions from being committed. Furthermore, encapsulating rollback logic within the exception block ensures that any error, regardless of its nature, is managed uniformly.

Another best practice in error handling is to incorporate logging into the exception management process. While printing errors to the console can be useful during development, integrating a logging framework provides better traceability in production environments. Python's built-in `logging` module offers robust logging capabilities, allowing developers to record errors with various levels of priority and to log additional contextual information that can be invaluable during debugging sessions. The following example illustrates the integration of the `logging` module:

```python
import sqlite3
import logging

logging.basicConfig(level=logging.INFO,
                    format="%(asctime)s [%(levelname)s] %(message)s",
                    datefmt="%Y-%m-%d %H:%M:%S")

try:
    connection = sqlite3.connect("example.db")
    cursor = connection.cursor()
    cursor.execute("CREATE TABLE IF NOT EXISTS Departments (id
     INTEGER PRIMARY KEY, name TEXT UNIQUE)")
    connection.commit()
except sqlite3.Error as error:
    logging.error("SQLite error occurred: %s", error)
    connection.rollback()
finally:
    if connection:
        connection.close()
```

This example configures the logging system to output messages that include timestamps and error levels. Rather than simply printing er-

188

rors to the console, the code logs them at the error level, ensuring that serious issues are recorded with proper context for later review.

It is also advisable to handle exceptions during both the connection and disconnection phases. While the focus is often on operations performed after a connection is established, failure to properly close a connection can lead to resource leaks that affect the database and the overall system performance. Implementing the connection closing logic within a finally block guarantees that the connection is closed regardless of whether an error has occurred. This strategy is particularly effective when used in combination with Python's context managers, which automatically manage the setup and teardown of database connections. An example using the with statement is as follows:

```
import sqlite3

try:
    with sqlite3.connect("example.db") as connection:
        cursor = connection.cursor()
        cursor.execute("INSERT INTO Departments (name) VALUES ('
    Engineering')")
        # No explicit commit needed; the context manager handles it.
except sqlite3.Error as error:
    print("Error during execution within context manager:", error)
```

The use of the context manager simplifies exception handling by ensuring that the connection is properly closed, even if an exception is thrown within the block. It encapsulates both the commit and rollback processes, providing a cleaner and more maintainable error management approach.

Another important aspect of exception handling is the management of potential resource leaks beyond just database connections. For instance, when working with cursors, it is beneficial to ensure that any allocated resources are released properly after their use. Python's garbage collection typically handles this automatically, but explicitly closing cursors can increase clarity and reduce the chances of unpredictable behavior, particularly in long-running applications. When multiple cursors are in use, handling exceptions at the cursor level can also provide more granular control over error management.

Error handling should also account for specific scenarios such as malformed SQL queries. When constructing dynamic queries, it is easy to inadvertently introduce syntax errors. In such cases, catching errors like sqlite3.ProgrammingError can be helpful. For example, a function designed to perform a dynamic query might include a try-except block to catch syntax-related issues:

```
def execute_dynamic_query(query, params=None):
    try:
        connection = sqlite3.connect("example.db")
        cursor = connection.cursor()
        if params:
            cursor.execute(query, params)
        else:
            cursor.execute(query)
        connection.commit()
        return cursor.fetchall()
    except sqlite3.ProgrammingError as pe:
        print("Programming error in SQL query:", pe)
    except sqlite3.Error as e:
        print("General SQLite error during dynamic query:", e)
        connection.rollback()
    finally:
        if connection:
            connection.close()

# Example usage with a malformed query
bad_query = "SELEKT * FROM Employees"  %>%  "This should trigger a
    syntax error"
execute_dynamic_query(bad_query)
```

In this function, the query is executed with an awareness of potential programming errors. The tailored except clauses provide precise error messages that indicate whether the error is due to a syntax issue or a more general database problem. The consistent use of rollback in error scenarios ensures that even if a dynamic query fails, the database remains consistent.

As development projects scale, integrating exception handling within higher-level application structures becomes increasingly important. For instance, when building a data access layer, centralized handling of database exceptions can prevent redundant code and improve maintainability. An effective strategy is to define a dedicated wrapper or helper function that encapsulates database interactions and uniformly handles exceptions. Such a helper function might look as follows:

```
def execute_sql_command(command, params=None):
    try:
        connection = sqlite3.connect("example.db")
        cursor = connection.cursor()
        if params:
            cursor.execute(command, params)
        else:
            cursor.execute(command)
        connection.commit()
        return cursor.fetchall()
    except sqlite3.Error as e:
        print("Error executing command:", e)
        connection.rollback()
        return None
    finally:
        if connection:
            connection.close()

# Using the helper function
result = execute_sql_command("SELECT * FROM Employees WHERE salary >
    ?", (60000,))
if result is not None:
    for row in result:
        print(row)
```

By abstracting the connection, execution, and cleanup processes, the helper function reduces code duplication and ensures consistent error handling across various parts of the application. This pattern is particularly advantageous when multiple modules or components interact with the database, as it centralizes the error management logic and simplifies troubleshooting.

In addition to active error handling during database operations, it is imperative for applications to exhibit transparency regarding error states.

When errors occur, propagating sufficient information to higher-level application components or logging systems facilitates prompt resolution and informed decision-making. This may involve re-raising exceptions after logging them or converting raw database exceptions into application-specific exceptions that better communicate the context of the failure.

Finally, aligning with the principle of defensive programming, it is wise to assume that errors will occur and to design code that recovers gracefully from such events. This attitude fosters a development environment where potential issues are anticipated, and appropriate recovery mechanisms such as retries, fallbacks, or alternative workflows are implemented. By proactively managing exceptions and errors through careful coding practices, developers contribute to the stability, security, and overall resilience of data-driven applications.

A thorough understanding of how exceptions flow during database operations, coupled with the systematic use of try-except-finally blocks and context managers, forms the backbone of reliable SQLite interactions in Python. Such robust error handling mechanisms ensure that applications can manage unexpected events without compromising data integrity or user experience.

5.5. Using Python Context Managers

Python context managers provide a powerful construct for resource management, particularly in the realm of database operations with SQLite. Utilizing the with statement when working with the sqlite3 module enhances code readability, reliability, and ensures the proper release of resources such as database connections and cursors. Context managers automatically handle both the initialization and cleanup of resources, reducing the risk of resource leaks and simplifying error handling.

When a connection to an SQLite database is established using a context manager, the __enter__ and __exit__ methods encapsulate the setup and teardown of the connection. The __enter__ method returns the connection object, while the __exit__ method is invoked at the end of the block, ensuring that the connection is closed regardless of whether the operations within the block succeed or raise an exception. This design pattern streamlines the code and embeds robust resource management directly into the control flow.

Consider the following example that demonstrates the basic usage of a context manager for database operations:

```
import sqlite3

with sqlite3.connect("example.db") as connection:
    cursor = connection.cursor()
    cursor.execute("""
        CREATE TABLE IF NOT EXISTS Products (
            id INTEGER PRIMARY KEY,
            name TEXT UNIQUE,
            price REAL
        )
    """)
    cursor.execute("""
        INSERT INTO Products (name, price) VALUES (?, ?)
    """, ("Gadget", 19.99))
    # No explicit commit is necessary; the context manager handles it
    .
```

In this code, the with statement ensures that the connection is automatically committed if the block executes without errors, or rolled back if an exception is raised. Developers do not need to explicitly call commit() or rollback(), which simplifies transaction management and reduces boilerplate code.

Another benefit of context managers is the reduction of repetitive code. In traditional implementations, developers often include try-finally blocks to ensure proper cleanup of resources. With context managers, however, the logic for cleanup is abstracted within the manager's implementation, leading to cleaner and more maintainable code. The following snippet illustrates how context managers replace explicit resource handling:

```
# Traditional approach without context manager
import sqlite3

connection = sqlite3.connect("example.db")
try:
    cursor = connection.cursor()
    cursor.execute("INSERT INTO Products (name, price) VALUES (?, ?)
    ", ("Widget", 29.99))
    connection.commit()
except sqlite3.Error as e:
    print("Error during operation:", e)
    connection.rollback()
finally:
    connection.close()

# Revised approach using a context manager
with sqlite3.connect("example.db") as connection:
    cursor = connection.cursor()
    cursor.execute("INSERT INTO Products (name, price) VALUES (?, ?)
    ", ("Widget", 29.99))
```

The revised approach is more succinct, automatically managing transactions and resource deallocation. This shift not only improves code clarity but also minimizes the risk of forgetting to close a connection or failing to rollback a transaction in case of an error.

The default behavior of the `sqlite3` context manager is designed to be safe for most use cases. When the block terminates normally, the connection commits all changes. Conversely, if an exception occurs within the block, all pending changes are rolled back, preserving the integrity of the database. This automated error handling mechanism helps developers write safer and more predictable code, especially in complex database operations.

Context managers also provide a unified way to manage additional resources that might be associated with database operations. For example, managing file operations alongside database transactions is a common scenario in data processing applications. By combining context managers for both file and database operations, developers can ensure that critical resources are released in the correct order. The following example demonstrates a combined usage:

```
import sqlite3

with sqlite3.connect("example.db") as connection, open("
    products_report.txt", "w") as report:
    cursor = connection.cursor()
    cursor.execute("SELECT id, name, price FROM Products")
    rows = cursor.fetchall()

    # Write a header for the report
    report.write("{:<5} {:<20} {:<10}\n".format("ID", "Name", "Price
    "))
    report.write("-" * 40 + "\n")

    for row in rows:
        report.write("{:<5} {:<20} {:<10.2f}\n".format(row[0], row
    [1], row[2]))
```

In this scenario, both the database connection and the file are managed by their respective context managers. This pattern ensures that even if an error occurs during data retrieval or while writing the report, both the connection and the file handle are properly closed. The simplicity of this syntax encourages developers to adopt comprehensive resource management practices across different parts of their applications.

Beyond the sqlite3.connect context manager, developers can create custom context managers to handle more granular or specialized resource management tasks. For instance, wrapping cursor operations within a separate context manager can provide additional control over error logging or even custom commit behaviors. Python's contextlib module, which provides utilities for creating context managers, makes this process straightforward. Consider the following custom context manager for a cursor:

```
import sqlite3
from contextlib import contextmanager
```

```
@contextmanager
def get_cursor(db_file):
    connection = sqlite3.connect(db_file)
    cursor = connection.cursor()
    try:
        yield cursor
        connection.commit()
    except sqlite3.Error as error:
        print("An error occurred during cursor operation:", error)
        connection.rollback()
        raise
    finally:
        cursor.close()
        connection.close()

# Usage of the custom context manager
with get_cursor("example.db") as cursor:
    cursor.execute("SELECT * FROM Products")
    results = cursor.fetchall()
    print(results)
```

In this custom context manager, the function get_cursor abstracts both the connection and cursor management. It commits changes if the operations succeed and rolls back in the event of an error. Additionally, it ensures that both the cursor and the connection are closed once the block is exited. This pattern encapsulates error handling and resource management, further reducing the likelihood of errors related to resource misuse and increasing overall code modularity.

The design of context managers encourages a declarative style of programming where resource management is explicitly tied to the block structure of the code. This approach simplifies reasoning about the lifecycle of objects such as database connections and cursors. Developers no longer need to worry about explicitly calling cleanup routines, which leads to fewer bugs and more predictable behavior.

In environments involving concurrent or multi-threaded operations, using context managers can help manage connections in a safer manner. Since SQLite supports multi-threaded access with careful configuration, ensuring that each thread acquires and releases its connection properly becomes critical. The use of context managers in thread-based applications minimizes race conditions and promotes a clean separation of resources among threads.

Furthermore, adopting context managers can improve error tracing and logging by ensuring that cleanup operations are centralized. When an exception is raised within a context-managed block, the context manager's __exit__ method can be designed to log detailed information about the error before performing cleanup actions. This centralized logging mechanism can be crucial for debugging complex applications with multiple interacting components.

In practical application development, the consistent use of context managers for SQLite operations leads to code that is less prone to errors due to forgotten cleanup calls. It improves the overall structure of the code and encourages developers to adopt practices that promote stability and reliability. The reliability of resource cleanup along with automated transaction management makes context managers an essential tool in a developer's toolkit.

The advantages of context managers extend to scenarios where operations need to be retried upon failure. By encompassing retry logic within the context manager itself, developers can create robust systems that attempt to reconnect or reinitialize resources automatically following transient failures. Although such implementations require careful design to avoid excessive retries or masking critical errors, the context manager pattern provides a natural framework for these advanced operations.

In summary, using Python context managers for SQLite operations offers multiple advantages: automatic resource cleanup, simplified transaction management, improved code readability, and enhanced error handling. The with statement makes it straightforward to integrate these benefits into everyday coding practices, thereby reducing the risk of resource leaks and ensuring consistency throughout the application. Whether managing a single database connection or coordinating multiple resources, context managers serve as an effective pattern for achieving robust and maintainable code in Python applications that interface with SQLite.

5.6. Implementing Parameterized Queries

Parameterized queries are a critical component in ensuring secure and reliable interactions with databases, particularly when handling user-provided input. This technique separates the SQL command structure from the data, thereby protecting the application against SQL injection attacks. SQL injection, a prevalent security vulnerability, occurs when attackers manipulate the SQL query through specially crafted input. Parameterized queries prevent such manipulation by binding parameters to placeholders in the SQL command rather than concatenating strings dynamically.

The fundamental concept behind parameterized queries is to use placeholders, typically represented by question marks (?), in place of literal data values within the SQL statement. The sqlite3 module interprets these placeholders and later binds the values provided by the developer in a separate argument. This approach ensures that the SQL engine treats the input parameters strictly as data and not as executable SQL code. The following code snippet illustrates a simple insert operation using a parameterized query:

```
import sqlite3

connection = sqlite3.connect("example.db")
cursor = connection.cursor()

# Parameterized SQL statement with placeholders for values
insert_query = "INSERT INTO Users (username, email) VALUES (?, ?)"
data = ("john_doe", "john.doe@example.com")
cursor.execute(insert_query, data)
```

198

```
connection.commit()
connection.close()
```

In this example, the use of placeholders ensures that regardless of the content of john_doe or the email address, the SQL engine does not parse them as part of the command structure. This protects against any malicious input that might attempt to alter the behavior of the query.

Parameterized queries are not only essential for insert operations, but they are equally valuable for update, delete, and select operations. When updating records, one might structure the query as follows:

```
update_query = "UPDATE Users SET email = ? WHERE username = ?"
data = ("new.email@example.com", "john_doe")
cursor.execute(update_query, data)
```

This pattern enforces the separation of the SQL command logic from the underlying data, greatly reducing the risk posed by untrusted input. Moreover, it simplifies error handling, since the SQL engine provides a clear error output when there is a mismatch between the number and type of placeholders and the supplied data.

A significant advantage of using parameterized queries is the mitigation of SQL injection attacks. By adhering strictly to the parameterized query format, developers can ensure that every input parameter is sanitized by the SQLite engine. This sanitization process means that inputs such as ; DROP TABLE Users; are treated as literal string values, not as commands to terminate the current statement and execute additional commands. The following illustrative example shows how an input string with potential injection content is securely handled:

```
# Potentially dangerous user input
malicious_input = "john_doe'; DROP TABLE Users; --"

# Even if malicious_input is provided, parameterized query treats it
    as data instead of SQL command
select_query = "SELECT * FROM Users WHERE username = ?"
cursor.execute(select_query, (malicious_input,))
```

199

In this scenario, the malicious input is safely encapsulated as a string, preventing the attack vector from being exploited. The SQL engine interprets the input as a value to be matched against the `username` column and not as a command to drop the table.

Another important use case for parameterized queries arises when dealing with batch operations. The `executemany()` method in the `sqlite3` module leverages parameterized queries to execute the same SQL command with multiple sets of parameters efficiently. This is particularly useful for inserting or updating multiple rows in a single operation, reducing the overhead of multiple individual transactions. The following code demonstrates how batch insertion can be implemented securely:

```
# List of tuples representing data for multiple users
users = [
    ("alice", "alice@example.com"),
    ("bob", "bob@example.com"),
    ("charlie", "charlie@example.com")
]

insert_query = "INSERT INTO Users (username, email) VALUES (?, ?)"
cursor.executemany(insert_query, users)
connection.commit()
```

The `executemany()` function generates a prepared statement and binds each tuple of data to the placeholders, ensuring that all data is safely and efficiently inserted into the database. This approach not only enhances security but also improves performance by reducing the number of round-trips between the application and the database.

Parameterized queries also provide benefits in terms of code clarity and maintainability. By separating SQL commands and data, developers can easily inspect the structure of their queries, debug issues related to parameter binding, and update the logic without affecting the data handling portions of the code. This separation is especially helpful in larger codebases where SQL commands may be dynamically generated or used in various contexts.

An additional aspect worth noting is the handling of different data types. The SQLite engine, when using parameterized queries, can automatically convert Python data types to their corresponding SQLite types. For example, Python integers, floats, and strings are directly mapped to their SQLite counterparts. Special care can be taken when dealing with date and time objects; developers can use the `sqlite3.PARSE_DECLTYPES` option during connection to enable SQLite's type detection for more complex types. Consider the following example:

```
import datetime

connection = sqlite3.connect("example.db", detect_types=sqlite3.
    PARSE_DECLTYPES)
cursor = connection.cursor()

# Create a table with a datetime column
cursor.execute("""
    CREATE TABLE IF NOT EXISTS LogEntries (
        id INTEGER PRIMARY KEY,
        message TEXT,
        log_time TIMESTAMP
    )
""")

# Insert a record with the current datetime using a parameterized
    query
current_time = datetime.datetime.now()
insert_query = "INSERT INTO LogEntries (message, log_time) VALUES (?,
    ?)"
cursor.execute(insert_query, ("System started", current_time))
connection.commit()
```

In this example, the `detect_types` parameter ensures that SQLite will correctly store and retrieve the datetime object, preserving the fidelity of time-related data without requiring additional conversion code.

Beyond individual query operations, parameterized queries can be encapsulated within higher-level functions or methods to create a secure data access layer. This abstraction not only encourages consistent use of parameter binding throughout the codebase but also centralizes error handling and logging for database operations. An example of such an abstraction might look like this:

```python
def execute_query(query, params=None):
    try:
        connection = sqlite3.connect("example.db")
        cursor = connection.cursor()
        if params:
            cursor.execute(query, params)
        else:
            cursor.execute(query)
        connection.commit()
        result = cursor.fetchall()
        return result
    except sqlite3.Error as e:
        print("Database error:", e)
        return None
    finally:
        if connection:
            connection.close()


# Example usage of the helper function
user_query = "SELECT * FROM Users WHERE email LIKE ?"
pattern = ("%@example.com%",)
users = execute_query(user_query, pattern)
if users:
    for user in users:
        print(user)
```

This helper function standardizes parameterized query execution and error management. By doing so, it reduces redundancy and enforces security measures across multiple components of the application. Any updates or improvements to query security can be made in one centralized location, simplifying maintenance.

While the advantages of parameterized queries are clear, developers should also be aware of potential pitfalls. One common mistake is failing to match the number of placeholders with the provided parameters. Such mismatches result in runtime errors, which can interrupt the flow of the application. It is important to ensure that the structure of the SQL command and the tuple of parameters are aligned precisely. Another potential oversight is the misuse of dynamic SQL construction in conjunction with parameterized queries. Developers must avoid partially constructing SQL strings with user data; instead, the entire query should be defined with placeholders, and all dynamic data should be passed as parameters.

Additionally, performance considerations may arise when handling extremely large batches of data. Although parameterized queries inherently improve security and efficiency by reducing parsing overhead, developers should remain mindful of potential bottlenecks when thousands of parameters are processed in a single call. In such cases, it may be beneficial to break batch operations into smaller transactions to optimize memory usage and ensure consistent performance.

The integration of parameterized queries into SQLite operations reflects a best practice that benefits both the security and robustness of an application. By enforcing a clear separation between SQL command structures and data values, applications become less susceptible to injection attacks, and the code is more maintainable and easier to understand. Developers should consistently use this pattern across all types of SQL operations—whether inserting new records, updating existing data, or querying for specific information.

Parameterized queries play a vital role in developing secure SQLite applications in Python. They provide a robust defense against SQL injection by ensuring that data is always treated as a literal value rather than executable code. This separation not only enhances security but also simplifies code structure and improves maintainability. By incorporating parameterized queries into batch operations and abstracting them into helper functions, developers can achieve a high level of consistency and efficiency in their database interactions. The careful implementation of these techniques is an integral aspect of best practices for secure and effective SQLite usage in Python applications.

5.7. Working with SQLite and Pandas

Integrating Pandas with SQLite provides a powerful toolset for data analysis, enabling developers to leverage the simplicity of SQLite for data storage combined with the advanced data manipulation capabilities of Pandas. This integration is particularly advantageous when dealing with structured data that requires both persistent storage and extensive analysis. Given the groundwork laid in previous sections on establishing SQLite connections, executing SQL commands, and handling query results, the transition to using Pandas for further analysis becomes both natural and efficient.

Pandas offers several built-in functions to facilitate interaction with SQLite databases. The most notable functions are `read_sql_query` and `read_sql_table`, which allow users to load data directly from an SQLite database into a Pandas DataFrame. A DataFrame is a powerful data structure that provides methods for filtering, grouping, and transforming data, making it ideal for exploratory data analysis and reporting. The simplicity of these functions reduces the overhead associated with manually iterating over query results as discussed in previous sections.

To begin, one can use the `read_sql_query` function to execute a SQL SELECT command and read the resulting data into a DataFrame. The following code snippet illustrates how to perform this integration:

```python
import sqlite3
import pandas as pd

# Establish a connection to the SQLite database
connection = sqlite3.connect("example.db")

# Define a SQL query to fetch data from a table; for instance, the
    Employees table
query = "SELECT id, name, department, salary FROM Employees"
# Read data into a DataFrame
df_employees = pd.read_sql_query(query, connection)
```

```
# Display the first few rows of the DataFrame
print(df_employees.head())

# Always close the connection when done
connection.close()
```

This code retrieves all rows from the Employees table and loads them into a DataFrame. The use of head() is a common pattern to preview the structure and contents of the DataFrame, facilitating rapid understanding of the dataset before further analysis.

Pandas not only reads data but also enables writing a DataFrame back to an SQLite database. The to_sql method is instrumental in this regard, as it can seamlessly insert an entire DataFrame into a specified database table. This capability is particularly useful for applications that involve data transformation, where the data is first manipulated in Pandas and then persisted back into a database for reporting or archival purposes. The code below demonstrates how to write data from a DataFrame to SQLite:

```
import sqlite3
import pandas as pd

# Create a sample DataFrame
data = {
    'name': ['Alice', 'Bob', 'Charlie'],
    'department': ['HR', 'Finance', 'Engineering'],
    'salary': [62000, 58000, 80000]
}
df_new_employees = pd.DataFrame(data)

# Connect to the database and write the DataFrame to a new table
    called NewEmployees
with sqlite3.connect("example.db") as connection:
    df_new_employees.to_sql("NewEmployees", connection, if_exists="
    replace", index=False)
```

In this example, the if_exists="replace" parameter ensures that if the table already exists, its contents will be replaced with the new DataFrame. The parameter index=False prevents the DataFrame's

205

index from being written as a separate column, thereby preserving the intended table schema.

Another significant aspect of using Pandas for data analysis with SQLite data involves the manipulation and transformation of DataFrames once the data is loaded. Common operations such as filtering, grouping, and aggregation are straightforward using Pandas and can complement the SQL-based extraction of data. For instance, one might want to compute summary statistics such as the average salary by department. The following code snippet illustrates how to perform such an aggregation:

```
# Assuming df_employees is already loaded as shown earlier
average_salary_by_dept = df_employees.groupby("department")["salary
    "].mean()
print(average_salary_by_dept)
```

This approach leverages the power of Pandas groupby operations, which can be more flexible and faster for iterating over in-memory data compared to executing multiple SQL queries. When dealing with large datasets, it is often beneficial to push as much computation as possible into the database query through SQL; however, for exploratory analysis and iterative development, Pandas offers a more interactive environment.

Combining SQL queries with Pandas DataFrame manipulation opens the door for hybrid workflows. In many cases, the initial query can act as a filter to retrieve only the relevant subset of data, which is then further refined using Pandas. Consider a scenario where an analyst wants to examine employees in a specific department with salaries above a certain threshold. This can be accomplished by first narrowing down the data using a SQL query and then applying additional Pandas filters:

```
# Construct SQL query with a condition
query = "SELECT id, name, department, salary FROM Employees WHERE
    department = 'Engineering'"
df_engineering = pd.read_sql_query(query, connection)
```

```
# Further filter using Pandas
filtered_df = df_engineering[df_engineering["salary"] > 75000]
print(filtered_df)
```

By applying both SQL and Pandas filters, the resulting workflow becomes more efficient: the SQL query limits the amount of data transferred from disk, while Pandas handles the finer details of the analysis. This division of labor minimizes memory usage and enhances performance.

Pandas also offers tools for data visualization, which can further enrich the data analysis experience. Once the data is loaded into a DataFrame, libraries such as Matplotlib or Seaborn can be employed to generate plots and charts. For example, visualizing the distribution of salaries across departments may provide actionable insights. The following example demonstrates how to create a simple bar plot:

```
import matplotlib.pyplot as plt

# Compute average salary by department using Pandas
salary_by_dept = df_employees.groupby("department")["salary"].mean()

# Create a bar plot of average salary by department
salary_by_dept.plot(kind="bar", color="skyblue", title="Average
    Salary by Department")
plt.xlabel("Department")
plt.ylabel("Average Salary")
plt.show()
```

The ability to chain these operations end-to-end—from data extraction via SQLite, through data manipulation with Pandas, to visualization—demonstrates a seamless and powerful workflow for data analysis in Python.

When working with SQLite and Pandas, an important consideration is data type compatibility. SQLite is a typeless database system compared to more strictly typed relational databases, so it may store all data as text or numeric types depending on the input. Pandas, on the other hand, infers data types when constructing DataFrames. In cases

207

where the inferred data types are not as expected, it may be necessary to explicitly cast DataFrame columns to desired types using methods such as astype(). For example, if a numerical column is read as an object due to inconsistencies in the data, converting it can be achieved as follows:

```
# Convert the 'salary' column to float if it is not already
df_employees["salary"] = df_employees["salary"].astype(float)
```

Another aspect of integrating Pandas with SQLite involves managing data updates. The iterative process of reading data into a DataFrame, performing transformations, and then writing the updated data back to the database supports a dynamic workflow for applications that require continuous data synchronization. Consider a situation where a data cleansing operation results in corrected salary figures. After processing the corrections using Pandas, one can update the SQLite database tables as demonstrated below:

```
# Assume df_corrected contains the updated salary data
with sqlite3.connect("example.db") as connection:
    # Write the corrected DataFrame to a temporary table
    df_corrected.to_sql("Employees_Corrected", connection, if_exists
    ="replace", index=False)

    # Use a SQL command to replace data in the original table with
     corrected values
    cursor = connection.cursor()
    cursor.execute("""
        UPDATE Employees SET salary = (
            SELECT salary FROM Employees_Corrected
            WHERE Employees.id = Employees_Corrected.id
        )
    """)
    connection.commit()
```

This example demonstrates how data cleansing and transformation using Pandas can be reintegrated into the SQLite database. The ability to write DataFrame contents as lookup tables or temporary holding areas further extends the flexibility of the overall workflow.

For larger datasets, performance considerations become paramount. Although Pandas is optimized for performance with in-memory data, SQLite offers the advantage of handling larger-than-memory datasets through disk storage. Combining these two requires mindful querying: using SQLite to pre-filter data can greatly reduce the size of the DataFrame loaded into Pandas. Additionally, setting appropriate indices in SQLite can expedite query performance, which in turn improves the responsiveness of subsequent Pandas operations.

Finally, working with SQLite and Pandas in a collaborative environment requires robust error handling and logging, similar to methods discussed in earlier sections. Using try-except blocks around database connections and query executions, together with comprehensive logging of data processing steps, ensures that issues are identified early and addressed promptly. This is particularly important in production environments where consistent and reliable data updates are essential for business-critical operations.

The synergy between SQLite and Pandas creates a compelling environment for end-to-end data analysis in Python. By capitalizing on SQLite's lightweight and portable storage, alongside Pandas' powerful data manipulation and visualization tools, developers can build efficient, scalable, and secure data-driven applications. This integration supports workflows ranging from exploratory data analysis and ad hoc reporting to dynamic data cleansing and transformation, reinforcing the versatility of Python as a tool for both application development and data science.

Chapter 6

Managing SQLite Databases with Python

This chapter provides insights into programmatically creating and deleting SQLite databases and tables using Python. It emphasizes efficient connection management, data insertion, and updates. Strategies for implementing database backup and restoration are presented, alongside techniques for enforcing data validation and integrity. Additionally, it covers scheduling database tasks, enabling seamless, automated management of SQLite environments within Python applications.

6.1. Creating and Deleting Databases Programmatically

Programmatically creating and deleting SQLite databases using Python is a fundamental operation that enables developers to automate database lifecycle management within larger applications and testing frameworks. Python's built-in `sqlite3` module provides a simple interface to create new databases by simply establishing a connection to a file. When a connection is made to a SQLite database file that does not exist, SQLite automatically creates the file. This behavior is essential for constructing dynamic systems where database files may be created on demand without any preliminary file setup.

The creation process begins with importing the `sqlite3` module and instantiating a connection to the desired database file. The act of connecting invokes the API to generate a new database if necessary. This process can be managed entirely within a Python script. For instance, the following code snippet illustrates the standard approach for creating a database:

```python
import sqlite3

def create_database(db_path):
    try:
        # Establish connection; creates database file if it does not
        exist.
        connection = sqlite3.connect(db_path)
        print("Database created and successfully connected to",
        db_path)
    except sqlite3.Error as error:
        print("Error while connecting to sqlite", error)
    finally:
        if connection:
            connection.close()

db_path = 'example_database.db'
create_database(db_path)
```

In this example, the create_database function takes a file path as input, attempts to establish a connection, and subsequently closes it. Closing the connection is crucial; this practice not only frees up system resources but also ensures data integrity by finalizing any pending transactions. The clear separation of connection and disconnection operations aids in debugging and improves code maintainability over time.

While creating a database is as simple as connecting to a file, deletion must be done externally since SQLite does not provide a native SQL command to delete a database. Deletion involves removing the corresponding file from the file system. This process can be seamlessly integrated into Python scripts using built-in modules such as os or pathlib. One must incorporate error handling to manage common issues, such as attempting to delete a file that does not exist. The following example demonstrates a straightforward deletion of a SQLite database file:

```
import os

def delete_database(db_path):
    try:
        if os.path.exists(db_path):
            os.remove(db_path)
            print("Database file", db_path, "has been deleted.")
        else:
            print("Database file", db_path, "does not exist.")
    except OSError as error:
        print("Error deleting database file", db_path, ":", error)

db_path = 'example_database.db'
delete_database(db_path)
```

The deletion function first checks if the specified file exists, ensuring that the operation does not cause unwanted exceptions. Using os.path.exists prevents errors when the file is already absent. Additionally, wrapping the deletion in a try...except block captures any unexpected issue that might arise during file system manipulation, offering a robust solution for automated maintenance scripts.

Managing database files programmatically opens several opportunities for automation. Developers can integrate these functions into larger workflows such as setup and teardown processes for testing environments. When running unit tests that require isolated test instances, creating and deleting databases on the fly minimizes manual intervention and ensures that tests run in a controlled, temporary environment.

This approach enhances test reproducibility and avoids issues stemming from stale data persisting between tests.

Moreover, creating a temporary database to evaluate new schema designs can be achieved using Python's `sqlite3` module. Rather than modifying a production database, developers can simulate scenarios by generating a temporary database, performing schema modifications, and then deleting the database once tests are complete. Handling database creation and deletion in a self-contained manner streamlines the development workflow. This practice is highly recommended in continuous integration pipelines and during prototyping phases where rapid iterations are necessary.

It is important to note that while the act of connecting to a file for creation is straightforward, the decision to delete a database should be taken with caution, specifically in production environments. Automated deletion should include safeguards such as confirmation prompts or verification steps to minimize the risk of accidental data loss. In mission-critical applications, additional logging may be implemented to audit when and how database files are removed, ensuring that any deletions are traceable and reversible, if necessary.

Efficient connection management is another aspect that directly interacts with database creation and deletion. Establishing connections in a controlled environment allows for a clear understanding of resource usage and ensures proper shutdown sequences in scripts. Best practices involve utilizing context managers provided by Python, such as the `with` statement, to automatically manage connection lifecycle. Although the simple examples shown here manage connections explicitly, adopting context managers in larger projects can reduce boilerplate code and eliminate potential forgetting of closing connections. A code example using context managers is provided below:

```
import sqlite3

def create_database_with_context(db_path):
```

```
try:
    with sqlite3.connect(db_path) as connection:
        # The connection is automatically closed after the block
        print("Database", db_path, "has been created and is
active within context.")
    except sqlite3.Error as error:
        print("Failed to create the database", db_path, "due to error
    :", error)

db_path = 'context_based_database.db'
create_database_with_context(db_path)
```

Using a with block ensures that even if an error occurs during database interactions, the connection is properly closed. This pattern is not only a safer method but also the recommended practice in professional codebases.

Another advantageous aspect of managing SQLite databases programmatically is the ease with which these operations can be extended to work with multiple databases simultaneously. This capability allows a script to manage entire suites of databases for testing or to segregate data logically within different file stores. Developers can iterate over a list of database names, performing creation or deletion operations in a loop. For example, consider the following code snippet that demonstrates handling multiple databases:

```
import sqlite3
import os

database_names = ['db1.db', 'db2.db', 'db3.db']

def create_multiple_databases(db_names):
    for db in db_names:
        try:
            with sqlite3.connect(db) as connection:
                print("Created database:", db)
        except sqlite3.Error as error:
            print("Error creating database", db, ":", error)

def delete_multiple_databases(db_names):
    for db in db_names:
        try:
            if os.path.exists(db):
```

```
            os.remove(db)
            print("Deleted database:", db)
        else:
            print("Database file", db, "does not exist.")
    except OSError as error:
        print("Error deleting database", db, ":", error)

create_multiple_databases(database_names)
delete_multiple_databases(database_names)
```

This code illustrates how one can use loops to automate the creation and deletion processes across several databases concurrently. Automating these tasks minimizes manual oversight and allows developers to integrate these actions into broader application setups or cleanup routines effectively.

While Python and SQLite offer a relatively simple interface for performing these operations, it is crucial to handle exceptions appropriately to avoid data corruption or inadvertent deletion of important files. Each stage—connection, transaction handling, file manipulation—should include robust error checking mechanisms. Integrating logging, whether using Python's logging module or third-party libraries, can provide valuable insights during runtime and facilitate debugging when issues arise.

Testing is an integral part of programming, and creating databases programmatically lends itself to scenarios where repeatability is critical. Automated tests often rely on temporary databases to simulate real-world scenarios without the need for permanent storage modifications. By deleting the test database at the end of a test run, developers ensure a clean state for subsequent tests. Tools such as pytest or unittest in Python can incorporate setup and teardown routines that make use of these functions for effective testing. A simplified representation of such usage in a testing scenario is outlined below:

```
import sqlite3
import os
import unittest
```

216

```
class TestDatabaseOperations(unittest.TestCase):
    db_path = 'test_database.db'

    def setUp(self):
        self.connection = sqlite3.connect(self.db_path)

    def tearDown(self):
        self.connection.close()
        if os.path.exists(self.db_path):
            os.remove(self.db_path)

    def test_connection_and_creation(self):
        self.assertTrue(os.path.exists(self.db_path))

if __name__ == '__main__':
    unittest.main()
```

This testing framework demonstrates how utilizing programmatic creation and deletion of SQLite databases supports the automation of test scenarios, further reinforcing best practices in both development and maintenance procedures.

The presented approaches to create and delete SQLite databases leverage Python's simplicity and efficiency while ensuring that resource management remains paramount. Automated database file management reduces the overhead associated with manual data handling and supports robust application architectures that require dynamic database interaction. Integrating these techniques into development workflows not only improves productivity but also enhances data security by enforcing strict connection control and ensuring that databases are not left open longer than necessary.

Adopting safe practices for file deletion, such as verifying file existence before removal and wrapping operations in error handling constructs, reduces the risk of accidental data loss. Furthermore, employing context managers solidifies the structure of the code by ensuring that database connections are gracefully managed, even in the presence of runtime exceptions. The examples provided throughout this section serve as a guide for implementing these best practices effectively.

6.2. Managing Database Connections Efficiently

Efficient management of database connections is critical in any application that interacts with SQLite. Whether a project involves creating temporary databases for testing or managing persistent data stores, controlling connections directly impacts resource consumption, application performance, and data integrity. In Python, the sqlite3 module provides a straightforward interface to connect to, interact with, and close SQLite databases. However, the ease of establishing a connection should be complemented by careful strategies for closing and managing these connections, ensuring that applications do not inadvertently leave connections open or encounter resource exhaustion.

One of the primary concerns when handling database connections is ensuring that each connection is closed promptly after its purpose is served. Long-lived connections may lead to file locks or memory leaks, especially in environments where multiple processes or threads may access the database. Traditional approaches involve explicitly calling the close() method on the connection object once database operations are completed. The following example demonstrates a conventional pattern for managing connections:

```
import sqlite3

def execute_query(db_path, query):
    connection = None
    try:
        connection = sqlite3.connect(db_path)
        cursor = connection.cursor()
        cursor.execute(query)
        connection.commit()
    except sqlite3.Error as error:
        print("Database error:", error)
        if connection:
            connection.rollback()
```

```
    finally:
        if connection:
            connection.close()

db_path = 'application.db'
query = "CREATE TABLE IF NOT EXISTS users (id INTEGER PRIMARY KEY,
    name TEXT);"
execute_query(db_path, query)
```

In this snippet, the use of a try...finally block ensures that the connection is closed regardless of errors during query execution. The explicit call to rollback() in the exception handling section further enforces transaction consistency. While this approach is effective, it can become repetitive as similar patterns are implemented throughout a codebase.

Python supports a more elegant solution via context managers, which streamline resource management by automatically handling the setup and teardown of connections. By leveraging the built-in with statement, developers can reduce boilerplate code and mitigate risks associated with forgetting to close connections. Consider the following example which demonstrates connection management using a context manager:

```
import sqlite3

def execute_query_with_context(db_path, query):
    try:
        with sqlite3.connect(db_path) as connection:
            cursor = connection.cursor()
            cursor.execute(query)
            # Changes are automatically committed when the block
    exits
    except sqlite3.Error as error:
        print("Database error using context manager:", error)

db_path = 'application.db'
query = "INSERT INTO users (name) VALUES ('Alice');"
execute_query_with_context(db_path, query)
```

In this pattern, the with statement encapsulates the connection object.

The management of commits and rollbacks is integrated into the connection's context management protocol. When the block is exited, if no exceptions occur, the context manager commits the transaction; if an exception is encountered, it performs a rollback automatically. This approach not only simplifies code but also enhances reliability by ensuring that every connection is appropriately closed.

Context managers are particularly useful in applications with nested database operations. For instance, a script that requires multiple sequential operations can be organized into separate context-managed blocks, reducing the risk of partial commits or unclosed connections. Consider the scenario where a series of operations must be performed: creating a table, inserting multiple rows, and then reading back the data. Organizing each operation into distinct context blocks improves clarity and guarantees that each connection is terminated after use.

```python
import sqlite3

def create_table(db_path):
    with sqlite3.connect(db_path) as connection:
        connection.execute("CREATE TABLE IF NOT EXISTS products (id
    INTEGER PRIMARY KEY, name TEXT, price REAL);")
        print("Table 'products' created.")

def insert_data(db_path, data):
    with sqlite3.connect(db_path) as connection:
        cursor = connection.cursor()
        cursor.executemany("INSERT INTO products (name, price) VALUES
    (?, ?);", data)
        print("Data inserted into 'products' table.")

def query_data(db_path):
    with sqlite3.connect(db_path) as connection:
        cursor = connection.cursor()
        cursor.execute("SELECT * FROM products;")
        rows = cursor.fetchall()
        print("Fetched data from 'products' table:")
        for row in rows:
            print(row)

db_path = 'shop.db'
data = [('Apple', 0.99), ('Banana', 0.59), ('Cherry', 2.99)]
create_table(db_path)
```

```
insert_data(db_path, data)
query_data(db_path)
```

This example highlights the benefit of compartmentalizing database operations. Each function deals with a single task and encapsulates its own connection lifecycle, making the code modular and easier to maintain. It also emphasizes the systematic closing of connections, which reduces the possibility of errors when multiple operations are chained together.

Beyond ensuring that connection objects are closed, efficient management of database connections also involves handling exceptions at an appropriate level. Database operations can fail for multiple reasons, including file permission issues, deadlocks in concurrent environments, or syntax errors in SQL statements. A robust system should handle these exceptions gracefully by logging errors, rolling back partial transactions, and providing mechanisms for retry or user notification. Ensuring that error handling is integrated into the connection management strategy can prevent data corruption and maintain the integrity of operations.

For applications that involve long-running processes or repeated database interactions, abstraction layers or helper functions for connection management can standardize the way connections are handled across the project. By adhering to a common pattern, developers reduce the risk of logic errors or resource leaks. For example, a dedicated helper function that consistently creates and returns a connection object can be used throughout the codebase. Such a function might include additional error logging and reporting capabilities, as illustrated below:

```
import sqlite3

def get_connection(db_path):
    try:
        connection = sqlite3.connect(db_path)
```

```
            return connection
    except sqlite3.Error as error:
        print("Error establishing connection:", error)
        raise

def perform_operation(db_path, query, parameters=None):
    connection = None
    try:
        connection = get_connection(db_path)
        cursor = connection.cursor()
        if parameters:
            cursor.execute(query, parameters)
        else:
            cursor.execute(query)
        connection.commit()
    except sqlite3.Error as error:
        print("Operation failed:", error)
        if connection:
            connection.rollback()
    finally:
        if connection:
            connection.close()

db_path = 'enterprise.db'
query = "UPDATE customers SET status = ? WHERE id = ?;"
params = ('active', 101)
perform_operation(db_path, query, params)
```

This pattern centralizes error handling and ensures that each connection follows the same lifecycle protocol. Encapsulation of the connection logic minimizes duplication and eases the process of debugging issues when they arise. As the system scales or processes become more complex, having a unified approach to managing connections will significantly reduce maintenance overhead.

In multi-threaded environments, the nuances of SQLite's connection handling become more pronounced. SQLite by default does not support shared connections across threads. Therefore, if an application employs concurrency—whether through threading or asynchronous programming—each thread must manage its own connection to the database. Although connection reusability in these contexts is limited by SQLite's design, establishing a connection per thread is straightforward, yet demands careful handling to avoid conflicts and ensure thread safety. Developers should consider using thread-local storage to maintain individual connections for each thread, suiting the designed concurrency model.

The complication of asynchronous operations further necessitates careful management of database connections. When using asynchronous frameworks such as `asyncio` along with libraries that provide asynchronous support for SQLite, developers must adapt their connection management strategies to the event-driven paradigm. Even in these cases, the principles remain the same: ensure that connections are established just in time for operations and closed right after completion, minimizing the time a connection remains open. Although a deeper discussion of asynchronous database operations goes beyond the immediate scope, the emphasis should be on acquiring and releasing resources efficiently.

Monitoring and logging connection events are additional practices that enhance the efficiency of managing database connections, particularly in production environments. By integrating logging at key points—when connections are opened, when transactions are committed or rolled back, and when connections are closed—developers can gain insights into the runtime behavior of their applications. This continuous monitoring helps identify patterns such as uncommitted transactions or prolonged connection durations that could lead to performance bottlenecks. Python's built-in `logging` module can be seamlessly integrated into connection management routines, providing a detailed audit trail for database interactions.

Despite the relative simplicity of connecting to an SQLite database, developers must remain vigilant about resource management. Given that SQLite operates on a file-based system, mishandling a connection might lead not only to resource leaks but also to file locks that block other processes from accessing critical data. By implementing standardized patterns and context managers as demonstrated in the previous examples, developers can efficiently manage connections, avoid common pitfalls, and guarantee a smooth operation of their applications.

Incorporating best practices in managing and closing database connections leads to robust applications that handle errors gracefully, optimize resource usage, and maintain data integrity. These measures, while occasionally overlooked in simple scripts, become essential in larger applications where database interactions are frequent and complex. The repeated use of context managers, centralized helper functions, and consistent error handling protocols collectively contribute to a high-quality codebase that is both maintainable and scalable.

The techniques presented in this section support efficient resource utilization by ensuring that database connections are created only when needed and terminated immediately after completing their tasks. The established patterns further minimize the risk of leaving connections open inadvertently, which could otherwise lead to performance degradation or data inconsistencies. This disciplined approach to connection management is an integral part of developing Python applications that interact with SQLite databases reliably and securely.

6.3. Automating Table Creation and Deletion

Automating the creation and deletion of tables within SQLite databases using Python is instrumental in streamlining development workflows, especially in environments that require frequent schema changes or testing setups. This automation not only minimizes manual intervention but also ensures that database schemas remain consistent across different stages of development. Python's `sqlite3` module offers an accessible interface to perform these operations, while robust scripting and error handling patterns guarantee that automated processes function reliably.

A common scenario in automation involves setting up a database schema by creating tables before executing operations such as data insertion, querying, or complex transformations. In testing frameworks, for example, each test run may require a fresh database schema to maintain isolation and repeatability. Conversely, dropping tables may be necessary for resetting the database state, particularly during iterative development cycles. Developing scripts that encapsulate these operations minimizes redundancy and reduces the possibility of human error.

Automation begins by constructing SQL statements for both table creation and deletion. The SQL syntax for creating a table in SQLite is simple and must be executed by a valid connection. The SQL command typically defines the table name, columns, data types, and optional constraints such as primary keys or unique constraints. For example, the following SQL command creates a table named employees with defined columns:

```
CREATE TABLE IF NOT EXISTS employees (
    id INTEGER PRIMARY KEY,
    name TEXT NOT NULL,
    department TEXT,
    salary REAL
);
```

Integrating this SQL command into a Python script involves establishing a connection using the sqlite3 module and then executing the command with a cursor object. The automation script should utilize error handling to manage potential issues, such as syntax errors or conflicts when the table already exists. The following code snippet demonstrates this approach:

```
import sqlite3

def create_table(db_path, create_statement):
    try:
```

225

```
        with sqlite3.connect(db_path) as connection:
            cursor = connection.cursor()
            cursor.execute(create_statement)
            print("Table created successfully.")
    except sqlite3.Error as error:
        print("Failed to create table:", error)

db_path = 'company.db'
create_statement = """
CREATE TABLE IF NOT EXISTS employees (
    id INTEGER PRIMARY KEY,
    name TEXT NOT NULL,
    department TEXT,
    salary REAL
);
"""
create_table(db_path, create_statement)
```

This function, `create_table`, employs a context manager to ensure that the connection is closed automatically after the SQL command is executed. The inclusion of the conditional clause IF NOT EXISTS in the SQL command prevents errors when the table already exists. This robust approach is critical in automated environments where multiple scripts or processes might attempt to create the same table concurrently.

Deletion of tables, often referred to as "dropping" tables, is another essential operation that is part of automation workflows. Similar to creation, the SQL command for dropping a table must be executed safely. In SQLite, the DROP TABLE command removes an entire table and any associated data. When automating table deletion, it is advisable to incorporate the conditional clause IF EXISTS to avoid errors in instances where the table may have been previously removed. The following function demonstrates a script for dropping a table:

```
import sqlite3

def drop_table(db_path, table_name):
    drop_statement = f"DROP TABLE IF EXISTS {table_name};"
    try:
        with sqlite3.connect(db_path) as connection:
```

```
        cursor = connection.cursor()
        cursor.execute(drop_statement)
        print(f"Table '{table_name}' dropped successfully.")
    except sqlite3.Error as error:
        print(f"Failed to drop table '{table_name}':", error)

table_name = 'employees'
drop_table(db_path, table_name)
```

By defining the table name dynamically and concatenating it into the SQL command, the function `drop_table` facilitates the deletion of any specified table. The IF EXISTS clause ensures that the command fails gracefully when the table does not exist, making the script safe for repeated execution within continuous integration pipelines or automated testing cycles.

Automating these operations within a broader workflow often entails handling multiple tables simultaneously. In many applications, a complete schema consists of several related tables, which may need to be created in batch mode during the initial setup or dropped as part of a cleanup routine. Developers can encapsulate the logic for batch operations into functions that iterate over a list of tables and execute the required SQL commands. For instance, the following snippet illustrates the automation of creating multiple tables:

```
import sqlite3

def create_multiple_tables(db_path, table_statements):
    try:
        with sqlite3.connect(db_path) as connection:
            cursor = connection.cursor()
            for statement in table_statements:
                cursor.execute(statement)
            print("All tables created successfully.")
    except sqlite3.Error as error:
        print("Error creating tables:", error)

table_statements = [
    """
    CREATE TABLE IF NOT EXISTS employees (
        id INTEGER PRIMARY KEY,
        name TEXT NOT NULL,
```

```
        department TEXT,
        salary REAL
    );
    """,
    """
    CREATE TABLE IF NOT EXISTS departments (
        dept_id INTEGER PRIMARY KEY,
        dept_name TEXT NOT NULL
    );
    """
]

create_multiple_tables(db_path, table_statements)
```

This approach enhances scalability by abstracting the creation process into a function capable of iterating over any number of SQL statements. Such modular design practices improve maintainability and allow for the incremental expansion of the schema without deviating from automated procedures.

Automation frameworks also frequently incorporate logging to track the success or failure of table operations. Integrating Python's logging module with the database automation process provides an audit trail that is particularly useful during development and in production environments. Logging facilitates debugging by systematically recording operation events and any errors encountered. A modified version of the table creation function with logging might appear as follows:

```
import sqlite3
import logging

logging.basicConfig(level=logging.INFO, format='%(asctime)s - %(
    levelname)s - %(message)s')

def create_table_with_logging(db_path, create_statement):
    try:
        with sqlite3.connect(db_path) as connection:
            connection.execute(create_statement)
            logging.info("Table created successfully using statement:
    %s", create_statement)
    except sqlite3.Error as error:
        logging.error("Failed to create table: %s", error)
```

```
create_table_with_logging(db_path, create_statement)
```

Incorporating logging not only aids in monitoring the flow of table operations but also supports dynamic debugging when automated scripts encounter issues in different operational contexts. The logged messages contribute to both proactive maintenance and reactive analysis when errors occur.

Automation of table management also adapts naturally to environments such as continuous integration and deployment (CI/CD) pipelines where database state must be predictable between deployment phases. Automated scripts for creating and dropping tables can be executed as part of pre-deployment checks or post-deployment cleanup routines. This automation ensures consistency between development, staging, and production environments. Additionally, when used alongside migration tools, automated table operations can support more complex schema evolutions that accommodate new features while preserving backward compatibility.

Error handling remains a central consideration in this automation. Robust scripts always incorporate exception handling to manage intermittent failures, such as corrupted database files or conflicting table definitions. In robust systems, an error in one table operation should not prevent subsequent operations from executing. Modularizing the table automation functions to return status codes or throw controlled exceptions allows for graceful error recovery and logging. For instance, the table creation process can be modified to catch and report errors without halting the entire script:

```python
import sqlite3

def safe_create_table(db_path, create_statement):
    try:
        with sqlite3.connect(db_path) as connection:
            connection.execute(create_statement)
            return True
    except sqlite3.Error as error:
```

```
        print("Error encountered during table creation:", error)
        return False

success = safe_create_table(db_path, create_statement)
if success:
    print("Table setup completed.")
else:
    print("Table setup encountered problems; review error logs for
      details.")
```

This structure allows automated systems to continue executing subsequent tasks even when a single table creation fails, which is especially useful in complex deployments where partial failures are acceptable within certain bounds.

In environments where schema evolution is frequent, additional layers of abstraction can be implemented using a versioning framework. Developers might maintain a collection of SQL scripts corresponding to different versions of the database schema, and the automation logic can apply incremental changes based on version comparisons. This modular design, paired with automated table creation and deletion scripts, supports seamless schema migrations by ensuring that the database structure can be both updated and rolled back as necessary.

The strategies for automating table creation and deletion discussed in this section exemplify core principles of reliable software design: modularity, error handling, and efficient resource management. The implementation of these operations using Python and SQLite not only accelerates the development cycle but also reduces the risk of errors escalating into larger system failures. By automating repetitive tasks, developers can allocate more time to higher-level logic, ensuring that the underlying database schema remains consistent and robust.

Integrating these automated processes into larger workflows effectively supports development agility and improves scalability. The examples provided illustrate a range of techniques from basic SQL execution to advanced error handling, logging, and dynamic schema management. This disciplined approach to database automation is central in modern application development, ensuring that the database layer remains as agile and reliable as the application code itself.

6.4. Inserting and Updating Data through Scripts

Programmatically inserting and updating data is one of the core functionalities when interfacing with SQLite databases in Python. This process relies on Python's robust `sqlite3` module to execute SQL statements directly from scripts, allowing developers to automate data manipulation tasks efficiently. Integrating insert and update operations into scripts facilitates rapid development cycles, enables automated testing, and ensures consistency within the database by reducing manual intervention.

A fundamental principle when inserting data into SQLite is the use of parameterized queries. Parameterized queries not only simplify the insertion process but also provide a safeguard against SQL injection by safely binding input values to placeholders in the SQL statement. An example of a basic insert operation is illustrated below. In this example, a new record is added to a table using a parameterized SQL statement:

```
import sqlite3

def insert_record(db_path, name, department, salary):
    query = "INSERT INTO employees (name, department, salary) VALUES
    (?, ?, ?);"
    try:
        with sqlite3.connect(db_path) as conn:
            cursor = conn.cursor()
            cursor.execute(query, (name, department, salary))
            conn.commit()
            print("Record inserted successfully.")
    except sqlite3.Error as error:
        print("Error while inserting record:", error)

db_path = 'company.db'
insert_record(db_path, "Alice Johnson", "Engineering", 85000.00)
```

231

In this snippet, the use of the `with` statement ensures that the connection is properly closed after the execution of the query. The `cursor.execute()` method binds the provided values to the placeholders in the SQL command, while `conn.commit()` finalizes the transaction. Error handling within a try-except block captures any issue that may arise during the operation, such as constraint violations or connection errors.

For scenarios involving bulk data insertion, Python's `executemany()` method offers a more efficient approach. Instead of iterating over a large list of records and executing the insert statement multiple times, `executemany()` batches the operations, reducing the overhead associated with repeated SQL interpretation. Consider the following example using `executemany()`:

```python
import sqlite3

def bulk_insert_records(db_path, records):
    query = "INSERT INTO employees (name, department, salary) VALUES
        (?, ?, ?);"
    try:
        with sqlite3.connect(db_path) as conn:
            cursor = conn.cursor()
            cursor.executemany(query, records)
            conn.commit()
            print(f"{cursor.rowcount} records inserted successfully
    .")
    except sqlite3.Error as error:
        print("Error during bulk insert:", error)

records = [
    ("Bob Smith", "Marketing", 65000.00),
    ("Carol White", "Finance", 72000.00),
    ("Dave Brown", "Engineering", 88000.00)
]

bulk_insert_records(db_path, records)
```

The use of a list of tuples to store records allows the function to handle an arbitrary number of rows, making it well-suited for integrating with data ingestion pipelines or ETL (Extract, Transform, Load) pro-

cesses. This method further emphasizes the utility of batching operations wherever possible for improved performance.

Updates to existing data are equally crucial in applications where data
evolves over time. The update operation typically involves modifying
values in specific columns based on certain conditions. A common
pattern is to use parameterized queries for updates to ensure that the
data passed to the SQL statement is safely bound. The following code
demonstrates how to update a record within a table:

```
import sqlite3

def update_record(db_path, employee_id, new_salary):
    query = "UPDATE employees SET salary = ? WHERE id = ?;"
    try:
        with sqlite3.connect(db_path) as conn:
            cursor = conn.cursor()
            cursor.execute(query, (new_salary, employee_id))
            conn.commit()
            if cursor.rowcount == 0:
                print("No records updated; check if the employee ID
exists.")
            else:
                print("Record updated successfully.")
    except sqlite3.Error as error:
        print("Error during update operation:", error)

employee_id = 1
new_salary = 90000.00
update_record(db_path, employee_id, new_salary)
```

This function updates the salary of an employee identified by
`employee_id`. The use of `cursor.rowcount` provides a simple
mechanism to verify whether the update affected any rows, acting as
a check for the existence of the record. The transaction is committed
only after the update is executed, ensuring data consistency in a
multi-user environment.

In many practical applications, data updates may involve multiple
fields or conditional changes applied to a set of records. For example, an operation might increase the salary of all employees in a given

department by a fixed percentage. This can be implemented using a dynamic update operation that handles multiple rows at once:

```
import sqlite3

def raise_department_salary(db_path, department, increment):
    query = "UPDATE employees SET salary = salary + ? WHERE
     department = ?;"
    try:
        with sqlite3.connect(db_path) as conn:
            cursor = conn.cursor()
            cursor.execute(query, (increment, department))
            conn.commit()
            print(f"Salaries updated for {cursor.rowcount} employee(s
    ) in the {department} department.")
    except sqlite3.Error as error:
        print("Error updating salaries:", error)

raise_department_salary(db_path, "Engineering", 5000.00)
```

This broader update operation leverages the SQL capability to compute new values directly within the query, avoiding the need to fetch the existing salary values before updating them. Using aggregate operations in SQL enhances performance, especially when multiple records are updated simultaneously.

Efficiency in data insertion and updating can also be improved by managing transactions effectively. Grouping multiple insert or update operations within a single transaction reduces the frequency of commit operations, which can be performance intensive in disk-based databases. The following example demonstrates how to manage a transaction that involves both insertion and updating within one context:

```
import sqlite3

def transaction_example(db_path, new_records, salary_updates):
    try:
        with sqlite3.connect(db_path) as conn:
            cursor = conn.cursor()

            # Inserting new records
            insert_query = "INSERT INTO employees (name, department,
    salary) VALUES (?, ?, ?);"
```

234

```
                cursor.executemany(insert_query, new_records)

                # Updating salary for a set of employees
                update_query = "UPDATE employees SET salary = ? WHERE id
        = ?;"
                for employee_id, new_salary in salary_updates:
                    cursor.execute(update_query, (new_salary, employee_id
        ))

                # Commit occurs automatically when exiting the with block
        if no exceptions are raised.
                print("Transaction completed: inserted and updated
        records.")
        except sqlite3.Error as error:
            print("Transaction failed:", error)

new_records = [
    ("Eve Black", "HR", 58000.00),
    ("Frank Green", "IT", 75000.00)
]

salary_updates = [
    (1, 92000.00),
    (3, 95000.00)
]

transaction_example(db_path, new_records, salary_updates)
```

This example highlights the power of transactions in managing multiple data manipulation operations atomically. If any part of the transaction fails, the entire operation can be rolled back, ensuring that the database remains in a consistent state. Moreover, grouping operations together minimizes the overhead associated with multiple commit calls.

Maintaining robust error handling is essential when automating data insertion and updating tasks. Aside from catching database-specific errors with sqlite3.Error, developers should consider implementing logging to track the status of operations. Logging critical events, such as the start and end of transactions or the occurrence of errors, aids in troubleshooting and maintaining a clear audit trail of database interactions. An integrated logging mechanism can be added to insertion and updating scripts as follows:

```
import sqlite3
import logging

logging.basicConfig(level=logging.INFO, format='%(asctime)s - %(
    levelname)s - %(message)s')

def insert_with_logging(db_path, name, department, salary):
    query = "INSERT INTO employees (name, department, salary) VALUES
    (?, ?, ?);"
    try:
        with sqlite3.connect(db_path) as conn:
            cursor = conn.cursor()
            cursor.execute(query, (name, department, salary))
            conn.commit()
            logging.info("Inserted record: %s, %s, %s", name,
    department, salary)
    except sqlite3.Error as error:
        logging.error("Insert operation failed: %s", error)

def update_with_logging(db_path, employee_id, new_salary):
    query = "UPDATE employees SET salary = ? WHERE id = ?;"
    try:
        with sqlite3.connect(db_path) as conn:
            cursor = conn.cursor()
            cursor.execute(query, (new_salary, employee_id))
            conn.commit()
            if cursor.rowcount == 0:
                logging.warning("No record found with id: %s",
    employee_id)
            else:
                logging.info("Updated employee id %s to new salary %s
    ", employee_id, new_salary)
    except sqlite3.Error as error:
        logging.error("Update operation failed: %s", error)

insert_with_logging(db_path, "Grace Hopper", "IT", 98000.00)
update_with_logging(db_path, 2, 70000.00)
```

By incorporating logging into data manipulation routines, developers can monitor operations in real-time and retrospectively analyze logs to diagnose issues in production environments. Detailed logs help to pinpoint the source of errors, whether they arise from incorrect SQL syntax, invalid data types, or connection problems.

Automation of data insertion and update operations also opens avenues for integration with higher-level frameworks and libraries. For example, applications that use Object-Relational Mapping (ORM) libraries such as SQLAlchemy can benefit from these scripting techniques during bulk operations or migrations. Although the focus here is on direct interactions with `sqlite3`, the underlying concepts of transaction management, error handling, and the use of parameterized queries are adaptable to various database interfacing libraries in Python.

By employing these techniques, developers can achieve a high degree of control over how data is managed within their SQLite databases. The detailed examples provided herein serve as templates for robust, efficient, and secure data manipulation. Such methods ensure that each insert or update operation is executed reliably, that transactions are managed to preserve consistency, and that errors are systematically captured and addressed throughout the application lifecycle.

6.5. Backup and Restore Procedures

Implementing reliable backup and restore procedures for SQLite databases is essential to ensure data durability and recoverability. Python provides robust features through the `sqlite3` module to facilitate these operations, allowing database files to be backed up and restored programmatically. Given that SQLite databases are file-based, backup procedures may involve either file-level copying or, more elegantly, the use of the built-in backup API provided by recent versions of SQLite and Python. This section outlines techniques to perform backup and restore tasks effectively, with detailed examples and best practices.

The recommended approach for backing up an SQLite database is to use the `backup()` method available on the `sqlite3.Connection` object. This API performs a hot backup of the database, meaning that the source database remains available for read and write operations while the backup is being made. The `backup()` method creates a replica of the database in a destination connection. The following example demonstrates performing a backup operation using a context manager to guarantee that both connections are managed correctly:

```
import sqlite3

def backup_database(source_db, backup_db):
    try:
        with sqlite3.connect(source_db) as src_conn:
            with sqlite3.connect(backup_db) as bkp_conn:
                src_conn.backup(bkp_conn)
                print(f"Backup successful: {source_db} -> {backup_db
    }")
    except sqlite3.Error as error:
        print("Backup failed:", error)

source_db = 'production.db'
backup_db = 'production_backup.db'
backup_database(source_db, backup_db)
```

In this script, the source and destination databases are opened concurrently within `with` blocks, ensuring that resources are freed automatically upon completion. The hot backup process mitigates downtime and interruption to other operations accessing the source database. Incorporating error handling through try-except blocks captures any issues that might occur during the backup process, such as file access errors or corrupt database states.

Backup procedures can also be integrated into broader system processes, such as scheduled tasks or maintenance windows. When backups are performed programmatically, it is common practice to log the status of backup operations. Logging details—such as the time of backup, the source, and destination file names—aid in monitoring the health of the backup process. The following sample extends the previous example by incorporating logging:

```
import sqlite3
```

```
import logging

logging.basicConfig(level=logging.INFO, format='%(asctime)s - %(
    levelname)s - %(message)s')

def backup_database_with_logging(source_db, backup_db):
    try:
        with sqlite3.connect(source_db) as src_conn:
            with sqlite3.connect(backup_db) as bkp_conn:
                src_conn.backup(bkp_conn)
                logging.info("Backup successful: %s -> %s", source_db
, backup_db)
    except sqlite3.Error as error:
        logging.error("Backup failed: %s", error)

backup_database_with_logging('production.db', 'production_backup.db')
```

When incorporating these routines into a production application, it is advisable to parameterize the file paths and backup intervals. Combining these mechanisms with a scheduler—such as `cron` on Unix-based systems or the `schedule` library in Python—provides continuous backup protection. Additionally, combining backups with file archiving or compression can reduce storage requirements, especially in environments with frequent backups.

In some scenarios, direct file-level copying may be employed as a complementary backup method. This approach involves copying the SQLite database file to a designated backup location while ensuring data consistency. However, file-level copies can be problematic if the database is actively being written to, as this may create an inconsistent backup. To address this, file-level copying is best performed either when the database is not in use or by utilizing SQLite's locking mechanisms. One method to ensure a consistent file copy is to temporarily pause write operations or to perform the copy immediately after initiating a checkpoint. The following example illustrates a simple file-level copy using Python's `shutil` module:

```
import shutil
import os
```

```
def copy_database_file(source_db, backup_db):
    if os.path.exists(source_db):
        try:
            shutil.copy2(source_db, backup_db)
            print(f"Database file copied successfully: {source_db} ->
        {backup_db}")
        except IOError as error:
            print("File copy failed:", error)
    else:
        print("Source database file does not exist:", source_db)

copy_database_file('production.db', 'production_filebackup.db')
```

While the file-copying method is simpler, it is generally less preferred than the built-in backup API due to the risk of capturing an inconsistent state.

Restoring a database from a backup typically involves the inverse operation. The restoration procedure is often as straightforward as replacing the current database file with a backup copy. Alternatively, one might use the backup API to transfer data from the backup database to the production database. The following example illustrates the use of the backup method to restore a database. Here, the backup database acts as the source and the production database serves as the destination:

```
import sqlite3

def restore_database(backup_db, target_db):
    try:
        with sqlite3.connect(backup_db) as src_conn:
            with sqlite3.connect(target_db) as tgt_conn:
                src_conn.backup(tgt_conn)
                print(f"Restoration successful: {backup_db} -> {
        target_db}")
    except sqlite3.Error as error:
        print("Restoration failed:", error)

restore_database('production_backup.db', 'production.db')
```

In this restoration script, the backup file is read via a source connection, and its contents are transferred into a target connection representing

240

the production database. This method provides a controlled mechanism to repopulate a database while ensuring that only valid and complete data is restored.

An alternative restoration technique is to perform a file-level overwrite. This involves replacing the production database file with the backup copy. Caution is advised as this method disrupts any ongoing processes that depend on the production database. The procedure generally involves closing all active connections and then replacing the database file. The following example demonstrates this using the os and shutil modules:

```
import os
import shutil

def restore_database_file(backup_db, target_db):
    if os.path.exists(backup_db):
        try:
            if os.path.exists(target_db):
                os.remove(target_db)
            shutil.copy2(backup_db, target_db)
            print(f"Database restored from file: {backup_db} -> {
target_db}")
        except IOError as error:
            print("Database file restoration failed:", error)
    else:
        print("Backup file does not exist:", backup_db)

restore_database_file('production_filebackup.db', 'production.db')
```

In this context, the backup file is used to overwrite the target database file. This method requires the application to be in a maintenance mode or to perform the restoration during off-peak hours to minimize disruptions.

Integrating backup and restore procedures into your application should also take into consideration the frequency of backups, retention policies, and validation of backup integrity. Automated scripts can be scheduled to perform regular backups at predetermined intervals. Additionally, implementing routines to verify the integrity of backups, such as opening the backup database and running quick queries, ensures that the resulting files are not corrupted. The additional verification step could be implemented as follows:

```
import sqlite3

def verify_backup(backup_db):
    try:
        with sqlite3.connect(backup_db) as conn:
            cursor = conn.cursor()
            cursor.execute("PRAGMA integrity_check;")
            result = cursor.fetchone()
            if result[0] == "ok":
                print("Backup integrity check passed.")
            else:
                print("Backup integrity check failed:", result)
    except sqlite3.Error as error:
        print("Error during integrity check:", error)

verify_backup('production_backup.db')
```

This integrity check involves executing the `PRAGMA integrity_check` command, which is a lightweight mechanism provided by SQLite to test the structural integrity of the database. A successful check confirms that the backup is reliable, while any deviations are immediately reported—allowing for prompt corrective measures.

Another important consideration is the handling of transactions during backup operations. In highly transactional environments, it might be necessary to temporarily pause operations to ensure consistency when using file-level backups. The backup API, however, inherently manages transactions to a degree by ensuring a point-in-time snapshot of the database is captured. Nonetheless, coordinating backups with application-level transactions can further reduce the risk of incomplete backups.

The ability to perform backup and restore operations programmatically introduces a level of automation and resilience critical for enterprise applications. Automated backup scripts can be integrated within

242

deployment pipelines, scheduled via operating system task schedulers, or managed by external orchestration tools. These strategies collectively minimize downtime and ensure that critical data can be recovered rapidly in the event of hardware failures, software errors, or security breaches.

The examples and techniques presented in this section demonstrate the essential practices for implementing effective backup and restore procedures. By leveraging the features provided by Python's `sqlite3` module, developers can construct robust solutions that offer both file-based and API-driven backup mechanisms. The integration of logging, error handling, and data integrity checks ensures that backup operations do not adversely affect the application and remain reliable over time. This disciplined approach to backup and restore processes forms a critical component of comprehensive data management strategies in modern applications.

6.6. Implementing Data Validation and Integrity Constraints

Data validation and integrity constraints are essential mechanisms for maintaining the accuracy and consistency of data stored within an SQLite database. Enforcing these constraints at the database level ensures that invalid, duplicate, or inconsistent data never becomes a permanent part of the dataset, reducing potential errors in application logic and downstream processes. This section details techniques for specifying validation rules and integrity constraints using SQL and Python, and discusses strategies for combining database-level checks with application-level safeguards.

SQLite supports a variety of integrity constraints, including primary keys, foreign keys, unique constraints, NOT NULL constraints, and

243

CHECK constraints. When designing a table, these constraints are declared as part of the table schema. For instance, consider a table definition for an `employees` table that enforces data integrity through multiple constraints. The following SQL command illustrates this:

```
CREATE TABLE IF NOT EXISTS employees (
    id INTEGER PRIMARY KEY,
    name TEXT NOT NULL,
    email TEXT UNIQUE NOT NULL,
    department TEXT,
    salary REAL CHECK(salary > 0)
);
```

In this schema, the `id` column is designated as the primary key, ensuring uniqueness and serving as the main identifier. The `name` and `email` columns are defined with a NOT NULL constraint to prevent missing data, while the `email` column also uses a UNIQUE constraint to avoid duplicate email entries. The `salary` column incorporates a CHECK constraint to ensure that only positive salary figures are allowed. Such constraints minimize the need for manual data validation and prevent many common errors before data reaches the application layer.

Implementing these constraints in a production environment requires that the application not only defines the correct SQL syntax but also ensures that these rules are enforced during all database operations. Python's `sqlite3` module allows developers to execute SQL commands that both create tables with these constraints and handle exceptions that occur when violations are attempted. For example, when inserting a record that violates a CHECK or UNIQUE constraint, SQLite will raise an error that can be caught using Python's exception handling mechanisms:

```
import sqlite3

def insert_employee(db_path, name, email, department, salary):
    query = """
    INSERT INTO employees (name, email, department, salary)
    VALUES (?, ?, ?, ?);
    """
```

```
try:
    with sqlite3.connect(db_path) as conn:
        conn.execute("PRAGMA foreign_keys = ON;")
        cursor = conn.cursor()
        cursor.execute(query, (name, email, department, salary))
        conn.commit()
        print("Employee inserted successfully.")
except sqlite3.IntegrityError as error:
    print("Integrity error during insertion:", error)
except sqlite3.Error as error:
    print("Database error:", error)

db_path = 'company.db'
# Attempt to insert a valid record
insert_employee(db_path, "John Doe", "john.doe@example.com", "
    Engineering", 75000.00)
# Attempt to insert a record that violates the CHECK constraint (
    salary must be > 0)
insert_employee(db_path, "Jane Smith", "jane.smith@example.com", "HR
    ", -5000.00)
```

In this example, the function `insert_employee` executes an insertion query within a context-managed connection. The usage of `PRAGMA foreign_keys = ON;` ensures that if foreign key constraints are defined elsewhere, these are enforced. The exception handling blocks are critical for catching integrity violations such as providing a negative salary or duplicate email address, thereby enhancing the robustness of the script.

Foreign key constraints play a significant role in maintaining referential integrity between related tables. When a table references another, the foreign key constraint ensures that the referenced record exists before an insert or update is allowed. To illustrate, consider a scenario where an `employees` table references a `departments` table:

```
CREATE TABLE IF NOT EXISTS departments (
    dept_id INTEGER PRIMARY KEY,
    dept_name TEXT UNIQUE NOT NULL
);

CREATE TABLE IF NOT EXISTS employees (
    id INTEGER PRIMARY KEY,
    name TEXT NOT NULL,
```

```
    email TEXT UNIQUE NOT NULL,
    dept_id INTEGER,
    salary REAL CHECK(salary > 0),
    FOREIGN KEY(dept_id) REFERENCES departments(dept_id)
);
```

By leveraging foreign keys, the application is forced to insert valid department keys in the employees table. Python scripts should enforce such relational integrity by ensuring that the corresponding records are created in the parent table before any dependent record is added. A typical workflow might first insert departments and then link employees to the valid department identifier. The following Python code demonstrates how to gracefully manage this relationship:

```python
import sqlite3

def insert_department(db_path, dept_name):
    query = "INSERT INTO departments (dept_name) VALUES (?);"
    try:
        with sqlite3.connect(db_path) as conn:
            cursor = conn.cursor()
            cursor.execute(query, (dept_name,))
            conn.commit()
            print(f"Department '{dept_name}' inserted successfully.")
    except sqlite3.Error as error:
        print("Error inserting department:", error)

def insert_employee_with_dept(db_path, name, email, dept_id, salary):
    query = """
INSERT INTO employees (name, email, dept_id, salary)
VALUES (?, ?, ?, ?);
    """
    try:
        with sqlite3.connect(db_path) as conn:
            conn.execute("PRAGMA foreign_keys = ON;")
            cursor = conn.cursor()
            cursor.execute(query, (name, email, dept_id, salary))
            conn.commit()
            print("Employee inserted successfully with department
    relation.")
    except sqlite3.IntegrityError as error:
        print("Integrity error during employee insertion:", error)
    except sqlite3.Error as error:
        print("Database error during employee insertion:", error)
```

```
db_path = 'company.db'
insert_department(db_path, "Engineering")
# Assuming department id 1 corresponds to 'Engineering'
insert_employee_with_dept(db_path, "Alice Brown", "alice.
    brown@example.com", 1, 82000.00)
```

Application-level data validation complements database constraints by preemptively filtering data before it reaches the database layer. Implementing validations in Python can reduce the number of operations that lead to a database error. This is particularly useful when input comes from user interfaces, file sources, or external APIs. For instance, a simple function to check the validity of an email address or a salary value might be implemented as follows:

```
import re

def is_valid_email(email):
    pattern = r'^[\w\.-]+@[\w\.-]+\.\w+$'
    return re.match(pattern, email) is not None

def validate_employee_data(name, email, salary):
    if not name.strip():
        return False, "Name cannot be empty."
    if not is_valid_email(email):
        return False, "Invalid email format."
    if salary <= 0:
        return False, "Salary must be a positive number."
    return True, "Data is valid."

# Example usage:
validity, message = validate_employee_data("Mark Taylor", "mark.
    taylor@example.com", 70000.00)
print(message)
```

By validating data in the application layer, developers can provide more informative feedback to users and reduce the load on the database by preventing invalid transactions. In cases where both application-level and database-level validations exist, the application validation is typically performed first, followed by enforcement via database constraints. This layered approach reduces redundant error handling while ensuring that integrity is maintained under all

247

circumstances.

Triggers further enhance data integrity by automatically performing actions when certain database events occur. For example, a trigger can be used to prevent the insertion of duplicate records by sanitizing input data or by enforcing more complex business rules than those expressible with simple constraints. A trigger might be defined in SQLite as follows:

```
CREATE TRIGGER validate_salary_insert
BEFORE INSERT ON employees
FOR EACH ROW
BEGIN
    SELECT
    CASE
        WHEN NEW.salary <= 0 THEN
            RAISE (ABORT, 'Salary must be greater than zero')
    END;
END;
```

This trigger operates before each insert operation on the employees table, ensuring that any attempt to insert a non-positive salary results in an immediate abort of the transaction. While triggers add an extra layer of constraint enforcement, they should be used judiciously as their debugging and maintenance can be more complex.

It is also important to consider that altering a table to add or modify constraints may require careful migration strategies. SQLite does not support a direct ALTER TABLE command to add constraints to an existing table. Instead, one must typically create a new table with the desired schema, copy the data from the existing table, and then replace the old table. Python scripts can automate this process, ensuring that data is migrated correctly without interruption.

Integrating comprehensive validation and integrity constraints into your application also involves providing clear feedback when operations fail. Detailed logging and error messages help developers quickly identify and rectify issues. For example, centralized error logging can

248

track integrity constraint violations and provide context for recurring issues:

```python
import logging

logging.basicConfig(level=logging.INFO, format='%(asctime)s - %(
    levelname)s - %(message)s')

def safe_insert_employee(db_path, name, email, department, salary):
    is_valid, message = validate_employee_data(name, email, salary)
    if not is_valid:
        logging.error("Validation failed: %s", message)
        return
    try:
        with sqlite3.connect(db_path) as conn:
            conn.execute("PRAGMA foreign_keys = ON;")
            cursor = conn.cursor()
            cursor.execute(
                "INSERT INTO employees (name, email, department,
salary) VALUES (?, ?, ?, ?);",
                (name, email, department, salary)
            )
            conn.commit()
            logging.info("Employee '%s' inserted successfully.", name
    )
    except sqlite3.IntegrityError as error:
        logging.error("Integrity error: %s", error)
    except sqlite3.Error as error:
        logging.error("Database error: %s", error)

safe_insert_employee(db_path, "Samuel Green", "samuel.green@example.
    com", "Marketing", 68000.00)
```

Combining detailed application-level validations with robust database constraints creates a resilient multi-layered defense against data anomalies. This comprehensive approach ensures that even if one level of validation fails or is bypassed, the other level still preserves the integrity of the data. By enforcing these rules programmatically through Python, developers maintain a high degree of confidence in the correctness and stability of their data operations.

The methods described in this section exemplify best practices for implementing data validation and integrity constraints in SQLite databases using Python. Establishing clear constraints at the database level, supplementing these with proactive application-level checks, and employing triggers where necessary all contribute to a system that minimizes data errors, enhances user feedback, and simplifies maintenance. Appropriate error handling and logging ensure that any integrity violations are promptly detected and addressed, ultimately resulting in a robust and reliable data management strategy.

6.7. Scheduling Database Tasks with Python

Automating and scheduling database tasks is a critical element of modern database management, ensuring that routine operations are performed reliably and without manual intervention. Python offers several tools and libraries that can be used to schedule tasks such as backups, data cleanup, and routine maintenance actions. Utilizing these scheduling tools can lead to improved performance, consistency in data management, and enhanced recovery strategies in case of unforeseen disruptions.

One common library for scheduling tasks in Python is schedule. This lightweight in-process scheduler allows developers to define jobs that run at specific intervals. The library is well-suited for tasks such as initiating backups, purging old records, or triggering vacuum and reindex operations on an SQLite database. A typical use case might involve scheduling a backup routine to run at a fixed time daily. For example, the following script demonstrates how to schedule a backup task that is set to execute every day at 02:00 AM:

```
import schedule
import time
import sqlite3
import logging

logging.basicConfig(level=logging.INFO, format='%(asctime)s - %(
    levelname)s - %(message)s')
```

```
def backup_database(source_db, backup_db):
    try:
        with sqlite3.connect(source_db) as src_conn:
            with sqlite3.connect(backup_db) as bkp_conn:
                src_conn.backup(bkp_conn)
                logging.info("Backup completed: %s -> %s", source_db,
    backup_db)
    except sqlite3.Error as error:
        logging.error("Backup failed: %s", error)

def scheduled_backup():
    source_db = 'production.db'
    backup_db = 'production_backup.db'
    backup_database(source_db, backup_db)

# Schedule the backup job for every day at 02:00 AM
schedule.every().day.at("02:00").do(scheduled_backup)

if __name__ == "__main__":
    logging.info("Starting scheduled jobs...")
    while True:
        schedule.run_pending()
        time.sleep(60)
```

In the above code, the `backup_database` function performs the backup operation as described in earlier sections. The `scheduled_backup` function consolidates the backup parameters, and the `schedule.every().day.at("02:00").do(scheduled_backup)` line registers the task to be executed daily at the specified time. The infinite loop continuously checks for pending tasks, ensuring that jobs are executed as scheduled.

In more complex environments, database maintenance tasks may include multiple operations such as data integrity checks, table optimizations (e.g., a VACUUM command in SQLite), and routine cleanup of temporary tables. Using the `schedule` library, multiple tasks can be defined and scheduled simultaneously. Consider an example where, in addition to database backups, a regular cleanup routine is also scheduled:

```
def clean_temporary_tables(db_path):
    try:
```

```
        with sqlite3.connect(db_path) as conn:
            cursor = conn.cursor()
            cursor.execute("DROP TABLE IF EXISTS temp_data;")
            conn.commit()
            logging.info("Temporary tables cleaned up successfully.")
    except sqlite3.Error as error:
        logging.error("Cleanup failed: %s", error)

def scheduled_cleanup():
    db_path = 'production.db'
    clean_temporary_tables(db_path)

# Schedule cleanup every day at 03:00 AM, following the backup
    process
schedule.every().day.at("03:00").do(scheduled_cleanup)
```

This pattern of defining discrete functions for each task and then scheduling them contributes to a modular design that is both maintainable and scalable. Tasks are executed in sequence based on their respective schedules, and any errors during execution are logged in detail to facilitate troubleshooting.

Another robust alternative for scheduling database tasks is the Advanced Python Scheduler (APScheduler). APScheduler provides a more flexible and feature-rich environment for scheduling tasks, supporting various scheduling strategies such as cron-style scheduling, interval-based triggers, and date-based jobs. APScheduler is particularly useful in applications that require persistent job stores, complex scheduling patterns, or integration with web frameworks. An APScheduler-based approach to scheduling a backup job can be seen in the following example:

```
from apscheduler.schedulers.blocking import BlockingScheduler
import sqlite3
import logging

logging.basicConfig(level=logging.INFO, format='%(asctime)s - %(
    levelname)s - %(message)s')

def apscheduler_backup():
    source_db = 'production.db'
    backup_db = 'production_backup.db'
```

```
    try:
        with sqlite3.connect(source_db) as src_conn:
            with sqlite3.connect(backup_db) as bkp_conn:
                src_conn.backup(bkp_conn)
                logging.info("APScheduler backup completed: %s -> %s
    ", source_db, backup_db)
    except sqlite3.Error as error:
        logging.error("APScheduler backup failed: %s", error)

if __name__ == "__main__":
    scheduler = BlockingScheduler()
    # Scheduling backup every day at 02:00 AM using cron trigger
    scheduler.add_job(apscheduler_backup, 'cron', hour=2, minute=0)
    logging.info("APScheduler running. Press Ctrl+C to exit.")
    try:
        scheduler.start()
    except (KeyboardInterrupt, SystemExit):
        logging.info("APScheduler shutdown initiated.")
```

In this APScheduler example, the backup operation is set to execute daily at the specified time using a cron trigger. APScheduler's BlockingScheduler runs a blocking event loop, which is ideal for scripts dedicated solely to the scheduling of tasks. The use of logging provides continuous feedback on job execution and any encountered errors.

In addition to backup routines, scheduling database tasks can also encompass more interactive maintenance activities. For instance, periodic integrity checks can be scheduled to run the SQLite PRAGMA integrity_check command. This can be combined with automated reporting to notify administrators in the event of any integrity issues. An example of such a task might be:

```
def integrity_check(db_path):
    try:
        with sqlite3.connect(db_path) as conn:
            cursor = conn.cursor()
            cursor.execute("PRAGMA integrity_check;")
            result = cursor.fetchone()
            if result[0] == "ok":
                logging.info("Database integrity check passed.")
            else:
                logging.warning("Database integrity check failed: %s
    ", result)
```

253

```
    except sqlite3.Error as error:
        logging.error("Integrity check error: %s", error)

# Schedule an integrity check every Sunday at 04:00 AM
schedule.every().sunday.at("04:00").do(lambda: integrity_check('
    production.db'))
```

This task ensures that the database is inspected for consistency and structural issues on a weekly basis. Automating such checks can be crucial in production environments to preemptively catch problems before they impact overall performance or data availability.

It is also important to note that scheduling tasks directly within Python scripts is not the only approach. In production environments, system-level task schedulers such as cron on Unix-based systems or the Task Scheduler on Windows can be employed to invoke Python scripts at predetermined intervals. This method decouples scheduling from the application, providing an external mechanism to manage task execution. However, integrating scheduling within Python offers advantages in terms of portability, ease of deployment, and the ability to dynamically modify schedules based on application logic.

For instance, a Python script that is called by a cron job might simply delegate work to the scheduler library or directly invoke backup and maintenance functions. By combining external schedulers with application-level scheduling libraries like APScheduler or schedule, developers can create a robust infrastructure that handles both periodic and ad-hoc execution seamlessly.

Moreover, logging and error handling are vital components of a well-designed scheduling system. By integrating detailed log messages into each scheduled task, developers gain visibility into the performance and reliability of automated operations. This transparency is crucial for quick diagnosis and resolution of issues. In scenarios where tasks fail, alerting mechanisms (such as sending emails or notifications via third-party services) can be integrated with the scheduling framework to ensure that administrators are promptly informed about failures.

The development of reusable scheduling modules further enhances the maintainability of database management workflows. Functions encapsulated in self-contained modules can be imported and used across multiple projects, promoting consistency in how tasks such as backups, cleanups, and integrity checks are performed. The modularity of these scripts allows for the easy addition of new tasks as system requirements evolve.

Scheduling database tasks with Python provides a powerful approach to automate various routine and complex operations. Libraries like `schedule` and APScheduler enable developers to integrate backup procedures, cleanup routines, and integrity checks directly within their Python applications. These tools offer flexible scheduling strategies, seamless integration with logging frameworks, and a high degree of control over task execution. By leveraging these capabilities, developers can significantly reduce manual maintenance overhead, enhance data consistency, and ensure that critical database tasks are performed in a timely and reliable manner.

Chapter 7

Performance Optimization in SQLite

This chapter focuses on optimizing SQLite performance, covering query performance analysis, index utilization, and query plan interpretation. It discusses techniques for enhancing data insertion and update operations, memory and disk usage optimization, and managing concurrency and locking issues. Additionally, it explores the use of PRAGMA statements to fine-tune database settings, ensuring efficient SQLite operations for varied applications.

7.1. Understanding Query Performance

Query performance in SQLite is influenced by a combination of logical query structure, database schema design, and the underlying hardware characteristics. In SQLite, as in many relational database systems, the cost of processing a query is primarily determined by how the

257

database engine accesses and manipulates the stored data. Although SQLite is designed for simplicity and efficiency, even small inefficiencies in query construction or data organization can lead to noticeable performance degradation, especially with larger datasets. A clear understanding of these factors is essential for building applications that require optimal response times and resource usage.

At the core of understanding query performance is the concept of query planning. When a query is issued, SQLite's query planner evaluates various execution strategies and selects the one that minimizes resource usage and computational cost. This process involves determining whether to perform a full table scan, utilize available indexes, or apply other optimization techniques such as early filtering or join reordering. For simple queries, the optimal strategy may be straightforward; however, as queries become more complex and involve multiple tables or subqueries, the number of potential plans increases, necessitating careful tuning to avoid unnecessary overhead.

Factors affecting query execution speed can be broadly categorized into issues related to the query itself and characteristics of the database environment. The complexity of the SQL statement plays a central role in performance. For instance, poorly constructed WHERE clauses, excessive use of subqueries, and unoptimized joins can heavily burden the query planner. The selectivity of conditions—the fraction of rows that meet the criteria specified in the query—determines whether an index scan or a full table scan will be used. High selectivity conditions typically benefit from index usage, while low selectivity may result in scanning a significant portion of the table, thus increasing execution time.

Database schema design is another critical component. Normalization and proper indexing not only maintain logical consistency but also enhance efficiency. Indexes serve as auxiliary data structures that significantly expedite lookups by reducing the number of rows examined during query execution. However, the presence of too many indexes can lead to increased overhead during data modifications, as each change requires updating the index structures. This trade-off between read and write performance needs careful management. In some cases, denormalization might be beneficial to reduce join complexity at the expense of storage space and potential data redundancy.

Memory allocation and disk access speed are further contributors to query performance. Caching mechanisms, both at the operating system level and within SQLite, can greatly reduce latency by keeping frequently accessed data in memory. SQLite employs an internal cache to minimize disk I/O operations. However, if the dataset exceeds available memory, disk reads will slow down query processing significantly. This is particularly noticeable in scenarios involving large databases or limited hardware resources. Understanding the interplay between cache size, disk speed, and query execution pathways allows developers to fine-tune performance by adjusting cache configurations or restructuring queries to access data in a more cache-friendly manner.

Analyzing query plans using SQLite's built-in EXPLAIN and EXPLAIN QUERY PLAN commands provides critical insights into the execution strategy chosen by the database engine. These commands return detailed information about the steps taken during query execution, allowing developers to identify potential performance bottlenecks. For example, an index not being used in a query plan might indicate that the query conditions are not selective enough or that the index was defined on an inappropriate column. The output from these commands should be studied carefully, with particular attention paid to the order of operations and the estimated cost of each step. Code examples can illustrate how this analysis is performed. Consider the following Python snippet employing the sqlite3 module:

```
import sqlite3

# Connect to the SQLite database
```

```
conn = sqlite3.connect('example.db')
cursor = conn.cursor()

# Query to check the query plan for an example SELECT statement
query = "EXPLAIN QUERY PLAN SELECT * FROM users WHERE age >= ?"
cursor.execute(query, (30,))
for row in cursor:
    print(row)

conn.close()
```

This example demonstrates how to retrieve and print the query plan, providing information that can be used to decide whether the query is utilizing indexes effectively or performing a full table scan. Analyzing the output assists in determining subsequent steps such as index creation, query refactoring, or other adjustments to improve performance.

The structure of the database and the arrangement of fields also play significant roles in query performance. When tables are designed with logical groupings and proper indexing, the query planner can more effectively reduce the search space. For instance, composite indexes—indexes that cover multiple columns—can be particularly useful when queries filter on several columns simultaneously. However, these indexes need to be structured in a way that respects the order and usage patterns of the columns. An inappropriately ordered composite index may not be leveraged effectively, forcing the query planner to revert to less efficient strategies.

It is also necessary to consider the impact of SQL functions and expressions within queries. Functions that are computationally expensive, when used excessively or inappropriately within WHERE clauses, can increase the processing overhead for each row examined. Similarly, the use of user-defined functions (UDFs) introduced via SQLite extensions should be evaluated for performance impact, especially for operations on large result sets. Balancing the need for flexibility in query development with the imperative of performance optimization is a recurrent challenge.

Error handling and query rewriting are other aspects of enhancing query performance. Invalid or suboptimal queries often result from overgeneralized SQL statements that fail to utilize available optimization opportunities. Developers must review and test queries with edge-case data to ensure they perform well under diverse conditions. Maintenance tasks such as reindexing tables or vacuuming the database can also contribute to improved performance, as they help in reorganizing data storage and minimizing fragmentation. These maintenance actions typically complement the insights gained from analyzing query execution plans, thereby providing a holistic approach to performance tuning.

Scalability challenges, though less prominent in SQLite compared to enterprise-level database systems, remain relevant as the volume of data increases or when the database is subject to numerous concurrent accesses. SQLite's locking mechanism, which serializes write operations, may impact performance under high contention scenarios. This effect amplifies the importance of query efficiency in read-heavy operations. By minimizing the computational burden of each query, developers can reduce the duration of locks held on the database, thereby improving overall system responsiveness.

Algorithmic improvements in the query planner have been the subject of continuous development over various SQLite releases. Although the improvements are often automatic from the perspective of the application developer, understanding the principles behind these enhancements is insightful. Optimized join algorithms, more intelligent index selection strategies, and better estimation of query cost parameters are among the technical advancements that contribute to more efficient query processing. Engaging with the SQLite documentation and release notes can offer advanced users a deeper appreciation of how these internal mechanisms affect their specific queries.

Deep dives into performance analysis may reveal the importance of factors beyond the SQL query itself. Profiling tools and performance analysis techniques, for example, provide empirical data regarding query latency, memory usage, and disk I/O. Such tools can capture fine-grained metrics that support decision-making for further refinements. The interplay between empirical performance metrics and theoretical query planning continues to be an area of active research and practical interest. Additionally, automation in performance monitoring can be achieved by embedding performance logging within application code, enabling real-time adjustments and long-term improvements.

The multifaceted nature of query performance in SQLite underscores the need for a systematic approach to optimization. Each factor, whether it concerns query syntax, index design, or environmental parameters, contributes to the aggregate performance experienced by end users. Integrating best practices derived from empirical evidence into day-to-day development routines ensures that applications remain responsive and resource-efficient. A well-optimized query not only improves immediate execution speed but also minimizes the cumulative load on the system, thereby enhancing the longevity and scalability of the application.

7.2. Utilizing Indexes for Speed

Indexes are one of the most powerful tools available to optimize query performance in SQLite. By providing a rapid lookup mechanism based on key values, indexes reduce the need for full table scans and significantly enhance the responsiveness of database operations. A well-designed indexing strategy directly translates into reduced query latency and, in many cases, lower resource consumption. The trade-offs associated with indexing mainly involve additional storage space and overhead during data modifications. For these reasons, it is important to structure indexes with a clear understanding of the queries that the application requires.

SQLite supports several types of indexes; the most common is the single-column index, created using the CREATE INDEX statement. This statement allows the developer to specify the table and column on which the index is to be built. Using indexes effectively depends on understanding the nature of the queries. For example, if many queries filter on a given column, an index on that column can drastically reduce the number of rows the database engine must inspect. Consider the following example that demonstrates the creation of an index on a user age column:

```
CREATE INDEX idx_users_age ON users(age);
```

In this case, queries that include conditions on the age field will be proportionally accelerated, particularly when the table contains a large number of records.

Composite indexes, which span multiple columns, allow for faster access when queries involve multiple fields simultaneously. The order of columns in a composite index is important as it dictates how the index can be used by the query planner. For instance, an index on both last_name and first_name can be very effective if most lookups include filtering by last name and then first name. However, if a query only filters by first name, this index might not be used as effectively. The following example shows the creation of a composite index:

```
CREATE INDEX idx_users_name ON users(last_name, first_name);
```

Proper management of indexes involves not only creating them but also monitoring their usefulness over time. SQLite provides diagnostic facilities such as the EXPLAIN QUERY PLAN command to inspect whether a query is leveraging an index as expected. When an index is not used, it may indicate that the query predicates do not align with the index structure, or that the index is not selective enough. An example of checking the query plan for a lookup using an index is given below:

```
EXPLAIN QUERY PLAN SELECT * FROM users WHERE age >= 30;
```

The output of this command shows how SQLite plans to execute the query, determining whether the idx_users_age index is being utilized. The ability to analyze and interpret these plans ensures that developers can iteratively refine both their indexing strategy and query structure to achieve optimal performance.

Indexes must be maintained carefully, particularly in contexts where data is frequently inserted, updated, or deleted. Each change to the underlying table requires a corresponding update in all associated indexes, which can introduce overhead that impacts write performance. This overhead represents a trade-off between ensuring efficient data retrieval and maintaining efficient data modification operations. In applications with predominantly read-heavy workloads, extensive indexing is generally beneficial. Conversely, in write-intensive applications, it is important to evaluate whether the performance gains during reads justify the additional cost of maintaining the indexes.

SQLite also supports unique indexes, which enforce uniqueness of the indexed column values while providing the same performance benefits as standard indexes. Unique indexes are valuable in scenarios where data integrity is paramount. The following example illustrates creating a unique index on a user email column:

```
CREATE UNIQUE INDEX idx_users_email ON users(email);
```

In addition to ensuring that duplicate email addresses are not inserted into the database, the unique index also accelerates queries filtering on the email column. The choice between a unique and a standard index should be guided by the underlying data model and integrity constraints.

In certain cases, the performance benefits of indexes can be maximized by reorganizing table schemas. For instance, if a frequently accessed table is large and its rows are wide, it might be helpful to use a covering index. A covering index contains all columns referenced in the query, thus eliminating the need to go back to the original table after consulting the index. This technique can result in meaningful performance improvements by reducing disk I/O. Although SQLite does not support explicitly declared covering indexes, the concept is implemented automatically when the index contains all the data required by a query. Developers should analyze their queries to determine if the current indexes effectively cover the necessary columns.

Indexes have a direct impact on the query optimizer's ability to reorder joins and filter operations within complex queries. For queries that involve multiple joins, indexes on foreign key columns are essential. They optimize the join process by quickly locating related rows in the partner tables. For example, imagine a scenario where a `orders` table references a `customers` table via a foreign key on the customer ID. Creating an index on the `customer_id` column in the `orders` table can significantly enhance the speed of join operations:

```
CREATE INDEX idx_orders_customer_id ON orders(customer_id);
```

This index minimizes the overhead of joining the two tables by reducing the search space when matching records.

Maintenance of indexes is an iterative process; as the database evolves, certain indexes may become redundant or inefficient. Removing unused or redundant indexes is as important as creating new ones. The `DROP INDEX` statement is used to remove an index that is no longer beneficial:

```
DROP INDEX IF EXISTS idx_users_unused;
```

Consistently auditing the database's query performance using diagnostic tools and comparing execution plans before and after modifications is essential. Such regular audits ensure that the indexing strategy remains aligned with the evolving query patterns and data distribution.

The careful implementation of indexes can effectively address performance issues that arise due to inefficient data retrieval. However, the decision to create an index must always be weighed against its potential impact on the system's overall performance. In scenarios where queries are not time-critical or where data modifications are very frequent, excessive indexing could lead to unnecessary performance bottlenecks. Profiling tools and query log analyses provide empirical data to support informed decisions on index creation and deletion.

Index fragmentation is another factor that can degrade performance over time. When data is inserted, updated, or deleted, indexes can become fragmented, resulting in inefficient use of memory and longer search times. Periodic maintenance tasks such as vacuuming the database or reindexing specific tables help mitigate fragmentation issues. For instance, the command to reindex a table is straightforward:

```
REINDEX users;
```

This command rebuilds the indexes associated with the users table, ensuring a more efficient data retrieval path.

An ongoing challenge is balancing index creation with query optimization efforts. As database usage patterns become more complex, it is important to conduct experiments and benchmark different indexing strategies. In-depth query analysis may involve tuning the schema to match query patterns, for example by splitting tables into multiple, more focused tables when certain indexes prove beneficial only for specific subsets of data.

Understanding the underlying hardware and operating system characteristics further refines index strategies. Disk I/O latency, memory throughput, and even the file system structure can impact the ben-

266

efits realized from efficient indexing. Developers must take into account these factors when designing the database schema. By adjusting SQLite's cache size or configuring the appropriate page size, a developer can often amplify the impact of a well-designed indexing strategy. These system-level optimizations play a supporting role in maximizing the performance benefits of indexes.

The interplay between indexing and transaction management is critical, especially in applications that handle concurrent operations. While indexes expedite read operations, they also introduce overhead during transactions that modify data. In multi-threaded environments, the concurrent maintenance of indexes can lead to locking contention. SQLite's lightweight locking mechanism, which serializes writes, minimizes but does not eliminate performance issues during high-volume transactional workloads. It is therefore essential to consider locking behavior when determining the number and type of indexes to maintain.

In scenarios where the schema supports a mix of static and dynamic data, adaptive indexing strategies may be warranted. This could involve dynamically creating or dropping indexes based on usage patterns observed over time. Automated routines that monitor query performance and adjust indexes accordingly are an area of active research and experimentation. Such adaptive techniques ensure that index maintenance does not become a one-time design decision, but rather a component of ongoing performance management.

Each decision regarding index creation, maintenance, and removal should be guided by detailed analysis and empirical evidence. The benefits of indexing are realized only when the indexes are tailored to the specific query patterns and operational characteristics of the application. As queries evolve and the data grows, continuous monitoring using diagnostic tools, such as EXPLAIN QUERY PLAN and performance profiling, becomes indispensable. A rigorous approach to managing indexes results in a more responsive database that scales gracefully with increased demand.

This integrated approach to utilizing indexes for speed not only enhances query performance but also promotes a deeper comprehension of the underlying dynamics within SQLite. The principles discussed here extend beyond SQLite to other relational database systems, reinforcing the importance of indexing as a core aspect of efficient database design and operation.

7.3.   Analyzing Query Plans

The analysis of query plans is a critical step in identifying performance bottlenecks in SQLite. A query plan reveals the internal decision-making of the SQLite engine, including which indexes are used, how tables are scanned, and in what order operations are performed. By interpreting query plans, developers can identify inefficiencies and adjust their queries or schema structure accordingly. This section details the methodologies for analyzing query plans, explains the output of the tools provided by SQLite, and offers practical examples to illustrate effective techniques.

SQLite offers two principal commands for analyzing query plans: EXPLAIN and EXPLAIN QUERY PLAN. The command EXPLAIN produces a sequence of low-level virtual machine instructions that SQLite executes to complete a given query. Although comprehensive, the output of EXPLAIN is verbose and often requires significant expertise to decode directly. In contrast, EXPLAIN QUERY PLAN provides a higher-level summary of the steps taken by the SQLite query planner, making it more accessible for developers aiming to pinpoint problematic areas in their queries.

Using EXPLAIN QUERY PLAN is generally the first step in query plan analysis. The command returns a set of rows, each describing an operation such as a table scan or an index lookup. Each row typically includes an identifier for the operation and a brief description of what the operation entails. A typical output might indicate whether a table is being scanned entirely or if an index is used to restrict the number of rows to be examined. Developers must focus on a few key aspects: the type of scan performed (sequential vs. index), the order of table joins, and any expressions applied to filter data. These details combined offer a roadmap of the database engine's execution strategy.

A concrete example demonstrates the use of this command. The following Python code snippet uses the sqlite3 module and prints the query plan for a sample query filtering on a single column. This provides insight into whether the appropriate index is being utilized.

```
import sqlite3

# Establish connection to the SQLite database
conn = sqlite3.connect('example.db')
cursor = conn.cursor()

# Define a query to analyze its execution plan
query = "EXPLAIN QUERY PLAN SELECT * FROM orders WHERE order_date >=
    ?"
cursor.execute(query, ('2021-01-01',))
rows = cursor.fetchall()

# Print out each row of the query plan
for row in rows:
    print(row)

conn.close()
```

Interpreting the output of the above snippet involves understanding the nature of each described operation. For instance, if the output indicates a "SCAN TABLE orders" instead of "SEARCH TABLE orders USING INDEX", it implies that the query is executing a full table scan rather than utilizing an index, potentially leading to performance degradation if the table holds a large number of rows.

Beyond simply checking whether an index is used, it is important to understand the sequence in which operations are performed. In queries involving multiple tables and complex join conditions, the order of joins can greatly influence performance. Query plans can sometimes suggest that the database engine is not optimizing the join order to reduce the intermediate result set. In some cases, rewriting the query or modifying indexes may allow for a more efficient join order. For example, joining a smaller table first to filter a large dataset may reduce the number of rows that require processing in subsequent join operations.

Another important aspect of query plan analysis is the estimation of cost metrics. Although SQLite's query plan output does not provide explicit cost values like some other database systems, developers can infer performance issues from the types of operations indicated. Full table scans, multiple subqueries, or the absence of expected index scans raise red flags. Developers should also look for operations that involve sorting or grouping large datasets, as these can be computationally intensive. If these operations are executed without the advantage of an index, they can drastically decrease query performance.

When tuning a query, consider the following practical strategies based on the analysis of query plans. If a plan reveals full table scans where an index might be expected, it is prudent to verify that an index exists on the relevant columns. For example, adding an index on a date column in the orders table might change the query plan from a full scan to a more efficient index search. Moreover, if the output indicates that a composite index could be more effective, reconstructing or creating a new composite index may be beneficial. Evaluating the predicate's selectivity is also essential; a highly selective condition that reduces the number of rows results in a more efficient query plan.

Beyond single query analysis, systematic monitoring of query plans provides valuable insight into the evolving workload and data distribution over time. As tables become larger and as application behavior changes, the original query plan might become suboptimal. Routine analysis, either manually or via automated performance monitoring tools, can uncover gradual performance degradations. In such cases, actions such as reindexing or vacuuming the database to reduce fragmentation may be needed to restore optimal performance. The process of monitoring and adapting queries based on query plan analysis represents an iterative cycle that evolves with the application.

For complex queries, developers might also apply the EXPLAIN command to gain granular insights into the internal workings of SQLite's virtual machine. Although its output is more challenging to read, it provides a complete decomposition of the query execution process. This low-level output can be invaluable for debugging particularly difficult performance issues. The following code demonstrates how to use EXPLAIN:

```
import sqlite3

conn = sqlite3.connect('example.db')
cursor = conn.cursor()

# Execute the EXPLAIN command on a complex query
query = "EXPLAIN SELECT * FROM customers JOIN orders ON customers.id
    = orders.customer_id WHERE orders.amount > ?"
cursor.execute(query, (100,))
explain_rows = cursor.fetchall()

# Output each instruction from the virtual machine
for instruction in explain_rows:
    print(instruction)

conn.close()
```

The detailed output from EXPLAIN requires familiarity with SQLite's virtual machine opcodes. Common opcodes include OpenRead, Rewind, and Rowid, among others. Each opcode corresponds to a low-level operation and provides context about how data is accessed or manipulated. For instance, the OpenRead opcode indicates the start of a table or index scan, while Rewind initializes the cursor to the beginning of

271

the dataset. Analyzing the sequence and frequency of these opcodes can reveal inefficiencies in the query plan, such as unnecessary loops or redundant data accesses.

When combining the output from both EXPLAIN and EXPLAIN QUERY PLAN, a comprehensive understanding emerges. While the latter provides an overview of the query's structure, the former allows developers to pinpoint exact steps where performance might falter. This dual-level analysis is especially useful for queries with multiple joins, subqueries, or complex conditions. By cross-referencing both outputs, developers can validate whether theoretical improvements in the query plan indeed translate into practical performance gains.

Another dimension to consider is the influence of query rewriting on the performance as revealed by query plans. Often, minor modifications in the SQL statement result in a dramatically different execution strategy. Experimenting with alternative formulations of a query and comparing the resulting query plans can lead to significant performance improvements. For example, rewriting a query to use a JOIN rather than a subquery might lead to a more efficient plan that leverages indexes better. In instances where it is unclear which query structure is optimal, A/B testing and performance benchmarking become essential.

Synthetic tests and benchmarks provide additional guidance. Developers can create testing scripts that repeatedly execute target queries under controlled conditions and record execution times and plan changes over various iterations. This empirical approach assists in understanding the real-world implications of theoretical query plan modifications. As query patterns evolve, continued benchmarking ensures that the implemented optimizations remain effective and that the database engine's plan remains appropriate for the current workload.

Moreover, documentation and community forums offer supplementary insights into specific query plan anomalies. SQLite's official documentation provides detailed descriptions of how query plans are generated and interpreted. Additionally, community-driven sources, including blogs and open-source project archives, often document case studies where particular query structures resulted in suboptimal plans and how these issues were resolved. Engaging with such resources can reveal industry best practices and innovative strategies for addressing complex performance issues.

Analyzing query plans also involves monitoring the impact of schema changes. When modifications such as new indexes or altered table structures are introduced, re-running query plan analysis confirms whether the desired improvements are reflected. For example, after adding an index on a column frequently used in filtering, examining the updated query plan should show a transition from a full table scan to an indexed search operation. Such validation steps are critical to the iterative process of performance tuning.

Sysadmin-level adjustments, including modifications to memory allocation or page size configurations, also affect the query plan indirectly. These adjustments, while not directly visible in the query plan output, can influence the efficiency of disk I/O operations and alter how data is cached. Consequently, when query plans reveal performance issues related to data retrieval delays, verifying the underlying hardware and SQLite configuration offers an additional perspective for optimization.

In-depth analysis of query plans requires an integrated approach that balances diagnostic tools, empirical measurements, and theoretical knowledge. Techniques evolved from the combined output of EXPLAIN QUERY PLAN and EXPLAIN reinforce a methodical strategy to identify and correct performance bottlenecks. This systematic process—ranging from modifying SQL queries to reconfiguring database schema and system-level settings—facilitates the evolution of high-performance SQLite applications. The insights garnered through query plan analysis serve as a foundation for continuous improvements, ensuring that applications leverage the full spectrum of SQLite's optimization capabilities.

7.4. Optimizing Data Insertion and Updates

Optimizing data insertion and update operations in SQLite is crucial for applications that handle large volumes of data or require rapid and frequent modifications. Efficient data modification practices not only improve overall application performance but also reduce lock contention and enhance concurrency. This section explores techniques for accelerating insert and update operations, examining both SQL-level improvements and low-level configuration adjustments.

A fundamental technique to optimize insertions and updates is the effective use of transactions. SQLite is designed to offer atomicity for every individual write operation; if no explicit transaction is started, every SQL statement is implicitly wrapped in its own transaction. This behavior ensures data integrity but introduces significant overhead when many individual operations are performed. By explicitly grouping multiple modifications in a single transaction, the cost associated with transaction commit operations is amortized across all changes. Consider the following example, which demonstrates how to batch multiple insert operations within a transaction:

```
import sqlite3

conn = sqlite3.connect('example.db')
cursor = conn.cursor()

# Begin a transaction
cursor.execute("BEGIN TRANSACTION;")

# Insert multiple records efficiently
for i in range(1, 1001):
    cursor.execute("INSERT INTO records (data) VALUES (?)", (f"Item {
        i}",))
```

```
# Commit the transaction to save all changes at once
conn.commit()
conn.close()
```

This approach significantly reduces the cumulative commit time compared to performing 1,000 individual transactions. When updating records in bulk, a similar transactional approach should be applied to minimize overhead.

Using prepared statements is another important optimization technique. Prepared statements not only improve execution speed by reducing the parsing and compilation time for repeated queries but also help prevent SQL injection vulnerabilities. In Python and other languages with SQLite bindings, prepared statements can be created by using parameterized queries. By preparing the SQL statement once and executing it multiple times with different parameters, the database engine reuses the compilation artifacts, leading to faster execution. An example in Python is as follows:

```
import sqlite3

conn = sqlite3.connect('example.db')
cursor = conn.cursor()

# Using a prepared statement for bulk updates
cursor.execute("BEGIN TRANSACTION;")
update_stmt = "UPDATE records SET data = ? WHERE id = ?"
for record_id in range(1, 1001):
    new_data = f"Updated Item {record_id}"
    cursor.execute(update_stmt, (new_data, record_id))
conn.commit()
conn.close()
```

In the context of data modifications, the database schema and indexing strategy have a significant impact on performance. Indexes, while invaluable for read operations, can become a liability during bulk insert and update operations. Each insert or update that modifies an indexed column necessitates additional work to update the corresponding index. A common strategy to optimize bulk inserts or updates is to temporarily disable or drop indexes, execute the data modifications, and then rebuild the indexes. This approach is especially beneficial when inserting or updating very large datasets. Rebuilding indexes in bulk is often faster than incrementally maintaining them. The process involves dropping the indexes, performing the modification, and then recreating the indexes once the modifications are complete.

```
-- Dropping an index before bulk operations
DROP INDEX IF EXISTS idx_records_data;

-- Perform bulk insert or update operations here

-- Recreate the index after modifications are complete
CREATE INDEX idx_records_data ON records(data);
```

Adjusting SQLite's PRAGMA settings can also lead to improved insertion and update performance. Several PRAGMA commands adjust internal configurations that affect disk I/O behavior, caching, and transactional integrity. For instance, setting the synchronous PRAGMA to off or normal can increase write speed by reducing the durability guarantees at the risk of potential data loss in the event of a system crash. Another useful setting is the journal mode. While the default journal mode ensures safety by writing a rollback journal for each transaction, changing to the WAL (Write-Ahead Logging) mode or even the MEMORY journal may provide performance benefits in scenarios where durability is less critical.

```
-- Temporarily disable synchronous writes to increase performance
PRAGMA synchronous = NORMAL;

-- Switch the journal mode to Write-Ahead Logging
PRAGMA journal_mode = WAL;
```

It is important to note that adjustments to PRAGMA settings should be made with an understanding of the trade-offs between performance and data safety. Testing these changes under realistic workloads and failure scenarios is essential to ensure that performance gains do not compromise data integrity beyond acceptable limits.

The physical layout of data on disk, including database page size, also plays a role in optimizing data modifications. The default page size in SQLite is usually sufficient for most applications, but for specific scenarios involving very large insert or update operations, adjusting the page size can be beneficial. A larger page size reduces the overhead of page management during bulk modifications, while a smaller page size may reduce the amount of data that must be rewritten during each update. Experimentation with the PRAGMA page_size setting can yield insights into optimal configuration for particular workloads.

```
-- Set an optimal page size before creating tables and inserting data
PRAGMA page_size = 4096;
```

Optimizing update operations also involves critical consideration of table design and query formulation. When an update query is expected to modify a large number of rows, avoiding unnecessary columns in the update statement can reduce overhead. Updating only those columns that require a change avoids the cost associated with rewriting entire rows. Additionally, using conditional updates that precisely target the rows needing modification minimizes the execution overhead. Consider a scenario where an update should only be applied to rows satisfying a particular condition:

```
UPDATE records
SET data = 'Special Update'
WHERE condition_column = 'specific_value';
```

This targeted approach ensures that the database engine performs fewer writes and reduces lock contention. In contrast, blanket update operations without a WHERE clause can lead to full table scans and unnecessary rewriting of unaffected rows.

Optimizations can also be realized by reducing the number of round-trip communications between the application and the database engine. Rather than executing multiple independent SQL statements, batching

277

several modifications into a single SQL command can lead to performance improvements. In some cases, using SQL constructs such as the INSERT INTO ... SELECT statement can parallelize or combine operations, minimizing communication overhead.

Another underappreciated factor that impacts data modifications is memory management within SQLite. Allocating a sufficient cache size via PRAGMA cache_size can significantly reduce disk I/O during bulk operations. Increasing the cache size allows more data to reside in memory, which not only speeds up insert and update operations but also improves read performance immediately after modifications. Configuring this setting appropriately based on available system resources and workload patterns can yield measurable benefits.

```
-- Increase the cache size for improved performance during bulk
    operations
PRAGMA cache_size = 10000;
```

For developers working in environments where concurrent write operations occur, careful management of transactions is vital. SQLite uses a locking mechanism that allows multiple readers but serializes writes. When multiple processes attempt to write simultaneously, performance can degrade due to lock contention. One strategy to mitigate this issue is to batch multiple writes into a single transaction, reducing the frequency of lock acquisition and release. In addition, employing WAL (Write-Ahead Logging) mode can improve concurrency by reducing contention between readers and writers.

Profiling and measuring the performance of data insertion and update operations is key to understanding the impact of various optimization techniques. Time measurements in application code, along with query plan analysis, provide quantitative evidence of improvement. For example, developers may use time-stamped logging around transaction boundaries to capture the duration of bulk modifications. Combined with system monitoring tools, such data informs further adjustments

278

to PRAGMA settings or transaction management strategies.

Special considerations should be given to scenarios where data integrity and performance requirements conflict. For mission-critical applications that cannot risk data loss, maintaining full synchronous writes and a conservative journal mode may be non-negotiable. In these cases, optimizing the structure of SQL statements, using prepared statements, and adjusting transaction boundaries become the primary means to enhance performance. The careful layering of these techniques ensures that, even under the most stringent durability requirements, data modifications are performed as efficiently as possible.

The use of application-level caching mechanisms can further reduce the load on the database during high-frequency modifications. Caching temporarily uncommitted data on the client side, and then performing asynchronous bulk updates, is a strategy employed to smooth out peak loads. This method is particularly effective in environments where data consistency can be managed by the application logic, rather than relying solely on the database engine.

Optimizing data insertion and update operations involves a multifaceted approach that spans transaction management, prepared statement usage, schema design, and tuning of SQLite configuration parameters. By systematically applying these techniques, developers can achieve significant performance improvements, reducing both the runtime overhead and the operational locks that impede concurrent access. The strategies outlined here provide a comprehensive framework for enhancing data modification speed while balancing considerations of data integrity and concurrency.

7.5.   Memory and Disk Optimization Techniques

Efficient use of memory and disk resources is critical to maximizing SQLite performance, particularly in environments where data volumes are large or system resources are constrained. Balancing memory usage with disk access speeds requires a multifaceted approach that addresses configuration parameters, data layout, caching strategies, and hardware characteristics. This section details methods for optimizing memory utilization and disk I/O, emphasizing practical adjustments to SQLite's operational parameters and schema design to achieve improved performance.

A primary mechanism for managing memory in SQLite is the cache. SQLite employs an in-memory cache to store database pages, thereby reducing the frequency of disk access. The size of this cache can be adjusted using the PRAGMA cache_size command. Increasing the cache size allows more data to be held in volatile memory, which can be particularly beneficial for read-heavy workloads or applications that repeatedly access the same data. However, allocation must be balanced against available system memory to avoid detrimental swapping. The following code snippet demonstrates how to configure the cache size within an SQLite session:

```
PRAGMA cache_size = 10000;   -- Increase the number of pages held in
    memory
```

A related parameter is the PRAGMA page_size. The page size determines the granularity of data transfer between disk and memory. A larger page size can reduce the number of disk I/O operations when large amounts of data are being accessed sequentially but may lead to increased memory usage and wasted space if most queries operate on small subsets of data. Conversely, a smaller page size can reduce memory waste but increase the number of disk accesses required to fulfill a request. Determining an optimal page size is workload-dependent and may require empirical testing. Setting an appropriate page size before initializing the database is accomplished with the following command:

```
PRAGMA page_size = 4096;   -- Set page size to 4 KB, a common value
    balancing memory and I/O
```

Disk optimization is equally vital, particularly because disk I/O is orders of magnitude slower than memory operations. One of the most effective approaches to minimize disk access is the use of Write-Ahead Logging (WAL). WAL mode separates the writing process from the main database file, enabling simultaneous reads and writes while reducing the latency associated with frequent disk flushes. Activating WAL mode is straightforward and is achieved through the following PRAGMA statement:

```
PRAGMA journal_mode = WAL;
```

WAL mode not only improves concurrency but also minimizes disk writes by batching changes together, which further enhances overall system efficiency. It is important to recognize that changing the journal mode may have implications on durability and should be tested against application-specific requirements.

Memory usage is also optimized by judiciously selecting synchronous settings. The PRAGMA synchronous directive controls the balance between performance and durability. Setting synchronous to NORMAL or OFF can yield dramatic improvements in write speed by reducing the number of disk flushes, although this comes at the cost of increased risk of data loss during a crash. In testing environments or non-critical applications, it is common to use a lower synchronous setting to maximize throughput:

```
PRAGMA synchronous = NORMAL;
```

While reducing the synchronous level improves performance, it is crucial to evaluate the potential risks and include additional safeguards such as frequent backups or replication in production environments.

Disk fragmentation and the efficient organization of data on disk also impact performance. SQLite databases benefit from periodic maintenance routines that reorganize data storage. The VACUUM command rebuilds the database file, reducing fragmentation and consolidating free space into contiguous blocks. This operation can significantly speed up query execution, although it may require temporary downtime or increased I/O during its execution. The VACUUM command is executed as follows:

```
VACUUM;
```

Routine usage of VACUUM, combined with reindexing operations, contributes to sustained performance, particularly in databases with frequent insertions, updates, and deletions. Reindexing can rebuild fragmented indexes, ensuring that the query planner has access to optimal index structures for data retrieval.

Another aspect of disk optimization involves the storage format and file system characteristics. SQLite leverages the operating system's file caching mechanisms; thus, using fast storage media such as solid-state drives (SSDs) can considerably reduce latency for disk operations. Additionally, aligning the SQLite page size with the underlying file system block size can avoid unnecessary read-modify-write cycles, thereby increasing throughput and reducing wear on the storage device.

Memory consumption can also be controlled by mindful schema design. Denormalized tables, while potentially increasing storage requirements, can reduce the frequency and cost of expensive joins, thereby lowering the overall memory footprint during query execution. Similarly, using appropriate data types that match the expected range of data ensures that both memory and disk space are used efficiently. Choosing INTEGER instead of TEXT for numerical values, when possible, reduces storage size and improves processing speed.

For environments handling concurrent accesses, optimizing for memory and disk includes managing lock contention. SQLite uses a file lock-ing mechanism to maintain data integrity during writes, and inefficient management of these locks can lead to performance bottlenecks. Em-ploying WAL mode and adjusting the cache and synchronous settings can mitigate many of these issues by reducing the duration and fre-quency of exclusive file locks. Furthermore, using memory-based tem-porary storage for sorting operations can reduce disk spillover. The PRAGMA temp_store command allows developers to control whether temporary tables are stored in memory or on disk:

```
PRAGMA temp_store = MEMORY;
```

Storing temporary data in memory usually speeds up transactions that involve large sorts or intermediate results but should be used with cau-tion in systems where memory is limited.

Modern systems offer various strategies to profile memory and disk performance. Profiling tools and logging within the SQLite engine can help monitor the effectiveness of the configured PRAGMA settings. De-velopers should consider conducting benchmarks that compare query execution times under different configurations. For example, system-atically varying the cache size and measuring the impact on complex query performance can reveal optimal settings tailored to the specific workload. Combining these quantitative results with qualitative analy-sis from query plan examinations forms a comprehensive strategy for performance optimization.

Understanding the interplay between memory and disk access is essen-tial for diagnosing performance issues that may not be apparent from query-level analysis alone. For instance, when query execution times are unexpectedly high, a review of the disk I/O patterns using system monitoring tools can reveal underlying issues such as cache eviction or disk contention. Similarly, monitoring memory utilization in real-time can help identify whether the database or the operating system is under memory pressure, which may indirectly affect SQLite's performance.

SQLite's design philosophy emphasizes simplicity and portability, yet it provides ample configuration options to optimize resource usage. Experienced developers often leverage SQLite's flexibility by tuning multiple parameters in combination rather than in isolation. It is not uncommon for iterative testing and tuning to be necessary, with adjustments made based on workload patterns and the evolution of the application over time. In one scenario, a developer might begin by increasing the cache size, then move to adjusting the page size and journaling mode, and finally incorporate file system optimizations and hardware upgrades. Each of these layers contributes cumulatively to a well-tuned database system.

Combining these strategies with code-level optimizations further enhances performance gains. For example, when executing batch operations, grouping SQL statements to reduce context switching between the application and the SQLite engine can lead to a more efficient use of both memory and disk resources. An example of batching asynchronous writes that leverages these optimizations might look as follows:

```
import sqlite3
import time

conn = sqlite3.connect('example.db')
cursor = conn.cursor()

# Apply performance-enhancing PRAGMA settings
cursor.execute("PRAGMA cache_size = 10000;")
cursor.execute("PRAGMA page_size = 4096;")
cursor.execute("PRAGMA journal_mode = WAL;")
cursor.execute("PRAGMA synchronous = NORMAL;")
cursor.execute("PRAGMA temp_store = MEMORY;")

# Begin a transaction for batch inserts
cursor.execute("BEGIN TRANSACTION;")
start_time = time.time()

for i in range(1, 10001):
```

```
    cursor.execute("INSERT INTO logs (event) VALUES (?)", (f"Event {i
    }",))

conn.commit()
end_time = time.time()
print(f"Batch insert time: {end_time - start_time:.2f} seconds")

conn.close()
```

By combining transaction management with the aforementioned PRAGMA settings, the above script demonstrates how to execute batch operations efficiently, reducing disk writes and optimizing memory usage. Timely adjustments and iterative testing, as shown in the timing measurement, help in fine-tuning performance for the specific hardware and workload.

Overall, managing memory usage and optimizing disk access in SQLite involves both system-level configuration and application-level tuning. The techniques discussed in this section—ranging from adjusting PRAGMA settings such as `cache_size`, `page_size`, `journal_mode`, and `temp_store` to leveraging hardware improvements and application-level batching—form an integrated approach to enhancing performance. Optimizing both memory and disk utilization not only improves query execution times but also contributes to a more responsive and robust application, capable of scaling with increasing data volumes and operational demands.

7.6. Handling Concurrency and Locking

SQLite employs a simplified locking mechanism that prioritizes simplicity and reliability but poses challenges in multi-user environments. In many deployments, multiple processes or threads may attempt concurrent access to the database, making the effective management of locks critical to preserve performance and prevent contention. SQLite utilizes a locking hierarchy wherein readers do not block one another, but writers acquire an exclusive lock that temporarily prevents access by others. This section examines strategies to manage concurrency and mitigate locking contention, exploring configuration settings, transaction management techniques, and application-level strategies, and it provides practical code examples.

SQLite supports different locking modes designed to manage how database file locks are handled. The default mode enables a conservative locking strategy that minimizes data corruption risk at the cost of potential performance degradation when many write operations occur concurrently. Developers can make use of the PRAGMA locking_mode command to alter the behavior. For example, switching to an exclusive locking mode can reduce the frequency of lock acquisitions by a single process when multiple transactions are executed sequentially, but it inherently limits concurrent access:

```
PRAGMA locking_mode = EXCLUSIVE;
```

The proper application of locking modes depends on the workload characteristics. In read-intensive systems, a shared mode may suffice, while write-intensive environments may benefit from exclusive modes when access is controlled by a single process.

Another critical configuration option is the busy timeout, which determines how long SQLite waits before returning an error when a lock cannot be immediately acquired. The PRAGMA busy_timeout command sets this interval in milliseconds. Setting an appropriate busy timeout can smooth transient contention by giving concurrent operations time to complete. For instance, a timeout of 5 seconds can be configured as follows:

```
PRAGMA busy_timeout = 5000;
```

A higher busy timeout value can prevent unnecessary failures in high-concurrency scenarios, especially when write operations are infrequent but require a short wait.

Write-Ahead Logging (WAL) is a widely used feature that significantly improves concurrency in SQLite. In WAL mode, writers append changes to a separate log file rather than modifying the main database file directly. This separation allows readers to access the stable database while the log is being written, thereby reducing contention between readers and writers. Activating WAL mode is achieved by executing:

```
PRAGMA journal_mode = WAL;
```

Switching to WAL mode can enhance performance in multi-threaded or multi-process scenarios, particularly when read and write operations occur concurrently. It is important to note that WAL mode performs differently under various file system conditions and may need additional tuning depending on the underlying hardware.

Another factor contributing to reduced locking contention is the careful management of transactions. Since every write operation in SQLite requires acquiring an exclusive lock, grouping multiple modifications into a single transaction minimizes the overhead associated with acquiring and releasing locks repeatedly. Developing an efficient transaction strategy is key; wrapping a sequence of updates or inserts within a single transaction can have a substantial impact. The following Python example demonstrates efficient transaction management for batch updates:

```
import sqlite3

conn = sqlite3.connect('example.db')
cursor = conn.cursor()

# Set a busy timeout to allow time for lock acquisition
cursor.execute("PRAGMA busy_timeout = 5000;")
cursor.execute("PRAGMA journal_mode = WAL;")

# Begin a transaction to encompass multiple modifications
cursor.execute("BEGIN TRANSACTION;")
```

287

```
for i in range(100):
    cursor.execute("UPDATE counters SET value = value + 1 WHERE id =
    ?", (i,))
conn.commit()
conn.close()
```

By grouping updates into a single transaction, the code minimizes the exclusive locking period and reduces overall contention.

Concurrency challenges often arise in multi-threaded applications. SQLite offers several threading modes: single-thread, multi-thread, and serialized. The serialized mode, which is the default, ensures that SQLite will serialize access to database connections, thereby guaranteeing thread safety. Although this mode simplifies development by handling locking internally, it can introduce unnecessary overhead if external application logic already manages thread synchronization. In cases where an application can ensure that no two threads access the same database connection concurrently, the multi-thread mode eliminates some internal locking overhead. Configuring threading mode is done when opening the connection by passing appropriate flags, although this is typically managed by the language-specific SQLite binding.

Application-level strategies also play a role in reducing locking contention. For instance, splitting the workload across multiple databases, such as using separate files for different sets of data, can minimize conflicts. When data segmentation is feasible, distributing the workload across distinct SQLite files prevents a single file from becoming a bottleneck. Additionally, designing the application to favor read operations can alleviate locking issues, since read locks do not block other readers in SQLite. In systems where data freshness is not immediately critical, implementing a caching layer can offload read pressure from the main database, thereby reducing lock contention.

Optimization of SQL queries themselves can indirectly influence locking behaviors. Optimized queries that execute quickly hold locks for a shorter duration. This involves ensuring that queries are well-indexed and that unnecessary full-table scans are avoided. As discussed in earlier sections, query performance enhancements reduce the time locks are held, thereby enabling faster turnover for waiting transactions. The integration of these techniques creates a more responsive system even under heavy load.

Concurrency control can be further improved by using prepared statements. Prepared statements reduce the preparation overhead and streamline the execution of repeated queries, thereby shortening the duration each transaction holds exclusive locks. This efficiency is particularly beneficial in environments that perform repetitive modifications to the database. An example of using prepared statements in Python is shown below:

```
import sqlite3

conn = sqlite3.connect('example.db')
cursor = conn.cursor()

cursor.execute("PRAGMA busy_timeout = 5000;")
cursor.execute("PRAGMA journal_mode = WAL;")

# Wrap multiple insert operations in a single transaction
cursor.execute("BEGIN TRANSACTION;")
insert_stmt = "INSERT INTO logs (message) VALUES (?)"
for log in range(500):
    cursor.execute(insert_stmt, (f"Log entry {log}",))
conn.commit()
conn.close()
```

Prepared statements reduce the time spent in query preparation, which in turn diminishes the lock duration necessary for completing batch operations.

Concurrency management also benefits from handling errors gracefully. When lock contention occurs, SQLite returns a SQLITE_BUSY error. Application logic should catch these errors and implement a retry mechanism that waits for a short period before attempting to execute the failing operation again. This method helps to manage temporary spikes in contention without causing the application to fail. A simple retry loop might look as follows:

```python
import sqlite3
import time

conn = sqlite3.connect('example.db')
cursor = conn.cursor()
cursor.execute("PRAGMA busy_timeout = 5000;")
max_retries = 5
retry_count = 0

while retry_count < max_retries:
    try:
        # Begin a transaction for a critical update
        cursor.execute("BEGIN TRANSACTION;")
        cursor.execute("UPDATE items SET stock = stock - 1 WHERE id =
    1;")
        conn.commit()
        break
    except sqlite3.OperationalError as e:
        conn.rollback()
        retry_count += 1
        time.sleep(0.2)
conn.close()
```

Implementing error handling with retries allows the application to gracefully handle transient lock contention rather than failing immediately.

Advanced strategies include using a dedicated background process to handle writes. By delegating write operations to a single process, an application can centralize lock management, reducing the frequency of conflicting access patterns. Other processes can then operate in read-only mode and refresh their caches periodically. This pattern is particularly effective in high-traffic applications where data consistency requirements permit slight delays in write propagation.

In multi-user systems, ensuring that transactions are as short as possible is a vital best practice. Long-running transactions hold locks that can block other operations. Developers should design their application logic to read, modify, and write data in a concise manner. Breaking down complex operations into smaller, atomic transactions prevents lock escalation and minimizes waiting times for other queries.

Reducing lock contention also necessitates an understanding of the cost associated with different operations. Inserts and updates in tables with multiple indexes cause additional work due to the need to update index structures. When high concurrency is expected, it may be preferable to limit the number of indexes on frequently modified tables or perform index maintenance during off-peak times. Scheduling maintenance tasks such as index rebuilding during periods of low activity further reduces the possibility of contention during critical periods.

Hardware considerations and parallelism play effective roles in handling concurrency. Employing faster storage, higher core-count processors, and optimizing operating system-level disk caching can all contribute to reducing the severity and duration of locks. By tuning the file system and ensuring that the storage hardware is capable of sustaining high I/O rates, overall lock wait times can be minimized, enabling a smoother concurrency experience under load.

Finally, monitoring and profiling lock contention is crucial for diagnosing performance issues related to concurrency. System-level monitoring tools, as well as SQLite-specific logging options, can provide insights into how often locks are acquired and held, and which operations are most affected. Instrumentation and logging allow developers to corroborate theoretical optimizations with empirical data, facilitating continuous improvement in the handling of concurrency.

Applying these strategies in combination leads to a robust system design that minimizes contention. Through proper configuration using PRAGMA settings, efficient transaction management, well-structured application logic, and proactive error handling, SQLite can maintain high performance even in multi-user environments. The thoughtful integration of concurrency strategies, as detailed above, fosters a database system that not only ensures data integrity but also maximizes throughput and responsiveness in the face of competing demands.

7.7. Using PRAGMA Statements

PRAGMA statements serve as a powerful interface to SQLite's internal configuration, providing developers with the means to fine-tune the database engine for specific application requirements. These statements control a wide array of settings that govern behavior such as memory allocation, locking, journaling, and performance optimizations. Advanced users leverage PRAGMA commands to adapt SQLite to diverse workloads—from high-frequency insertions to intensive read operations and complex multi-user environments.

One fundamental use of PRAGMA statements is managing caching behavior. For instance, the `cache_size` PRAGMA controls the number of pages that SQLite holds in memory. By increasing the cache size, frequently accessed data remains in memory longer, reducing disk I/O and improving query response times. A typical usage to enlarge the cache in an SQLite session is shown below:

```
PRAGMA cache_size = 10000;
```

This configuration is particularly effective in read-heavy applications, as it minimizes the latency associated with repeatedly fetching data from disk. However, it is important to balance the cache size with the available system memory to prevent swapping, which could adversely impact performance.

Another critical configuration option is the `page_size` PRAGMA. The page size determines the block size for disk I/O operations. While the default page size is often appropriate for general use, custom applications may benefit from tuning this parameter to match their workload characteristics or the underlying file system block size. For example, setting a page size of 4096 bytes is common in many environments:

```
PRAGMA page_size = 4096;
```

Adjusting the page size correctly can reduce the number of I/O operations required for large sequential reads or writes, which is particularly beneficial when dealing with substantial data volumes.

Journaling mode and synchronous settings play a pivotal role in balancing performance and data integrity. SQLite provides multiple journaling modes, the most widely used being the default rollback journal and Write-Ahead Logging (WAL). The WAL mode offers significant concurrency improvements by allowing readers to access a stable version of the database concurrently with writers. Enabling WAL mode involves the following command:

```
PRAGMA journal_mode = WAL;
```

Switching to WAL mode is advantageous in multi-user environments where concurrent reading and writing occur consistently. Conversely, for applications prioritizing absolute durability over performance, retaining the default journal mode or exploring other modes such as MEMORY may be more appropriate.

The synchronous PRAGMA is closely related to journaling and controls the durability guarantee of write operations. By adjusting the synchronous setting, developers can trade off between performance and the risk of data loss in the event of a crash. A lower level of synchronization (e.g., NORMAL or OFF) can substantially speed up bulk insertions and updates by reducing the number of disk flushes performed. This command is typically executed as follows:

```
PRAGMA synchronous = NORMAL;
```

293

Such configuration is ideal in scenarios where the application can tolerate a short window of potential data loss, such as during non-critical data logging or caching tasks.

PRAGMA statements also govern settings that affect temporary storage. SQLite uses temporary files for operations such as sorting and creating temporary tables. These operations can be performed in memory to reduce disk I/O, provided there is sufficient available memory. The temp_store PRAGMA directs SQLite to store temporary tables either in memory or on disk:

```
PRAGMA temp_store = MEMORY;
```

Using in-memory temporary storage can result in faster execution times for operations that create large intermediate datasets. Nevertheless, this setting should be employed judiciously in memory-constrained environments where allocating substantial RAM for temporary data could compromise overall system performance.

Another area where PRAGMA statements offer fine-grained control is lock management and concurrency. The busy_timeout PRAGMA determines how long SQLite will wait for a lock before aborting an operation. This setting is particularly useful in multi-user environments where lock contention is common. A busy timeout of 5000 milliseconds, for instance, can be set using:

```
PRAGMA busy_timeout = 5000;
```

This command instructs SQLite to wait for up to 5 seconds when a conflicting lock is encountered, thereby reducing the likelihood of immediate failures during high concurrency. Properly calibrating the busy timeout can smooth out transient load spikes, allowing for graceful recovery from temporary lock contention.

Optimizing the physical layout and fragmentation of the database file can also be addressed through PRAGMA statements. The auto_vacuum

294

PRAGMA controls how SQLite manages free space within the database file. When auto-vacuum mode is enabled, SQLite automatically reclaims unused space after deletions, minimizing file fragmentation. The setting can be enabled with:

```
PRAGMA auto_vacuum = FULL;
```

While an auto-vacuum setting can optimize disk space usage and potentially improve access times by reducing fragmentation, it may introduce overhead during data modifications. Developers must weigh the benefits of reduced disk fragmentation against the performance costs of more frequent data reorganization.

PRAGMA directives also include settings tailored for specialized use cases such as encryption, debugging, and performance diagnostics. For example, the `integrity_check` command allows developers to quickly verify the consistency of the database file:

```
PRAGMA integrity_check;
```

Regular integrity checks can preemptively identify corruption issues before they escalate into major performance or data reliability problems. Such diagnostic commands are essential in environments where robust data integrity is a mission-critical requirement.

Using PRAGMA statements is not limited to adjusting runtime performance; they also facilitate the tuning of long-term database maintenance. For instance, the `reindex` command can rebuild indexes that have become fragmented over time due to extensive insert, update, or delete operations:

```
REINDEX;
```

Periodic reindexing, in combination with the VACUUM command, helps maintain optimal query performance by ensuring that data storage and index structures remain organized and efficient. The VACUUM command rebuilds the entire database file and can be invoked via:

```
VACUUM;
```

This command consolidates free space and defragments the database file, resulting in more efficient disk access patterns and potentially lower query latencies.

A dynamic aspect of PRAGMA statements is the ability to query current settings and behavior directly from the SQLite engine. Many PRAGMA commands can return the current value of a configuration option, allowing applications to verify that intended optimizations are in effect. For example, a Python application can query and print the current cache size as follows:

```
import sqlite3

conn = sqlite3.connect('example.db')
cursor = conn.cursor()

cursor.execute("PRAGMA cache_size;")
cache_size = cursor.fetchone()
print(f"Current cache_size: {cache_size[0]}")

conn.close()
```

This approach facilitates runtime diagnostics and dynamic adjustments based on observed performance characteristics.

When applying PRAGMA statements, developers must account for compatibility and version-specific behaviors. As SQLite evolves, certain PRAGMA settings may be added, modified, or deprecated. It is crucial to consult the official SQLite documentation when targeting a specific version to ensure that the configured settings behave as expected. Version control of the database engine and corresponding PRAGMA settings is an integral part of performance tuning and long-term maintenance practices.

Effective use of PRAGMA statements requires an integrated approach, where multiple settings are tuned in concert to produce the desired performance profile. For example, combining an increased `cache_size`, a tuned `page_size`, and an appropriate `synchronous` level can yield cumulative performance benefits that surpass adjustments made in isolation. An exemplary sequence of initialization commands might look like this:

```
PRAGMA cache_size = 10000;
PRAGMA page_size = 4096;
PRAGMA journal_mode = WAL;
PRAGMA synchronous = NORMAL;
PRAGMA temp_store = MEMORY;
PRAGMA busy_timeout = 5000;
```

This configuration stabilizes the database's performance by reducing disk I/O, improving concurrency through WAL mode, and managing locks via a generous busy timeout. Such configurations are often established at the beginning of a database session or within the application startup sequence, ensuring consistent behavior throughout the application's lifecycle.

PRAGMA statements offer a versatile and accessible method for fine-tuning SQLite's internal parameters to match the specific needs of an application. By understanding and judiciously applying these directives, developers can optimize memory utilization, disk access, concurrency, and overall query performance. The thoughtful configuration of PRAGMA settings forms a cornerstone of high-performance SQLite application design, enabling developers to strike an optimal balance between speed, reliability, and resource utilization.

Chapter 8

Security and Best Practices in SQLite

This chapter addresses SQLite security and best practices, focusing on preventing SQL injection through parameterized queries and input validation. It covers data encryption techniques, backup and disaster recovery planning, and maintaining data integrity with constraints. Effective management of database permissions, alongside regular maintenance and monitoring, is emphasized to ensure the reliable and secure operation of SQLite environments.

8.1. Securing SQLite Databases

Securing SQLite databases is a multifaceted task that involves managing access to the underlying database file and protecting the data stored within it through encryption mechanisms. Given that SQLite databases are file-based, the operating system's file permissions are a primary means of controlling access. However, additional measures such as encryption, application-level authentication, and key management must be integrated to ensure that sensitive information remains protected even if unauthorized access to the file system occurs.

Since SQLite does not include a built-in user authentication system, securing access to the database file itself relies heavily on the environment in which the database is deployed. Restricting file access through operating system-level permissions is one of the fundamental techniques. It is important to ensure that the database file is stored in a secured folder where only trusted users have read and write permissions. For example, Unix-based systems allow administrators to set file ownership and permissions using commands such as chmod and chown. This measure reduces the risk of unauthorized users accessing the file directly.

Application-level controls further enhance security by providing an additional barrier. Implementing application logic to verify user credentials before connecting to the database is a common strategy. Since SQLite itself does not enforce access control, the application must handle user authentication and authorization, often integrating with external identity providers or leveraging operating system user sessions. Combining the operating system's file permission model with robust application-level authentication mechanisms improves the overall security posture of the database system.

In many instances, protecting data in transit and at rest requires encrypting the database content. Encryption in SQLite can be implemented at different scopes. Full database encryption secures all data contained within the file, while column-level or table-level encryption targets only sensitive data fields. The SQLite Encryption Extension (SEE) provides one option to encrypt an entire database. However, its licensing terms may not be suitable for all projects. An alternative approach is to use third-party libraries such as SQLCipher, which is

300

built on top of SQLite and offers transparent, strong encryption using industry-standard algorithms.

A practical example using SQLCipher in Python illustrates the integration of encryption into SQLite connections. The following Python code snippet demonstrates how to open an encrypted SQLite database using the pysqlcipher3 package. This example assumes that the encryption library is properly installed and configured.

```python
import sqlite3

# For demonstration purposes, using SQLCipher to open an encrypted
    database
def connect_encrypted_db(db_path, key):
    conn = sqlite3.connect(db_path)
    cursor = conn.cursor()
    # Enable the key to unlock the database
    cursor.execute("PRAGMA key = '{}';".format(key))
    cursor.execute("PRAGMA cipher_page_size = 1024;")
    cursor.execute("PRAGMA kdf_iter = 64000;")
    cursor.execute("PRAGMA cipher_hmac_algorithm = HMAC_SHA1;")
    cursor.execute("PRAGMA cipher_kdf_algorithm = PBKDF2_HMAC_SHA1;")
    return conn

db_path = 'secure_database.db'
encryption_key = 's3cr3t_passw0rd'

conn = connect_encrypted_db(db_path, encryption_key)

# Example query execution using parameterized queries to ensure
        internal query safety
cursor = conn.cursor()
query = "SELECT * FROM sensitive_table WHERE user_id = ?;"
cursor.execute(query, (42,))
rows = cursor.fetchall()

conn.close()
```

In the above example, setting the encryption key through the PRAGMA command instructs SQLite to use the provided key for database decryption. The additional PRAGMA settings configure encryption parameters such as the cipher page size and the key derivation function iterations. Such settings are critical as they influence both the security and performance characteristics of the encryption.

It is important to note that when implementing encryption, key management becomes a central challenge. Hardcoding encryption keys within the application code—as illustrated in simple examples—is discouraged in production environments. Instead, keys should be securely stored, often using environment variables or external key management systems. This decouples the key from the source code and minimizes the risk of key exposure during source code access. Utilizing dedicated key management infrastructures, such as hardware security modules (HSMs) or cloud-based key management services, can further enhance data security.

Encryption also brings performance considerations. The computational overhead associated with encryption and decryption operations means that developers must balance security requirements with application performance. It is advisable to benchmark database operations under realistic workloads to ensure that encryption does not unduly impact the user experience. Additionally, while encryption shields stored data from unauthorized access, it does not inherently protect against other forms of attacks such as SQL injection. Developers must continuously employ best practices—such as parameterizing queries and rigorous input validation—to mitigate a broader array of security risks.

Another consideration in securing SQLite databases is the use of secure connections. Although SQLite is typically used for local storage and often does not involve network communication, scenarios where the database file is accessed over a network or integrated into a larger distributed system can introduce vulnerabilities. Here, ensuring that any data exchanged between the database and the application is secured through transport layer encryption (e.g., TLS) becomes crucial. Furthermore, regularly updating the SQLite engine to incorporate the latest security fixes is essential. Developers should subscribe to relevant security bulletins and integrate automated update mechanisms when feasible.

It is also recommended that developers perform periodic audits of the secure database environment. This involves verifying that file permissions remain appropriately restricted, ensuring that encryption keys have not been compromised, and testing that the encryption configuration meets the desired security standards. Automated tools that monitor file integrity and access logs can help identify anomalous behavior indicating potential security breaches or unauthorized access attempts.

Managing access control in SQLite can be supplemented with cryptographic measures. For applications that require more granular control over user permissions and data segmentation, implementing an intermediate layer that manages authentication, authorization, and logging is effective. Such an intermediary ensures that only authorized queries are executed on the database, and that there is an audit trail of all database interactions. This approach is particularly useful when the SQLite database is embedded within larger applications where multiple users or roles need differentiated levels of access.

Mechanisms such as role-based access control (RBAC) can be enforced at the application level. Although SQLite itself does not manage roles, a well-defined access control policy integrated into the application logic can simulate role-based permissions. This helps in evolving scenarios where data access needs to be dynamically controlled and logged. Logging is an integral part of maintaining secure databases. Without an audit trail, it is challenging to assess whether security policies are appropriately enforced or to detect potentially malicious activities. Implementing logging functions that record significant events, such as failed access attempts or modifications to security configurations, is recommended in environments where data sensitivity is high.

The combination of operating system-level security, robust encryption methods, and deliberate application-level controls forms the foundation of securing SQLite databases. It is critical that each element of the security strategy is maintained regularly and audited against evolving threat models. As database storage technologies and attack vectors continue to evolve, security policies must be revisited and updated to ensure that they remain effective. This includes both the underlying infrastructure that supports the SQLite database and the application logic that interfaces with it.

Developers are advised to leverage established libraries and frameworks that emphasize security. The use of well-reviewed encryption libraries reduces the risk of implementing encryption incorrectly. Additionally, code reviews and security testing procedures, such as vulnerability scanning and penetration testing, are indispensable practices. Such measures help to uncover potential flaws in how encryption keys are managed or how access controls are implemented. These practices further align with the overall emphasis on maintaining data integrity and ensuring that access to the database is strictly limited to authorized entities.

The diverse strategies discussed here—ranging from file permission management and application-level authentication to advanced encryption techniques—illustrate that securing SQLite databases requires a comprehensive approach. Each component of the security framework supports the others, creating multiple layers of defense. By integrating these practices, developers can achieve a high level of security for their SQLite environments, ensuring that sensitive data remains protected against unauthorized access and potential breaches.

8.2.   Preventing SQL Injection Attacks

SQL injection remains one of the most prevalent security threats to database-driven applications. Attackers exploit vulnerabilities in query construction, injecting malicious SQL code that can alter, delete, or reveal sensitive data. In the context of SQLite, prevention hinges on disciplined coding practices, particularly focusing on parameterized queries and rigorous input validation.

SQL injection vulnerabilities typically manifest when user input is directly concatenated into SQL statements. This unsafe practice can lead to unintended execution paths. An adversary might manipulate input to inject additional SQL commands or alter query logic. For example, a poorly constructed query that incorporates user-supplied data might inadvertently allow an attacker to bypass authentication checks or exfiltrate data. Parameterized queries mitigate this risk by separating SQL code from data. Database engines subsequently treat inputs as parameters rather than executable SQL code, ensuring that special characters or embedded commands do not alter query semantics.

Parameterized queries, also known as prepared statements, allow developers to define SQL queries with placeholders that are subsequently bound to data values. This mechanism lets the underlying database engine pre-compile query templates, providing a secure and efficient means to handle user input. When the query is executed, the engine recognizes these placeholders as data, eliminating the possibility of treating them as part of the SQL command. For instance, consider the process of fetching user information based on a provided user ID. Instead of concatenating the ID into a query string, developers can write a query with a placeholder for the parameter and then safely attach the user input.

```
import sqlite3

def fetch_user_details(user_id):
    conn = sqlite3.connect('application_database.db')
    cursor = conn.cursor()
    # Use a parameterized query with a placeholder
    query = "SELECT * FROM users WHERE id = ?;"
    cursor.execute(query, (user_id,))
    result = cursor.fetchone()
```

```
    conn.close()
    return result

# Example usage with a user-supplied parameter
user_input = 5  # This input should be sanitized prior to any further
    processing if needed
user_details = fetch_user_details(user_input)
print(user_details)
```

In this example, the query employs a question mark (?) as a place-holder for the user ID. The parameter, provided as a tuple, substitutes the placeholder during execution. This approach not only safeguards against SQL injection but also promotes code clarity by clearly delineating the query structure from its parameters.

Input validation is another critical line of defense. While parameterized queries effectively secure the SQL execution pathway, it is still essential to validate and sanitize all external inputs. Well-defined input validation prevents unexpected data from being processed by the application, reducing the risk of injection attacks and other vulnerabilities. Input validation encompasses checking that data conforms to expected formats, sizes, and types. For instance, if a user ID is numeric, the application should enforce this constraint before even reaching the SQL query execution stage. An effective strategy is to implement both server-side and client-side validations, ensuring that invalid inputs are caught early in the processing pipeline.

The following code snippet illustrates additional input validation checks performed on a user-supplied parameter before constructing a query. This example extends the previous snippet by incorporating validation logic to ensure that the input is a valid integer.

```
def is_valid_integer(value):
    try:
        int(value)
        return True
    except ValueError:
        return False
```

```
def fetch_user_details_with_validation(user_input):
    if not is_valid_integer(user_input):
        raise ValueError("Invalid user ID. An integer is required.")

    # Convert user input to an integer after validation
    user_id = int(user_input)

    conn = sqlite3.connect('application_database.db')
    cursor = conn.cursor()
    query = "SELECT * FROM users WHERE id = ?;"
    cursor.execute(query, (user_id,))
    result = cursor.fetchone()
    conn.close()
    return result

# Example usage with validated user input
user_input = "123"  # String input that represents an integer
if is_valid_integer(user_input):
    user_details = fetch_user_details_with_validation(user_input)
    print(user_details)
else:
    print("Provided input is not a valid integer.")
```

This code demonstrates how to integrate input validation with parameterized queries. The function is_valid_integer ensures that the input can be safely converted to an integer, thereby preventing malformed or malicious input from advancing to the query stage. This dual-layer approach fortifies the application against attacks that might exploit data type inconsistencies or unexpected string manipulations.

While parameterized queries and input validation form the crux of preventing SQL injection, additional defensive programming practices can further mitigate risks. For example, employing the principle of least privilege—whereby database accounts have only the permissions they require—can restrict the damage potential of a successful injection. If an application queries the database using an account with limited access, even a successful injection may not yield meaningful results.

Robust logging and error handling strategies also play a vital role in

307

maintaining a secure application. Logging unexpected inputs, failed queries, or unusual execution patterns can alert administrators to potential attack attempts. However, care must be taken not to log sensitive information. Error messages should be generic to avoid revealing internal database or application structure details that could aid an attacker.

Frameworks and libraries used for database interaction commonly provide built-in features that support parameterized queries. Developers are encouraged to leverage high-level abstractions where available, rather than constructing SQL strings manually. ORMs (Object-Relational Mapping frameworks) are particularly useful in this regard as they automatically bind parameters and often incorporate additional security checks. These frameworks significantly reduce the likelihood of human error by abstracting away the intricacies of raw SQL execution. Nonetheless, developers should possess a solid understanding of the underlying query mechanisms to avoid pitfalls when lower-level access is required.

Another aspect to consider is the evolution of query patterns within an application. As the system matures, new query constructs or complex filters may be introduced. Continuous code reviews and security audits help ensure that no new vulnerabilities are inadvertently introduced during maintenance or feature expansion. Automated static analysis tools can be integrated into the development pipeline to flag the use of unsafe query practices. Such tools analyze source code for common patterns that may lead to SQL injection vulnerabilities and provide actionable recommendations for remediation.

A practical application might involve dynamically constructed queries where various conditions are appended based on user selections. Even in these cases, it is essential to use parameterized queries. Consider a scenario where an application constructs queries based on multiple user filters. Instead of using string concatenation for each filter condition, each parameter should be individually bound to a prepared statement. This method maintains the integrity of the SQL command regardless of the number of conditions appended.

```
def search_users(name_filter, age_filter):
    conn = sqlite3.connect('application_database.db')
    cursor = conn.cursor()

    base_query = "SELECT * FROM users WHERE 1=1"
    parameters = []

    if name_filter:
        base_query += " AND name LIKE ?"
        parameters.append(f"%{name_filter}%")

    if age_filter:
        if not isinstance(age_filter, int):
            raise ValueError("Age filter must be an integer.")
        base_query += " AND age = ?"
        parameters.append(age_filter)

    cursor.execute(base_query, parameters)
    results = cursor.fetchall()
    conn.close()
    return results

# Example usage of the dynamic query function
results = search_users("Alice", 30)
print(results)
```

In this example, the query begins with a constant condition that always evaluates to true, providing a convenient starting point for appending additional filters. Each potential filter is checked and added to the query only if applicable, along with a corresponding parameter. Even with dynamic query construction, using parameterized queries preserves security by preventing the injection of harmful SQL code.

Attention to input length and format is another best practice to further enhance security. Limiting the maximum length of textual inputs can minimize the potential havoc caused by an injection attack. For instance, if an expected input should not exceed 100 characters, enforcing this limit at both the application and database levels prevents excessively long inputs that might strain the system or serve as a vector for malicious payloads.

The effectiveness of preventing SQL injection also depends on the overall security posture of the application environment. Regularly updating libraries and the SQLite engine ensures that known vulnerabilities are patched, reducing the risk that an attacker can exploit legacy code weaknesses. Moreover, secure coding guidelines should be part of the development process, with particular emphasis on the perils of concatenated SQL strings. Team training and adherence to code review protocols further reinforce these practices, ensuring that code committed to version control adheres to established security standards.

Continuous monitoring and penetration testing are invaluable tools in identifying weaknesses in database interaction code. Security testers can simulate SQL injection attacks to assess the robustness of parameterized queries and input validation measures. These tests help uncover edge cases that might have been overlooked during development. In environments with sensitive data, building a robust testing regimen helps maintain confidence that the security measures are correctly implemented and functioning as intended.

The integration of these strategies—parameterized queries, strict input validation, and supplementary security practices—results in a comprehensive defense against SQL injection attacks. These methods collectively ensure that the SQL query execution pathway is insulated from direct user manipulation. The principles outlined here are applicable to a wide spectrum of applications, reinforcing that secure code practices are foundational to overall system security. Through rigorous adherence to these guidelines, developers can effectively mitigate the risk of SQL injection and safeguard the integrity, confidentiality, and availability of their SQLite databases.

8.3. Implementing Data Encryption

Encrypting data at rest in SQLite is a critical measure to protect sensitive information from unauthorized access when physical access to the database file is gained. Unlike client-server database systems, SQLite stores its database as a single file on disk, making it an attractive target for attackers who gain access to the file system. Encrypting the database file mitigates such threats by rendering the data unintelligible without the proper decryption key.

One prominent method for encrypting SQLite databases is through the use of extensions such as SQLCipher. SQLCipher builds upon SQLite and provides full database encryption using Advanced Encryption Standard (AES) in CBC mode with a 256-bit key. Other options include the SQLite Encryption Extension (SEE), which is offered by the SQLite developers, though its licensing may restrict its use in some projects. Understanding these encryption alternatives is essential for selecting a method that best fits system requirements, performance considerations, and security policies.

The use of encryption changes the way applications interact with the database. When encryption is in place, any connection to the database must provide the correct decryption key. Without this key, the engine is unable to decrypt data, thereby negating any unauthorized attempts to access sensitive information. Integration of encryption into application code typically involves the execution of specific PRAGMA commands immediately after establishing a connection to the database.

A practical example of leveraging SQLCipher in a Python application shows how encryption is seamlessly integrated into SQLite connections. In the following Python code snippet, the connection to an encrypted SQLite database is initialized by setting several encryption-specific PRAGMA statements:

```
import sqlite3
```

311

```
def connect_encrypted_db(db_path, key):
    conn = sqlite3.connect(db_path)
    cursor = conn.cursor()
    # Issue PRAGMA commands to activate encryption
    cursor.execute("PRAGMA key = '{}';".format(key))
    cursor.execute("PRAGMA cipher_page_size = 1024;")
    cursor.execute("PRAGMA kdf_iter = 64000;")
    cursor.execute("PRAGMA cipher_hmac_algorithm = HMAC_SHA1;")
    cursor.execute("PRAGMA cipher_kdf_algorithm = PBKDF2_HMAC_SHA1;")
    return conn

db_path = 'encrypted_data.db'
encryption_key = 'strong_encryption_key_1234'
conn = connect_encrypted_db(db_path, encryption_key)
```

In this example, the PRAGMA command PRAGMA key is used to provide the decryption key whenever the connection is made. Additional PRAGMA settings configure encryption parameters such as cipher page size and key derivation iterations, which influence both performance and security strength. These settings are important because they control the resistance of the database encryption mechanism against brute force attacks while maintaining acceptable performance levels during data access operations.

Key management is a crucial component of any encryption strategy. The encryption key should never be hardcoded within the application's source code. Instead, it should be stored securely, using methods that prevent inadvertent exposure. Secure key management practices include storing keys in dedicated key management services, hardware security modules (HSMs), or secure vaults provided by cloud services. By decoupling the key from the application's codebase, the possibility of key leakage during code reviews or repository access is greatly reduced.

Ensuring compatibility and performance with encryption in place requires developers to carefully design their database access routines. Notably, encryption impacts both read and write performance. The extra computational overhead arising from encryption and decryption processes should be considered when designing the application, especially for systems with high transaction rates. Performance testing with encryption enabled is essential to identify any bottlenecks and optimize configuration parameters accordingly. In many cases, selecting an adequate cipher algorithm and tuning its parameters provides a balance between high security and application performance.

Data encryption in SQLite extends beyond encrypting a single file; it can also be implemented selectively. Some applications may require encrypting only specific tables or columns containing sensitive data. However, such granular encryption requires additional application logic and, in some cases, might be implemented using custom SQL functions or triggers that manage encryption and decryption. These approaches offer flexibility but demand a deeper understanding of encryption fundamentals to prevent mistakes that could compromise data confidentiality.

In scenarios where selective encryption is employed, developers must adopt careful practices to ensure that the encryption keys are managed appropriately for each sensitive field. For example, an application could encrypt a column containing social security numbers using a dedicated encryption function. When data is retrieved, the function decrypts the field before it is presented to the application or user. The following example illustrates a simplistic conceptual approach to encrypting and decrypting data in an SQLite table using Python. Note that in production, a robust and secure encryption library should replace any custom implementations.

```
from cryptography.fernet import Fernet

# Generate a key for encryption and decryption
# In a secure environment, store this key in a secure key management
    service
encryption_key = Fernet.generate_key()
cipher_suite = Fernet(encryption_key)
```

313

```
def encrypt_value(plaintext):
    # Converts plaintext to bytes and encrypts it
    return cipher_suite.encrypt(plaintext.encode('utf-8'))

def decrypt_value(ciphertext):
    return cipher_suite.decrypt(ciphertext).decode('utf-8')

def insert_sensitive_data(conn, sensitive_info):
    cursor = conn.cursor()
    encrypted_info = encrypt_value(sensitive_info)
    cursor.execute("INSERT INTO sensitive_data (info) VALUES (?);", (
     encrypted_info,))
    conn.commit()

def fetch_sensitive_data(conn, record_id):
    cursor = conn.cursor()
    cursor.execute("SELECT info FROM sensitive_data WHERE id = ?;", (
     record_id,))
    encrypted_info = cursor.fetchone()[0]
    return decrypt_value(encrypted_info)

# Example usage with an unencrypted SQLite database for demonstration
conn = sqlite3.connect('selective_encryption.db')
insert_sensitive_data(conn, "confidential_information")
data = fetch_sensitive_data(conn, 1)
print(data)
conn.close()
```

This example uses the cryptography library to encrypt and decrypt a specific column in a table. Though this method does not leverage SQLCipher's full-database encryption, it offers flexibility when only portions of the data require stringent protection. The choice between full-database encryption and selective column encryption depends on the application's architecture, performance requirements, and the sensitivity of the stored data.

Another aspect of implementing encryption is verifying that encryption policies are correctly enforced throughout the lifecycle of the database. Automated tests should ensure that any database backup or copy remains encrypted and that no unencrypted data is inadvertently exposed. Periodic audits and penetration testing help validate that encryption configurations have not been inadvertently altered and that no vulnerabilities exist in the encryption setup.

For applications that interact with SQLite databases using encryption, proper error handling and recovery mechanisms are essential. For instance, if an incorrect encryption key is provided or if the key is compromised, the application needs to handle decryption errors gracefully. In such cases, detailed yet secure logging is important to diagnose issues without exposing sensitive information. Developers should also explicitly manage situations where encryption settings might have changed between database versions, ensuring that encryption remains consistent and reliable across updates.

Advanced encryption techniques may also include techniques such as envelope encryption, where data is encrypted with a data encryption key (DEK) that is itself encrypted with a master key. This approach simplifies key rotation procedures and allows for granular access control. Employing envelope encryption with SQLite involves additional layers of key management, but it can improve the long-term security of stored data, particularly in high-security environments. When implementing envelope encryption, a secure and centralized mechanism for key rotation ensures that even if a single encryption key is compromised, the overall system remains secure.

Configuration management for encryption settings is also an important consideration. Parameters such as PRAGMA configurations in SQLCipher should be treated as part of the application's secure configuration. Secure configuration management systems, along with environment-based configuration files, can help prevent accidental exposure or misconfiguration of critical encryption parameters. Centralizing configuration management not only bolsters security but also simplifies deployment and disaster recovery planning, especially when encryption is a critical component of the data protection strategy.

Implementing data encryption in SQLite requires a multifaceted ap-

315

proach that integrates database-level encryption with application-level management and secure coding practices. The reliance on extensions such as SQLCipher provides robust, transparent encryption for the entire database, whereas selective column encryption using dedicated libraries offers flexibility in protecting only the most sensitive fields. Critical to both approaches is secure key management and careful performance monitoring. As encryption practices are implemented, thorough testing, auditing, and continuous monitoring ensure that the system remains secure against evolving threats while still delivering acceptable performance.

8.4. Backup and Disaster Recovery Planning

Maintaining reliable backups and preparing for disaster recovery are essential components of a secure and robust SQLite environment. Given that SQLite stores its data in a single file, backup processes are relatively straightforward compared to client-server databases, yet they require careful consideration to ensure that the data remains consistent, recoverable, and secure. A well-designed backup strategy encompasses regular backups, secure storage of backup files, and periodic testing of recovery procedures to verify that data can be restored within the desired time frame.

A key aspect of backup planning involves determining the appropriate frequency and method of backups. SQLite provides a built-in online backup API, which allows the creation of consistent snapshots of the database even while it is in use. Using the backup API minimizes downtime and avoids interference with application performance. The sqlite3_backup_init() C function, or its equivalent in high-level languages such as Python, offers a mechanism to create full backups by reading from the active database and writing to a new backup file. Integrating such functionalities in your application extends the concept of backups from simple file copies to dynamic, application-aware data protection.

When planning backups, the concept of Recovery Point Objective (RPO) and Recovery Time Objective (RTO) should guide backup frequencies and storage strategies. RPO defines the maximum period during which data can be lost in the event of a disaster, while RTO specifies the maximum allowable downtime before system functionality is restored. A backup strategy that balances these metrics is critical; frequent backups might reduce the RPO at the expense of system performance, whereas infrequent backups might result in data loss that exceeds acceptable limits. Therefore, selecting the appropriate backup strategy depends on the specific requirements of the deployment environment, the criticality of the data, and the expected load on the system.

In scenarios where data is dynamically changing, incremental backups become particularly useful. Incremental backups only save changes made since the last full backup, reducing the amount of data handled during each backup operation and accelerating the backup process. However, implementing incremental backups with SQLite requires careful orchestration since the default backup API creates complete copies of the database. Developers may opt for file-system level snapshotting or third-party tools designed for incremental backup management. Regardless of the method chosen, the backup process should be automated to reduce human error and guarantee regular creation of backup files.

The automation of backup processes is typically achieved through scheduled tasks. In a Python-based environment, developers can leverage scheduling libraries such as `schedule` or use native operating system tools like `cron` on Unix-like systems or Task Scheduler on Windows. Automating backups not only ensures consistency but also integrates recovery planning into the broader system maintenance rou-

317

tine. The following Python code snippet demonstrates a simple usage of SQLite's backup method to create a consistent copy of a database:

```python
import sqlite3
import time

def backup_database(source_db_path, backup_db_path):
    source_conn = sqlite3.connect(source_db_path)
    backup_conn = sqlite3.connect(backup_db_path)
    # Initiate the backup process
    with backup_conn:
        source_conn.backup(backup_conn, pages=1, progress=progress)
    backup_conn.close()
    source_conn.close()

def progress(status, remaining, total):
    print("Copied {} of {} pages...".format(total - remaining, total)
    )

if __name__ == "__main__":
    source_database = 'production_data.db'
    backup_database = 'backup_production_data.db'
    backup_database(source_database, backup_database)
    print("Backup completed at", time.strftime("%Y-%m-%d %H:%M:%S"))
```

In this example, the backup process is invoked by calling the backup method on a database connection, which copies pages from the source to the destination database. This structured approach provides real-time feedback via a progress callback function and ensures that the backup is performed within a managed transaction, preserving the integrity of the backup copy.

Beyond the creation of backup files, ensuring their secure storage is critical. Backups must be protected with the same level of security as the live database. Access controls on backup files, encryption of backup data both at rest and during transmission, and storing backups in physically secure locations are necessary measures. In environments where backups are transmitted offsite or to a cloud service, end-to-end encryption must be enforced. For encrypted databases, it is also essential that the backup procedures preserve encryption metadata so that the backups remain secure and compatible with the original encryption

318

settings.

Disaster recovery planning extends beyond the procedure of creating backups. It encompasses a holistic view of the steps required to restore functionality in the event of data loss or corruption. Developers and administrators should document disaster recovery procedures, specifying not only how the backups are to be restored but also how the application should be reconfigured in a disaster scenario. This documentation should include clear instructions for verifying the integrity of restored data and validating that all necessary system components are operational after recovery.

It is advisable to implement periodic disaster recovery drills. These drills simulate catastrophic events, allowing teams to practice restoring the database from backups and to identify any deficiencies in the recovery process. Such exercises not only boost confidence in the backup strategy but also help uncover latent errors or inefficiencies that might delay recovery. Logging and monitoring recovery drills provide valuable insights that can be integrated into future iterations of the disaster recovery plan. A structured testing regimen ensures that backups remain viable over time and that recovery procedures are updated to reflect changes in the database schema or application architecture.

In addition to full database backups, versioned backups play a pivotal role in disaster recovery. By maintaining multiple backup versions, organizations can revert to a backup taken before the occurrence of data corruption or an unintentional release of erroneous data. This versioning strategy is critical in mitigating the impact of user errors or malicious activity, as it provides a historical archive from which the system can be restored to a known good state. Storage systems that support versioning, whether on-premises or in cloud environments, should be integrated with the backup procedures to automate the retention and pruning of backup snapshots in accordance with organizational policies.

Moreover, backup and disaster recovery planning should be part of a broader risk management strategy. Performing a risk assessment to identify potential sources of data loss—ranging from hardware failures and natural disasters to cyber-attacks—can inform the frequency and type of backups needed. The risk assessment should guide investments in redundant systems, offsite backup storage, and automated monitoring solutions that alert administrators to any discrepancies or failures in backup execution. The integration of backup logs with centralized monitoring systems can also facilitate early detection of anomalies, thereby preventing minor issues from escalating into major disruptions.

Another point of analysis in backup planning is the challenge of ensuring consistency across distributed systems. While SQLite is typically deployed on a single host, modern applications may rely on SQLite databases integrated within multi-tier architectures or hybrid environments. In these cases, the synchronization of backups with other components of the system becomes crucial. Consistent backups across distributed systems ensure that all interdependent data can be restored simultaneously, preserving transactional consistency and data integrity. Coordination between different system components, possibly through orchestrators or integrated backup management tools, is therefore an essential aspect of disaster recovery in complex environments.

The continuous monitoring of the backup process is indispensable. Automated verification procedures should be established to check the integrity of backup files immediately after their creation. Tools that read backup logs and perform checksum validations help detect incomplete or corrupt backups before the backup window closes. In situations where periodic monitoring is not feasible, generating a summary report of each backup process can aid in post-mortem analysis and facilitate the tracking of backup success rates over time.

A comprehensive backup and disaster recovery plan in an SQLite environment is not static but evolves with the application itself. As the database schema changes and new features are introduced, the backup strategy must adapt accordingly. Iterative testing and regular updates to backup procedures are necessary to address new vulnerabilities and performance bottlenecks. Maintaining detailed documentation and performing routine code reviews of the backup scripts ensure that the processes remain aligned with the overall security posture of the application.

A final operational consideration is the coordination of backups with application maintenance windows. Since many backup operations can be performed while the database is online using the backup API, careful scheduling helps to reduce potential performance impacts during peak usage periods. However, when significant schema changes or application updates are planned, taking the database offline momentarily may provide a more secure and consistent snapshot of the data. Balancing the need for continuous operation with the requirements for reliable backups is an ongoing challenge that must be addressed through thoughtful planning and stakeholder communication.

The strategies for maintaining reliable backups and preparing for disaster recovery constitute an integral part of comprehensive data management. These strategies are designed to safeguard the integrity and availability of critical data, ensuring that organizations remain operational even in the face of significant disruptions. By employing automated backup routines, secure storage protocols, periodic testing, and continuous monitoring, administrators can create a resilient system capable of recovering from a variety of adverse scenarios.

8.5. Ensuring Data Integrity

Ensuring data integrity is paramount in maintaining the consistency and reliability of databases, particularly in systems where data is frequently modified and interrelated. In SQLite, enforcing data integrity is achieved primarily through the use of constraints, triggers, and transaction management. These mechanisms work in tandem to prevent invalid data entry, maintain referential consistency, and ensure that all database operations complete successfully or not at all.

Data integrity can be conceptually divided into several dimensions: entity integrity, referential integrity, and domain integrity. Entity integrity ensures that each record in a table is uniquely identifiable, typically through the use of primary keys. Referential integrity guarantees that relationships between tables remain consistent, generally enforced through foreign key constraints. Domain integrity, on the other hand, restricts the possible values that can be stored in a column; this is achieved by enforcing data types, default values, and check constraints.

SQLite supports these integrity constraints through SQL syntax extensions that are similar to those found in other relational database systems. For example, a table defined with a primary key constraint automatically enforces uniqueness and non-nullability of a column. Similarly, foreign key constraints can be defined to ensure that entries in a child table correspond to valid primary key values in a parent table. It is essential to note, however, that SQLite requires the explicit activation of foreign key support via a PRAGMA statement.

The following example demonstrates how to define tables with primary key, foreign key, and check constraints in SQLite. The primary table, orders, is linked to a table customers via a foreign key relationship. A check constraint is included in the orders table to ensure that the order total is always non-negative.

```
CREATE TABLE customers (
    customer_id INTEGER PRIMARY KEY,
    name TEXT NOT NULL,
    email TEXT UNIQUE NOT NULL
);

CREATE TABLE orders (
```

```
    order_id INTEGER PRIMARY KEY,
    customer_id INTEGER NOT NULL,
    order_date TEXT DEFAULT (datetime('now')),
    order_total REAL CHECK(order_total >= 0),
    FOREIGN KEY (customer_id) REFERENCES customers(customer_id)
);
```

In this schema, the customers table enforces entity integrity through a primary key and ensures that each email address is unique. The orders table not only uses a primary key but also enforces referential integrity by referencing the customer_id in the customers table. The check constraint on order_total ensures that no negative values are permitted.

Activation of foreign key constraints in SQLite is not automatic; it must be explicitly enabled using the following PRAGMA statement upon establishing a database connection:

```
import sqlite3

def get_connection(db_path):
    conn = sqlite3.connect(db_path)
    conn.execute("PRAGMA foreign_keys = ON;")
    return conn

db_path = 'integrity_example.db'
connection = get_connection(db_path)
```

The above Python code snippet establishes a connection to an SQLite database and immediately enables foreign key enforcement. This step is critical to ensure that any insertion, update, or deletion operations respect the referential constraints defined in the schema.

Transaction management in SQLite further reinforces data integrity by ensuring atomicity of operations. A transaction groups a sequence of operations, making sure that either all changes are committed or none at all. In the event of an error, a rollback operation ensures that the database state remains consistent. This mechanism is particularly important for multi-step operations that depend on the successful execution of each individual component.

323

Consider a Python example where several related operations – such as inserting a new customer and corresponding orders – are performed within a transaction:

```python
def create_customer_and_order(conn, customer_data, order_data):
    try:
        cursor = conn.cursor()
        # Begin transaction
        cursor.execute("BEGIN TRANSACTION;")

        # Insert customer record
        cursor.execute("INSERT INTO customers (name, email) VALUES
(?, ?);", customer_data)
        customer_id = cursor.lastrowid

        # Insert order record with foreign key reference to
customer_id
        order_data_with_customer = (customer_id,) + order_data
        cursor.execute("INSERT INTO orders (customer_id, order_date,
order_total) VALUES (?, ?, ?);", order_data_with_customer)

        # Commit transaction
        conn.commit()
    except Exception as e:
        # Rollback in case of error
        conn.rollback()
        raise e

# Example usage
customer_info = ('John Doe', 'john.doe@example.com')
order_info = ('2023-10-12', 150.75)
try:
    create_customer_and_order(connection, customer_info, order_info)
    print("Customer and order were created successfully.")
except Exception as error:
    print("Transaction failed: ", error)
```

This example emphasizes the importance of encapsulating related database operations within a single transaction. If any part of the process fails, the rollback ensures that partial data does not corrupt the overall database integrity.

Beyond built-in constraints and transactions, custom triggers can provide additional enforcement of integrity policies and business rules.

Triggers in SQLite are procedural code segments that automatically execute in response to certain events on a table. They can be used to enforce complex constraints that cannot be captured by standard SQL constraints alone. For instance, a trigger might be used to enforce a rule that prevents deletion of a customer record if pending orders exist.

```
CREATE TRIGGER prevent_customer_deletion
BEFORE DELETE ON customers
FOR EACH ROW
BEGIN
    SELECT
        CASE
            WHEN (SELECT COUNT(*) FROM orders WHERE customer_id = OLD
    .customer_id) > 0
            THEN RAISE(ABORT, 'Cannot delete customer with active
    orders.')
        END;
END;
```

This trigger prevents deletion of any customer records that are associated with existing orders. Such custom rules help enforce the business logic that is beyond the scope of traditional foreign key or check constraints, thereby ensuring consistency in how data is managed across various scenarios.

Ensuring data integrity also involves routine verification and validation procedures. Database administrators should periodically run integrity checks to ascertain that constraints are not violated and that relationships between tables remain consistent. SQLite's PRAGMA integrity_check command can be instrumental in this regard. Running this command returns a message indicating whether the database is free of errors or if issues have been detected.

```
PRAGMA integrity_check;
```

Incorporating such integrity checks into automated maintenance routines provides early detection of anomalies that might compromise data integrity. Regular audits, possibly integrated into continuous integration systems, help in maintaining a reliable database environment

325

and enable developers and administrators to address potential issues proactively.

Data consistency can also be enhanced using techniques such as optimistic and pessimistic concurrency control. While SQLite uses file locking to manage concurrency, application-level strategies can further minimize conflicts in heavily multi-user environments. For example, implementing versioning of records or timestamp checks can prevent race conditions where simultaneous updates might lead to inconsistent states.

When designing database schemas and interactions, careful planning is required to account for future changes. Schema migrations, although necessary for evolving applications, must be handled with precision to ensure legacy data remains consistent with new constraints. Version control for database schemas, combined with automated migration tools, helps maintain continuity and data integrity during development cycles. Best practices include verifying migration scripts in a staging environment before applying them to production systems, ensuring that both the structural and referential integrity of data are preserved.

Ensuring data integrity is more than enforcing constraints at the schema level; it is a comprehensive approach that integrates database design, application logic, continuous monitoring, and regular maintenance routines. By leveraging SQLite's robust support for primary keys, foreign keys, check constraints, transactions, and triggers, developers create systems that not only prevent data anomalies but also provide mechanisms to automatically correct or rollback undesirable changes. This multi-faceted approach underpins reliable database operations and forms the foundation of secure, consistent data management across the system.

Commitment to data integrity from the initial design phase of an application significantly mitigates risks associated with data corruption and invalid entries. Establishing a culture that emphasizes rigorous testing and audit trails ensures that integrity rules evolve alongside the application, adapting to new requirements while safeguarding historical consistency. Overall, the practices and examples detailed herein illustrate a layered and resilient strategy for ensuring data integrity, which is indispensable in any robust SQLite-based system.

8.6. Managing Database Permissions

SQLite, as a file-based database system, does not contain an internal user management and permission system akin to those found in client-server databases. Instead, managing database permissions in SQLite requires a multi-layered approach that leverages both operating system-level controls and application-level security frameworks. Understanding the interplay between these layers is essential to prevent unauthorized access and to ensure that only designated users can perform specific operations on the database.

At the operating system level, file permissions act as the primary line of defense. Because the SQLite database is stored in a single file, ensuring proper file system permissions is critical. Limiting access to this file by setting restrictive permissions prevents unauthorized reading, writing, or deletion of the database. For instance, on Unix-like systems the chmod and chown commands can be used to restrict access to the database file so that only the intended application process or a specific user account can interact with it. For example, the following shell command restricts the database file so that only the owner has read and write permissions:

```
chmod 600 /path/to/database.db
```

Such practices mitigate the risk of unauthorized file-level access and

safeguard the database from direct manipulation. Alongside file permissions, encryption is frequently employed to add an extra layer of
protection. When a database is encrypted with tools such as SQLCipher and the corresponding decryption key is managed securely, even
if an unauthorized party gains access to the file, reading or modifying
the contents remains infeasible without the key.

Beyond the operating system, application-level controls are indispensable. Since SQLite itself does not restrict user roles or permissions, the
hosting application must implement a rigorous mechanism for user authentication, authorization, and logging. This mechanism often takes
the form of role-based access control (RBAC), wherein users are assigned specific roles (such as administrator, editor, or viewer) and the
application enforces permissions based on these roles. This design ensures that each user can only perform operations that align with their
privileges.

One practical approach to implement RBAC in an application using
SQLite is to maintain tables that record users, roles, and permissions.
The application enforces these permissions before executing any critical database operation. The following example demonstrates a simplified Python implementation that integrates role-based checks before
executing a query:

```
import sqlite3

# Simulated database of users and roles
user_roles = {
    'alice': 'admin',
    'bob': 'editor',
    'charlie': 'viewer'
}

# Dictionary defining permissions for each role
role_permissions = {
    'admin': ['read', 'write', 'delete'],
    'editor': ['read', 'write'],
    'viewer': ['read']
}
```

```
def has_permission(user, action):
    role = user_roles.get(user)
    if role is None:
        return False
    return action in role_permissions[role]

def execute_query(user, query, params=()):
    if not has_permission(user, 'write') and query.strip().upper().
     startswith("INSERT"):
        raise PermissionError("User does not have permission to
     insert data.")
    if not has_permission(user, 'delete') and query.strip().upper().
     startswith("DELETE"):
        raise PermissionError("User does not have permission to
     delete data.")

    conn = sqlite3.connect('application_database.db')
    conn.execute("PRAGMA foreign_keys = ON;")
    cursor = conn.cursor()
    cursor.execute(query, params)
    conn.commit()
    conn.close()

# Example usage
try:
    execute_query('bob', "INSERT INTO articles (title, content)
     VALUES (?, ?);",
                    ("New Features", "Details about new features."))
except PermissionError as pe:
    print("Access denied:", pe)
```

In this example, the function has_permission checks the user's role against a predefined set of permissions. The execute_query function then enforces these permissions by verifying that the user is allowed to perform the requested action. Such application-level access control complements file and encryption mechanisms by ensuring that even if an attacker bypasses low-level security, they will not be able to execute sensitive operations through the application interface.

Another critical facet of managing database permissions is logging and auditing. It is important to maintain an audit trail that records significant database operations. Such logs should include details on who

329

accessed the database, what operations were attempted, and whether those operations succeeded or failed. Logging not only provides a forensic record of activities but also acts as a deterrent against malpractice. Integrating logging into the application layer, and especially monitoring anomalous patterns such as repeated failed access attempts, assists in early identification of potential breaches. Developers are advised to use centralized logging systems where database access logs can be collated with other system security logs.

Given the absence of built-in user management in SQLite, access control is often enforced indirectly by isolating different users into distinct application sessions. For example, different operating system users or different containers can be used to separate access to database files physically. In multi-user environments, it is common to deploy SQLite databases in environments where the operating system provides user isolation. This could involve segregating databases by client application, deploying within a container orchestrated by a tool such as Docker, or enforcing network-level access controls when the application is a part of a microservices architecture.

In environments where multiple applications share access to a single SQLite file, ensuring that each application adheres to a consistent security policy becomes challenging. It is then critical to adopt design principles that minimize cross-application access. One strategy is to use file-based encryption combined with a secure key management system so that each application or user possesses a unique mechanism for decrypting and encrypting data. For instance, keys can be generated and stored within a secure vault, and the application logic can retrieve the appropriate key based on the user's credentials before accessing the database.

For advanced use cases, developers can implement row-level security using custom triggers and views. Although SQLite does not provide direct support for row-level access control, creative application designs can emulate this behavior. For instance, a trigger could restrict modifications to certain rows based on the user's identity, while views can be defined to expose only a subset of data filtered according to the user's role. Consider the following trigger example that prevents a non-administrator from altering sensitive rows in a table:

```
CREATE TRIGGER prevent_unauthorized_update
BEFORE UPDATE ON sensitive_data
FOR EACH ROW
WHEN (SELECT role FROM user_info WHERE username = CURRENT_USER) <> '
    admin'
BEGIN
    SELECT RAISE(ABORT, 'Only administrators can update this data.');
END;
```

While SQLite does not natively support the CURRENT_USER function, this example illustrates the conceptual approach developers might adopt. Instead, application code must supply contextual information during execution, and database triggers can use this information to enforce custom security policies.

Combining these strategies into a coherent security framework requires consistent policies and practices. Developers should document the access control mechanisms employed, including the rationale behind chosen file permissions, encryption strategies, and application-level controls. In distributed environments, this documentation can form the basis of security audits and regular compliance reviews. Ensuring that permissions remain synchronized with policy changes over time is critical; periodic code reviews and security assessments serve as a means to validate that access controls remain robust against evolving threats.

Maintaining security in SQLite environments is not solely about imposing restrictions but also about validating that the mechanisms in place are effective. Regular testing, including penetration testing and routine audit procedures, should be performed to verify that the implemented access controls operate as expected. These tests help identify potential misconfigurations, such as accidentally overly permissive file access rights or flaws in role validation logic.

Managing database permissions in SQLite environments is a comprehensive endeavor that demands attention at both the operating system and application layers. Relying exclusively on SQLite's native capabilities is insufficient due to its lack of built-in user management; hence, a layered security approach is necessary. By combining firm file system permissions, robust encryption, stringent application-level access controls, and detailed logging, developers can create an ecosystem where database access is carefully regulated and continuously monitored.

Institutionalizing these practices involves not only technical measures but also the establishment of a security culture within the development team. Training developers to understand the implications of improper access control, performing code reviews to enforce secure coding practices, and integrating security testing into the development lifecycle are all integral to an effective permission management strategy. This comprehensive approach ensures that the SQLite database remains a trusted component within a larger system, secure against unauthorized access and capable of supporting the organizational policies and regulatory requirements imposed on sensitive data management.

The methods and examples discussed herein provide a blueprint for managing database permissions in SQLite environments. They illustrate how leveraging operating system controls, application-level role-based access management, dynamic triggers, and centralized logging contribute to a securely managed database. Through careful planning, continuous monitoring, and iterative improvements, organizations can ensure that the right users have the appropriate access while protecting the database from potential threats.

8.7. Regular Maintenance and Monitoring

Regular maintenance and monitoring are key practices for ensuring that SQLite databases continue to operate efficiently over time. Given the file-based nature of SQLite, a combination of routine maintenance tasks and continuous monitoring can preempt performance degradation, prevent data corruption, and ensure quick recovery in the event of unexpected disturbances.

One important maintenance task is database optimization. As applications continually modify the database, it is common for unused space and fragmentation to occur. The VACUUM command reorganizes the database file, reducing its size and potentially improving query performance. Executing VACUUM repacks the database into a minimal amount of disk space and defragments data pages, which is particularly beneficial in systems where numerous insertions, deletions, and updates occur over the application's lifetime.

```
VACUUM;
```

Automating the execution of such commands can help maintain performance. For example, scheduling a periodic vacuum operation during off-peak hours can prevent bloating of the database file. In a Python context, scheduling can be integrated using a cron job on Unix-based systems or with a scheduling library within the application. The following code snippet demonstrates how to invoke maintenance operations within an application:

```
import sqlite3

def perform_maintenance(db_path):
    conn = sqlite3.connect(db_path)
    cursor = conn.cursor()
    # Optimize the database by defragmenting and reclaiming unused
     space
    cursor.execute("VACUUM;")
    conn.commit()
    conn.close()
```

333

```
database_path = 'maintenance_example.db'
perform_maintenance(database_path)
```

Beyond the VACUUM command, other PRAGMA directives such as PRAGMA optimize and PRAGMA integrity_check serve critical roles during maintenance. The PRAGMA optimize command instructs SQLite to run various internal optimizations that might have been deferred, while PRAGMA integrity_check verifies the structural integrity of the database. Regularly scheduled integrity checks can detect corruption early, allowing administrators to act before data integrity is compromised.

```
PRAGMA integrity_check;
```

Automating these integrity checks and logging the results provides a trail of the database health status over time. For example, integrating these checks into a monitoring dashboard can alert administrators to anomalies, such as recurring integrity issues that might indicate underlying hardware problems or software misconfigurations.

Monitoring also involves keeping track of query performance and resource usage. As data volume increases, query execution times can become a critical metric affecting user experience. Collecting performance statistics, such as query response times, cache hit ratios, and I/O wait times, helps identify slow or resource-intensive operations. Tools or scripts that log query execution details can be used to pinpoint bottlenecks. An important strategy is to enable query logging in your application and use analysis tools to review the logs periodically.

In the context of SQLite, the EXPLAIN QUERY PLAN command can be employed to understand the effectiveness of the query plan generated by the SQLite engine. By evaluating the query plan, developers can determine if indexes are being used appropriately or if further schema adjustments are required. This process is fundamental to proactive performance tuning and can be integrated into regular maintenance schedules.

```
EXPLAIN QUERY PLAN SELECT * FROM orders WHERE order_total > 100;
```

Another critical aspect of maintenance is monitoring database file size and growth trends. SQLite databases have a tendency to grow with increased usage, especially when historical data accumulates over long periods. Regular analysis of file sizes allows administrators to plan for storage scaling or to implement purging and archiving strategies. Automated scripts can be designed to monitor file sizes and compare them against predefined thresholds, triggering alerts if the database grows beyond expected limits.

Routine backups, as discussed in previous sections, are part of the maintenance landscape. Verifying that backups are being created correctly and periodically testing restoration procedures is essential. Confidence in backup integrity is only possible with active monitoring of backup schedules and regular drills. A maintenance checklist should include verification of backup health through automated tests that restore data into a test environment and compare it against production criteria.

The following Python snippet illustrates a simple routine that monitors a database file for size changes and logs the results. This example is intended to be integrated into an overall monitoring system:

```
import sqlite3
import os
import time

def log_database_size(db_path, log_path):
    size = os.path.getsize(db_path)
    with open(log_path, 'a') as log_file:
        log_file.write(f"{time.strftime('%Y-%m-%d %H:%M:%S')} - Size:
    {size} bytes\n")

# Paths for the database and log file
database_path = 'maintenance_example.db'
log_file_path = 'db_size.log'
```

```
# Log the database size (this call can be scheduled or looped for
    continuous monitoring)
log_database_size(database_path, log_file_path)
```

In addition to low-level database operations, monitoring systems should capture system-level metrics such as available disk space, memory usage, and CPU load. These metrics are closely correlated with database performance, particularly in resource-constrained environments. A holistic monitoring approach ensures that administrators have an end-to-end view of both the database conditions and the underlying hardware performance.

The operational aspect of maintenance often involves periodic reindexing. Indexes, while critical for performance optimization, can become inefficient over time due to table updates and data modifications. Dropping and recreating indexes periodically helps optimize retrieval speeds. However, this should be approached with caution as rebuilding indexes can be resource-intensive and may temporarily affect database performance. An automated maintenance window, possibly during off-peak hours, is ideal for such activities.

In parallel with technical maintenance, establishing clear documentation and alerting procedures is fundamental to operational excellence. Administrators should have access to dashboards that consolidate health metrics, recent maintenance activities, and logs from automated integrity checks. Furthermore, integrating notifications via email or messaging platforms enables rapid response when anomalies are detected. For example, a monitoring system could be configured to send alerts if the PRAGMA integrity_check returns values other than the expected "ok" result.

Beyond the scope of performance and structural integrity, security monitoring forms a complementary aspect of maintenance. Logging user access, monitoring for unauthorized modifications, and tracking changes to critical tables are practices that enhance overall system se-

336

curity. The overlapping concerns of performance and security require that maintenance routines be designed with both perspectives in mind. Regular reviews of security logs may also reveal performance issues such as repeated failed access attempts or long-running queries associated with potential intrusion scenarios.

Scheduled maintenance tasks should be tailored to the specific usage patterns and growth trajectories of the application. For instance, high-transaction systems might require more frequent vacuum and reindexing, while read-heavy applications may benefit from periodic performance audits and cache optimizations. In any case, maintenance tasks should be automated as much as possible to minimize human error and guarantee that critical tasks are not overlooked.

Maintenance is not a one-time activity; it requires constant adaptation as applications evolve and data volumes grow. Versioning of database schemas, migration strategies, and regular updates of the SQLite engine are all part of a proactive maintenance strategy. Keeping the underlying SQLite library up-to-date ensures that performance improvements and bug fixes are applied promptly, reducing the risk of encountering known issues.

Finally, fostering a culture of regular maintenance and monitoring requires collaboration across development, operations, and security teams. Cross-functional teams can share insights from routine logs, performance metrics, and integrity checks to identify patterns and plan long-term improvements. This collaborative approach ensures that maintenance activities are aligned with business objectives and that potential issues are addressed before they escalate into critical failures.

By integrating these practices into a comprehensive maintenance and monitoring regimen, organizations can ensure that their SQLite databases remain adaptable, resilient, and efficient. A proactive approach to maintenance not only preserves performance over time but also underpins the overall security, reliability, and sustainability of the database environment.

Chapter 9

Handling Large Datasets with SQLite

This chapter explores managing large datasets in SQLite, focusing on overcoming limitations through efficient data import and export practices. It discusses optimizing table designs, memory usage, and indexing strategies for enhanced performance. Techniques such as batching for data operations and partitioning are presented to effectively distribute load and handle extensive datasets within SQLite.

9.1. Understanding SQLite Limitations

SQLite stands as an embedded relational database engine that is renowned for its simplicity and portability. Despite its many advantages, the engine exhibits inherent limitations when handling large datasets. SQLite is designed to operate as a single-file database, meaning that all objects are contained within one disk file. As dataset size increases, the consequences of this architecture, particularly in the realms of concurrency, memory management, and I/O performance, become increasingly pronounced.

One of the primary challenges arises from SQLite's locking mechanism. SQLite uses file-level locking to ensure data integrity during write operations. This locking strategy can lead to significant performance degradation in multi-threaded or concurrent access scenarios, especially when write-heavy workloads are involved. Since the database file is locked during write operations, other processes or threads attempting to write must wait, potentially causing delays. Although SQLite supports concurrent reads, the single-writer limitation makes write-intensive applications less efficient when compared to server-based databases that employ finer-grained locking strategies. Addressing this challenge often involves architecting the application to minimize write contention, such as by batching write operations or utilizing read replicas in scenarios where read-only access can be distributed.

In addition to concurrency issues, input/output (I/O) performance becomes a crucial factor when handling large datasets. SQLite's file-based design means that the performance is largely dependent on disk speed and system cache policies. When working with large datasets, the performance of disk reads and writes can become a bottleneck, particularly if the underlying storage medium is not optimized for random I/O. This bottleneck can be partially mitigated by tuning SQLite with prudent PRAGMA settings. For example, configuring the synchronization mode and journal mode can yield improvements in write performance, albeit at the potential cost of reduced data safety in the event of a crash. A typical approach to optimize I/O performance involves adjusting the following PRAGMA commands:

```
PRAGMA synchronous = NORMAL;
PRAGMA journal_mode = WAL;
```

The adjustments illustrated above shift SQLite towards a more performant configuration by reducing the strictness of the synchronization guarantee and adopting the Write-Ahead Logging (WAL) mode, which allows for greater concurrency. These settings, however, must be carefully evaluated against the data integrity requirements of the application.

Memory usage constitutes another critical area where limitations may present challenges. SQLite is designed to load portions of the database file into main memory to enhance query performance. However, as data volume increases, the memory footprint can become substantial, particularly for complex queries that require large temporary storage areas for sorting or aggregating data. In scenarios where available memory is limited, such queries may lead to swapping or even cause the database engine to exhaust available system resources. To alleviate such stress, careful query design and indexing strategies can be crucial. By creating indexes on columns frequently used in search conditions or joins, the engine can reduce the amount of data it must load, resulting in more efficient query execution.

Large datasets also necessitate attention to table design. Normalizing data minimizes redundancy, yet over-normalization might require excessive join operations that degrade performance on large tables. Conversely, denormalization can improve query speed by reducing the need for joins, but at the expense of increased storage size and potential data inconsistency. Balancing normalization and denormalization, while understanding the typical query patterns, is essential. Understanding the trade-offs involves analyzing query execution plans and optimizing indexes appropriately. For example, a conventional approach to improving performance is to combine denormalized structures with carefully designed indexes that optimize for the most common query patterns. This method can be validated by employing EXPLAIN QUERY PLAN output from SQLite to identify bottlenecks in query execution.

341

Examining the internal structure of SQLite, one discerns that each database page is a fixed-size block of data. When a row in a large table exceeds the size of an individual page or when numerous rows are being appended to a table concurrently, the frequency of page splits may escalate. This consequence increases disk I/O as the database engine reorganizes data across pages and files, further complicating efforts to maintain efficient performance. In addition, the B-Tree structures that underpin SQLite indices can become less efficient as the volume of records grows. Such structures demand more extensive rebalancing operations and can incur increased overhead during both read and write operations. Critical analysis of query performance and database size can help pinpoint when these structural limitations begin to degrade performance.

Another common challenge with large datasets is the overhead associated with transaction management. SQLite databases are transactional, ensuring atomicity for all changes, but this guarantee is implemented by writing transaction logs to disk. In environments with high-velocity data insertion or bulk modification, the overhead of transaction logging may outweigh the benefits provided by the safety and atomicity of these operations. Techniques such as statement batching and deferred transactions are recommended to reduce this overhead. For instance, rather than committing after every individual INSERT, grouping multiple INSERT operations into a single transaction can significantly improve throughput. The following code snippet illustrates how batching can be implemented in Python when using SQLite:

```
import sqlite3

connection = sqlite3.connect('large_dataset.db')
cursor = connection.cursor()
cursor.execute("BEGIN TRANSACTION;")

for i in range(10000):
    cursor.execute("INSERT INTO data_table(col1, col2) VALUES (?, ?)
    ;", (i, i * 2))
```

```
connection.commit()
connection.close()
```

Implementing write batching in the manner above minimizes the number of costly commit operations, thereby alleviating the bottleneck associated with transaction overhead.

Scalability limitations are another aspect that must be considered. Unlike server-based databases that can distribute processing across multiple CPU cores or nodes, SQLite is primarily single-threaded with respect to write operations. This centralization restricts the ability to leverage multi-core processors for write-intensive workloads. Although SQLite can be compiled with multi-threading support and does allow concurrent accesses under certain conditions, the inherent limitations of the single-writer approach remain a dominant factor. In systems where massive parallelism is required, one might consider offloading write operations to a more capable database engine. Within an SQLite context, mitigating these constraints often requires distributing the workload across multiple SQLite databases, each responsible for a portion of the dataset, and merging results as needed.

The limitations of SQLite become more evident when the database file grows in size. As the database file increases, backup strategies and migration plans must account for longer read and write operations. Moreover, file corruption can pose a serious risk in large database files. Despite SQLite's inherent safeguards, increased file sizes amplify the impact of any corruption, emphasizing the need for robust backup routines and possibly employing replication strategies even in a seemingly lightweight database system.

Addressing these limitations requires a combination of careful database schema design, deliberate tuning of SQLite settings, and an application-level awareness of concurrency and I/O constraints. Engineers are advised to evaluate the anticipated database workload

343

and implement proactive strategies, such as maintaining smaller, segmented databases or employing file partitioning when feasible. Although SQLite is not a panacea for all data storage challenges, understanding its boundaries allows developers to design systems that maximize performance and maintain reliability under heavy data loads. The optimization techniques discussed here provide valuable strategies for mitigating performance bottlenecks and handling large datasets effectively.

9.2.   Efficient Data Import and Export

Efficiently importing and exporting large volumes of data is critical in applications that use SQLite as a backend storage solution. Given SQLite's unique file-based design, the techniques for transferring substantial amounts of data require careful planning and an understanding of both SQLite's internal mechanisms and external data handling tools. It is important to coordinate import and export operations with tuning parameters that maximize disk I/O performance while minimizing overhead from transactional guarantees and indexing.

When importing data into SQLite, one of the most significant factors is the use of transactions. Commencing an import operation by explicitly beginning a transaction reduces the cost incurred by committing each individual operation. Even for bulk inserts from CSV files or other data sources, wrapping the operations in a single transaction can drastically reduce the number of disk flushes required during the write process. A typical strategy involves disabling features temporarily that might impede raw performance. For example, adjusting the PRAGMA settings to reduce disk synchronization overhead and then restoring them after the bulk operation is complete can provide enhanced performance.

A practical approach is to configure SQLite to use Write-Ahead Logging (WAL) mode during the import process as it can help manage concurrent reads while writes are occurring. Additionally, switching the synchronous setting to a less stringent mode during the data import operation can yield further speed improvements. The following snippet illustrates an import process in Python that employs these techniques:

```python
import sqlite3
import csv

# Connect to the SQLite database
connection = sqlite3.connect('large_dataset.db')
cursor = connection.cursor()

# Configure PRAGMA settings for performance
cursor.execute("PRAGMA journal_mode = WAL;")
cursor.execute("PRAGMA synchronous = OFF;")

# Prepare table for bulk insertion
cursor.execute("""
CREATE TABLE IF NOT EXISTS records (
    id INTEGER PRIMARY KEY,
    col1 TEXT,
    col2 TEXT,
    col3 INTEGER
);
""")

# Begin a single large transaction
cursor.execute("BEGIN TRANSACTION;")
with open('data.csv', 'r') as csvfile:
    reader = csv.reader(csvfile)
    for row in reader:
        cursor.execute("INSERT INTO records (col1, col2, col3) VALUES
        (?, ?, ?);", row)
cursor.execute("COMMIT;")

# Restore PRAGMA settings to ensure data integrity
cursor.execute("PRAGMA synchronous = NORMAL;")
connection.close()
```

This coding example highlights the importance of transaction control, PRAGMA configuration, and bulk insert operations. The use of batch operations minimizes the overhead per inserted row, a crucial factor when handling large datasets.

Exporting data from SQLite encounters a similar set of challenges. The

345

process demands the efficient reading of large volumes of data from the database file, and in many instances, the goal is to produce outputs in commonly accepted formats like CSV or JSON. Similar to bulk imports, the process must avoid unnecessary transactional overhead and extraneous data transformations that can slow down the extraction process. In scenarios where the data is being streamed for reporting or migration purposes, it is often beneficial to use optimized query patterns that minimize memory consumption. For example, reading data in manageable chunks prevents the application from exhausting system memory, thereby ensuring smoother export operations. An efficient export procedure may accompany pagination or limit-offset techniques in SQL.

A Python-based example for exporting a large SQLite table to CSV is provided below:

```python
import sqlite3
import csv

# Establish connection to SQLite database
connection = sqlite3.connect('large_dataset.db')
cursor = connection.cursor()

# Open CSV file for writing output
with open('exported_data.csv', 'w', newline='') as csvfile:
    csv_writer = csv.writer(csvfile)
    # Write header from table metadata
    cursor.execute("PRAGMA table_info(records);")
    header = [col[1] for col in cursor.fetchall()]
    csv_writer.writerow(header)

    # Efficiently stream rows from the database
    cursor.execute("SELECT * FROM records;")
    batch_size = 5000
    while True:
        rows = cursor.fetchmany(batch_size)
        if not rows:
            break
        csv_writer.writerows(rows)
connection.close()
```

This example manages memory consumption by reading data in

346

batches rather than attempting to load the entire dataset at once. By coupling batch reading with writing to a CSV file, the export operation becomes both efficient and scalable for large volumes of data.

In situations where data transformations are required during export, employing SQL's built-in functions to preprocess data can be beneficial. Complex transformations on the application side may be inefficient; therefore, using SQL expressions or triggering stored procedures can offload these computations directly to the database engine. Incorporating such strategies reduces network overhead and simplifies the export logic. Consider the need for a formatted export where dates or numerical values require standardization; embedding these operations into the SQL query ensures that data is properly formatted prior to extraction. For example, one might use SQL functions like `strftime` to format dates or use arithmetic expressions to derive new columns on the fly.

The performance of both data import and export inside SQLite can also be affected by indexing strategies. While indexes are vital for optimizing query performance in routine operations, they can hinder the speed of bulk imports and exports. Therefore, for a large data import, it is sometimes advisable to temporarily drop indexes and rebuild them post-import. This approach reduces the overhead involved in maintaining index integrity during every insert operation. However, careful planning is required as dropping indexes may temporarily affect query performance and application responsiveness. Once the data is immutably loaded and verified, the rebuilding of indexes can be performed with commands such as:

```
DROP INDEX IF EXISTS index_name;
-- After completing bulk import:
CREATE INDEX index_name ON records(col1, col2);
```

It is recommended to perform these operations during periods of low system activity to minimize the impact on concurrent operations.

Log file management is another aspect that bears consideration when working with large volumes of data. The extensive use of transactions during import or export operations might generate a significant amount of log data, and the size and location of these log files may affect overall performance. Managing temporary files, using in-memory databases for staging data, or adjusting logging levels can conserve disk space and improve operation speed. In addition, employing incremental backups or snapshot methodologies, especially during export operations, can help capture the state of the data without interrupting active transactions.

Performance tuning for both import and export also benefits from profiling queries and monitoring resource usage. SQLite provides the EXPLAIN QUERY PLAN statement to analyze the execution of queries, aiding in the identification of potential bottlenecks. By periodically analyzing query plans, developers can identify inefficient joins, missing indexes, or unexpected full-table scans. Such diagnostic information is essential for iteratively refining both import and export strategies. A brief command to analyze a potentially problematic query may appear as follows:

```
EXPLAIN QUERY PLAN SELECT * FROM records WHERE col3 > 1000;
```

The analysis provided by this command can guide modifications in the data schema or suggest a need for additional indexes to enhance performance.

Another best practice involves managing the schema evolution over time. As datasets grow and the structure of the data changes, maintaining a flexible schema that accommodates growth without necessitating complete table rebuilds is imperative. For example, adding new columns to a table or reorganizing columns for better cache utilization may be performed using SQLite's ALTER TABLE commands, which help mitigate migration challenges during export operations. A care-

348

ful schema migration plan ensures that data integrity is maintained and that both import and export processes are minimally disrupted.

The involvement of external utilities, such as the SQLite command-line shell, can further streamline the import and export of large data volumes. Tools such as `sqlite3` offer command-line options for exporting to CSV or importing from text files, which can be embedded as part of automated data pipelines. By integrating these tools with shell scripting or Python subprocesses, it is possible to schedule periodic bulk data transfers that respect the operational constraints of the system while maintaining consistency and performance.

System resource monitoring and load balancing strategies are also critical when orchestrating large-scale import and export operations. Scheduling tasks during off-peak hours and balancing the workload among available system resources prevents contention and maximizes throughput. Using operating system tools in conjunction with SQLite's internal logging can provide insights into disk I/O patterns, memory usage, and CPU load. Such information can subsequently be used to fine-tune the parameters of both PRAGMA settings and external processes.

It is essential to develop a robust error-handling strategy during import and export operations. Large-scale data transfers are susceptible to interruptions, partial data loads, or network failures. Implementing retry mechanisms, logging failures for subsequent analysis, and using temporary tables to stage data before a final commit are methods that enhance the reliability of data import/export processes. Failsafes can be incorporated, for instance, by validating the integrity of the data post-import through checksum comparisons or row count verifications.

Finally, automation of these data transfer processes contributes significantly to minimizing human error and increasing operational efficiency. Frameworks such as Apache Airflow, cron jobs, or even custom Python scripts can be used to build dependable pipelines for periodic data transfers. Automation not only ensures that import and export operations are performed consistently and securely but also allows for scalable adaptation as the dataset grows over time.

Each of these strategies, whether they involve tuning SQLite's internal parameters, utilizing bulk transactions, managing indexes during key operations, or automating processes for regular data transfers, contributes to a robust framework for managing large volumes of data in SQLite. Identifying the proper balance between performance and consistency is critical. Integrating these best practices minimizes resource contention and ensures that both import and export operations are executed in an efficient and reliable manner.

9.3. Optimizing Table Design

Optimizing table design is paramount for efficiently managing large datasets in SQLite. A well-structured table schema not only minimizes storage requirements but also enhances query performance and ensures data integrity. When handling extensive data, every detail of the table design—from data types, constraints, and indexes to normalization principles—plays a significant role in overall performance.

A methodical approach begins with a careful evaluation of the data's nature and use patterns. Selecting appropriate data types is essential. Overestimating field sizes or choosing generic types may lead to inefficient storage and increased disk I/O. For example, using INTEGER instead of TEXT for numeric data produces benefits in both storage and query efficiency. The following SQL snippet illustrates a tailored table definition that provides optimal storage by selecting data types that closely match the intended usage:

```
CREATE TABLE IF NOT EXISTS orders (
```

350

```
    order_id INTEGER PRIMARY KEY,
    customer_id INTEGER NOT NULL,
    order_date TEXT NOT NULL,
    total_amount REAL NOT NULL
);
```

Adhering to normalization rules is a common starting point in schema design. Normalization effectively reduces redundancy, prevents update anomalies, and eases maintenance. For large datasets, normalization may also reduce the amount of data that must be processed during operations such as updates and inserts. However, when working with SQLite and high-volume queries, strictly normalized schemas might require multiple join operations, potentially degrading performance. A balanced approach considers occasional denormalization, especially when queries routinely combine data from multiple tables. Denormalizing in controlled scenarios can eliminate the need for frequent joins by merging frequently accessed data into a single table. This trade-off between space and speed must be evaluated based on the specific workload and query frequency.

Partitioning data across multiple tables or using strategies like table partitioning within SQLite is another method to improve performance. By logically splitting a single large table into several smaller tables based on a column value (for example, years or geographical locations), one can reduce the query search space. Although SQLite does not natively support automatic table partitioning like some server-based solutions, the partitioning logic can be implemented in the application layer. This design technique allows the system to perform targeted queries on specific partitions, thereby reducing both memory usage and I/O delays. When data is partitioned manually, naming conventions and rigorous documentation are essential to ensure that application logic correctly directs queries to the appropriate partitions.

Indexing is a critical aspect of table design, particularly for accelerating queries on large datasets. Proper indexes dramatically reduce the time

351

required to locate specific data, but indexes also consume additional disk space and can slow down write operations. Therefore, it is crucial to analyze query patterns and only create indexes that deliver substantial performance improvements. Composite indexes, which cover multiple columns, can be especially useful when queries frequently filter by more than one column. An example of creating a composite index in SQLite is as follows:

```
CREATE INDEX IF NOT EXISTS idx_orders_customer_date
ON orders(customer_id, order_date);
```

This index assists in queries that filter orders by customer and date. It is important to revisit indexing strategies periodically; as data volume grows, the performance characteristics of indexes may evolve, requiring adjustments or additional indexes to maintain efficiency.

Another crucial consideration involves constraint definitions. Enforcing constraints, such as NOT NULL and foreign key relationships, contributes to data integrity, yet may introduce performance overhead if not managed carefully. In high-volume insert environments, temporarily deferring constraint checks can reduce insertion time, especially when importing data. SQLite supports deferred constraint enforcement, allowing the system to delay validation until the end of the transaction. This mechanism can be leveraged during bulk operations:

```
PRAGMA foreign_keys = OFF;
BEGIN TRANSACTION;
-- Bulk insert operations here
COMMIT;
PRAGMA foreign_keys = ON;
```

While disabling foreign keys temporarily must be executed with caution, it is a promising option for controlled data loads where integrity can be verified post-import.

Proper use of indexes and constraints dovetails into efficient query design. Combining well-designed schemas with optimized query patterns

ensures that the database engine performs minimal unnecessary operations. Query optimization can also be achieved by avoiding overuse
of subqueries and instead relying on well-structured joins. Observing
the EXPLAIN QUERY PLAN output facilitates pinpointing inefficiencies.
This iterative feedback loop between table design and query formulation is essential for refining performance. Consider the following command:

```
EXPLAIN QUERY PLAN
SELECT order_id, total_amount
FROM orders
WHERE customer_id = 1001
AND order_date BETWEEN '2021-01-01' AND '2021-12-31';
```

The insights from the query plan help in understanding whether the
existing indexes are used effectively or if further modifications are necessary.

Storage optimization techniques also extend to the way large objects
or binary data (BLOBs) are handled. Storing large multimedia files or
documents directly in the database can lead to bloated table sizes and
reduced performance. One effective strategy is to store large objects
outside the database and save only the file paths or references in the
corresponding table. This approach minimizes the load on SQLite's
file-based structure while maintaining data integrity and accessibility.

Handling temporal data efficiently is another design consideration.
Using standardized formats such as ISO 8601 for dates and times
permits straightforward comparisons and efficient sorting. In
SQLite, dates stored as TEXT in the ISO 8601 format (YYYY-MM-DD
HH:MM:SS.SSS) can be compared lexicographically, thereby enabling
indexes and range queries to work effectively. Consistency in date
storage prevents errors and reduces the complexity of temporal
queries.

The dynamic nature of data schemas necessitates a flexible approach to schema evolution. Large datasets may require modifications over time, such as adding new columns, altering existing constraints, or partitioning tables anew. Utilizing SQLite's ALTER TABLE commands permits incremental changes without requiring a complete rebuild of the database. Even though such operations can be disruptive if performed during peak usage, planning schema changes during off-peak periods ensures that operations remain minimally invasive. For example:

```
ALTER TABLE orders ADD COLUMN discount REAL DEFAULT 0;
```

This simple command alters the table with minimal disruption and maintains backward compatibility with existing data.

Normalization, indexing, and judicious application of constraints should always be weighed against the performance characteristics of the target queries. In high-transaction environments, it might be advantageous to denormalize certain tables to reduce the need for joins. For instance, if write operations are less frequent than reads and the query performance is critical, a pre-aggregated table that consolidates related data from multiple normalized tables may be preferable. Data redundancy in this scenario is an acceptable trade-off for significantly faster read queries, provided measures are in place to keep the aggregated table updated.

Monitoring and profiling query performance is indispensable throughout the life of a large dataset. SQLite's lightweight profiler and logging facilities offer real-time data that informs subsequent table design refinements. Using tools to monitor query latency, memory usage, and disk I/O patterns provides a factual basis for schema modifications. Data-driven adjustments—such as splitting a table when it exceeds critical size thresholds or reworking composite indexes based on usage statistics—ensure that the database adapts to evolving workloads.

Furthermore, table design optimization should consider the impact of table joins in complex queries. Nested joins and unindexed keys can

354

lead to inefficient execution plans. By analyzing the query plans and adjusting the schema for key columns, significant performance improvements can be obtained. Adding indexes to foreign key columns often results in quicker join operations and a reduction in lookup times across related tables.

The modern trend towards hybrid data storage also influences table design decisions. In cases where a single SQLite database becomes a bottleneck for read or write operations, it may be beneficial to delegate certain responsibilities to an in-memory database or a secondary lightweight data store. Such architectures can be incorporated into the table design strategy by migrating hot data to faster storage tiers while archiving historical data in the primary SQLite database. Clear demarcation between active and archival data can be maintained through carefully planned table structures.

Optimizing table design in SQLite involves a multi-faceted approach that spans the selection of appropriate data types, normalization versus denormalization strategies, effective use of indexes, and management of constraints. It requires ongoing evaluation and tuning, informed by query profiling and workload analysis. Strategies such as partitioning, deferred constraint enforcement during batch operations, and careful handling of large objects all contribute to a robust and scalable schema. These considerations, when implemented thoughtfully, offer a reliable path toward managing large datasets effectively in an SQLite environment.

9.4. Using Batching for Data Operations

Batching is a technique that groups multiple data operations into a single unit of work, reducing the number of individual transactions and the associated overhead that can occur when processing large datasets. This approach is particularly valuable in SQLite due to its file-based ar-

355

chitecture and single-writer mechanism. By minimizing the frequency of commit operations and aggregating similar commands, batching enhances performance and reduces latency for both insertions and updates.

When executing a series of data operations, each individual transaction incurs a fixed overhead related to disk I/O, locking, and journaling. By grouping these operations into one transaction, the system can reduce repeated overhead costs. For instance, in a scenario that involves inserting thousands of rows into a table, each separate commit operation would require a complete cycle of disk writes and index updates. Batching these insertions into a single transaction optimizes disk access patterns and limits the number of times the database engine must flush data to persistent storage. The following Python example demonstrates using batching for insert operations:

```python
import sqlite3

# Open connection to the SQLite database
connection = sqlite3.connect('batch_processing.db')
cursor = connection.cursor()

# Create table if it does not exist
cursor.execute("""
CREATE TABLE IF NOT EXISTS sensor_data (
    id INTEGER PRIMARY KEY,
    sensor_value REAL,
    timestamp TEXT
);
""")

# Use batching by grouping multiple inserts into one transaction
cursor.execute("BEGIN TRANSACTION;")
for i in range(10000):
    sensor_val = i * 0.5  # Example sensor reading
    time_stamp = f"2023-10-01 00:00:{i % 60:02d}"
    cursor.execute("INSERT INTO sensor_data (sensor_value, timestamp)
      VALUES (?, ?);", (sensor_val, time_stamp))
cursor.execute("COMMIT;")

connection.close()
```

In this example, the use of BEGIN TRANSACTION and COMMIT encapsulates 10,000 insert operations within a single transaction. Not only does this minimize the cumulative overhead of repeated commit operations, it also dramatically increases throughput when writing large volumes of data.

Batching can also be applied to update and delete operations. For example, consider a routine that processes a large batch of records to update their status based on certain criteria. Executing individual updates for each record could lead to significant performance degradation due to repeated disk writes. Instead, constructing an update statement that processes multiple rows together improves efficiency. The concept of batching for updates is similar to insertions: grouping multiple update statements within one transaction, as illustrated in the subsequent Python snippet:

```
import sqlite3

connection = sqlite3.connect('batch_processing.db')
cursor = connection.cursor()

# Begin transaction for batch update
cursor.execute("BEGIN TRANSACTION;")
# Simulate updating status for 5000 records based on a condition
for record_id in range(1, 5001):
    cursor.execute("UPDATE sensor_data SET sensor_value =
    sensor_value * 1.1 WHERE id = ?;", (record_id,))
cursor.execute("COMMIT;")

connection.close()
```

These update operations benefit from reduced overhead in the same manner as batch insertions. Execution time is further improved because the cost of rebalancing indexes and writing to the journal file is amortized over a larger set of operations.

Another effective use of batching is in scenarios where data is imported or exported incrementally. When data is being transferred from external sources into SQLite (or vice versa), processing records in defined,

manageable batches can avoid memory exhaustion or performance bottlenecks. This strategy is particularly useful when dealing with stream-
ing data or deploying data pipelines where network latency and intermittent connectivity can affect operation reliability. For example, reading and inserting records in batches can alleviate the risk of overwhelm-
ing the database engine and ensure consistent performance over prolonged operations.

Performance improvements can be observed by monitoring the number of disk flushes. In many cases, disk I/O is the limiting factor, so
reducing the frequency of expensive flush operations through batching
is a key advantage. Moreover, by tuning SQLite PRAGMA settings in
conjunction with batching, further optimizations can be achieved. For
instance, temporarily altering the synchronous setting to reduce the
number of disk syncs during batch operations can provide additional
speedup:

```
PRAGMA synchronous = OFF;
```

It is important to note that this PRAGMA adjustment, while beneficial
during batch processing, increases the risk of data loss in the event of
a failure during the transaction. Therefore, it must be used judiciously
and restored to a safer setting once batch operations are complete.

Batching is not limited to write operations. For data retrieval, particularly when processing large datasets, batching can help to manage
memory use. Instead of retrieving an entire large result set at once,
applications can fetch rows in smaller chunks. This approach is especially pertinent in languages like Python, where iterating over results
in batches using the fetchmany method helps to prevent memory over-
flow and keeps the application responsive. An example of batched retrieval is provided below:

```
import sqlite3

connection = sqlite3.connect('batch_processing.db')
```

```
cursor = connection.cursor()

# Execute a query that selects a large dataset
cursor.execute("SELECT * FROM sensor_data;")
batch_size = 1000

while True:
    batch = cursor.fetchmany(batch_size)
    if not batch:
        break
    # Process each batch of records incrementally
    for row in batch:
        # Process individual row (for example, analysis,
      transformation)
        pass

connection.close()
```

In this retrieval example, data is processed in increments of 1,000 rows, which helps maintain a manageable memory footprint even when the overall dataset is extensive.

Batching also proves significant when dealing with multi-step work-flows, where intermediate results are aggregated or transformed before final storage. In data transformation pipelines, storing temporary results in a staging table using batch operations can improve performance. For instance, if data needs to be validated, transformed, and then moved to a permanent table, performing these operations within a single batch minimizes synchronization delays across multiple operations. Creating a temporary staging table, processing data in batches, and then inserting the processed results into the main table is a common pattern:

```
CREATE TEMPORARY TABLE staging_sensor_data (
    sensor_value REAL,
    timestamp TEXT
);
```

Once the data is staged, further batch operations may be conducted to move data from the staging table to the main table. Such an approach enables error handling at each discrete stage, allowing for effective troubleshooting and rollback if necessary, without compromising the integrity of the permanent data store.

Using batching does introduce some challenges that need to be managed carefully. One of the key considerations is ensuring that the batch size is optimally chosen based on the system and workload characteristics. A batch size that is too large may lead to increased memory usage or longer periods of locked resources, which can affect concurrent operations. Conversely, a batch size that is too small may mitigate the performance gains associated with batching, as the overhead per transaction remains significant. Systematic testing and performance analysis are essential tools for fine-tuning the optimal batch size in any given environment.

Error handling in batched operations is another essential aspect. When processing data in large batches, a failure in any one of the operations may require the rollback of an entire batch if transactional integrity is desired. This all-or-nothing approach ensures data consistency, but it also necessitates the development of robust error detection and retry mechanisms. Implementing try-except blocks and rollback logic in the application code can allow for graceful recovery from transient errors while ensuring that partial batch operations do not leave the database in an inconsistent state. Consider the following pattern in a Python-based batch processing loop:

```python
import sqlite3

connection = sqlite3.connect('batch_processing.db')
cursor = connection.cursor()

try:
    cursor.execute("BEGIN TRANSACTION;")
    # Execute batch operations
    for i in range(5000):
        cursor.execute("INSERT INTO sensor_data (sensor_value,
        timestamp) VALUES (?, ?);", (i * 0.8, "2023-10-01 12:00:00"))
    cursor.execute("COMMIT;")
```

```
except Exception as e:
    cursor.execute("ROLLBACK;")
    print("Batch operation failed:", e)
finally:
    connection.close()
```

In this code snippet, the use of error handling ensures that if any part of the batch operation fails, the entire batch is reverted, preventing partial updates that could compromise data integrity.

Apart from write and update operations, batching is crucial for maintenance tasks such as cleaning or archiving data. Running regular cleanup operations in batches can keep the database from becoming bloated with outdated records. For example, instead of deleting millions of rows in one go, a cleanup script might delete records in smaller batches, allowing the database to recover between operations and maintain responsiveness. This incremental approach minimizes lock contention and enables the database to process user queries concurrently.

In operational environments, integrating batching within automated workflows or scheduled tasks can further improve overall efficiency. Batch processing systems can be configured to trigger during low-traffic periods, alleviating the impact on user operations during peak hours. Combining batching with robust logging and performance monitoring completes the picture by providing actionable insights into transaction times, error rates, and resource consumption.

The tactical use of batching for data operations is a powerful strategy to optimize performance, scale operations, and ensure stability when managing large datasets. By strategically grouping data modifications into transactional batches and tuning batch sizes according to workload characteristics, developers can achieve significant improvements in both throughput and system stability. This practice, when combined with careful error handling, real-time monitoring, and adaptive tuning of SQLite's configuration parameters, offers a solid framework for managing data efficiently in systems where large-scale operations are routine.

9.5. Managing Memory Usage

Efficient memory management is a critical aspect when working with substantial datasets in SQLite. As data volume increases, so does the demand on memory for query execution, temporary storage, and caching. Managing memory usage involves a multifaceted approach that includes the correct configuration of SQLite settings, optimal query design, and an understanding of how data is stored and manipulated within the engine.

SQLite allocates memory for various purposes such as caching database pages, storing temporary tables, and maintaining execution plans. The `cache_size` PRAGMA, for instance, controls the number of database pages that the SQLite engine stores in memory. By tuning this parameter, developers can balance between improved query performance and the available system memory. Setting a higher cache size can reduce disk I/O by keeping more pages in memory; however, this must be done with care to avoid excessive memory consumption. The following SQL command increases the cache size:

```
PRAGMA cache_size = 10000;
```

In addition to the cache size, the `temp_store` PRAGMA dictates where temporary tables and indices are stored during query processing. For large or complex queries, storing temporary objects in memory rather than on disk can significantly enhance performance. SQLite offers the option to store these temporary objects in memory by setting `temp_store` to MEMORY:

```
PRAGMA temp_store = MEMORY;
```

This setting is particularly useful during batch operations or when processing large join queries, as it minimizes disk access and leverages the faster access speed of RAM. However, caution is warranted when deploying this feature on systems with limited memory, as it may lead to exhaustion of available resources if not appropriately monitored.

Memory usage is also influenced by the design of the queries themselves. Complex queries that involve extensive sorting, grouping, or use of subqueries can require significant amounts of temporary memory. When executing a query that demands large amounts of memory, SQLite uses its internal temporary storage engine, which may spill over to disk if memory is insufficient. Analyzing the EXPLAIN QUERY PLAN output can help identify queries that are likely to consume excessive memory and allow for optimization efforts such as creating appropriate indexes or restructuring the query. For example, a query that involves sorting large datasets can benefit from indexes that reduce the volume of data needed for the sort operation.

Efficient use of prepared statements can further improve memory management. Prepared statements reduce overhead by reusing the same compiled SQL statement for multiple executions. In environments where similar queries are executed repeatedly, this practice not only reduces CPU usage but also minimizes memory allocation overhead associated with re-parsing and re-compiling the SQL statement. Consider the following Python snippet demonstrating the use of prepared statements:

```
import sqlite3

connection = sqlite3.connect('large_dataset.db')
cursor = connection.cursor()

# Prepare a statement for repeated execution
stmt = "INSERT INTO sensor_data(sensor_value, timestamp) VALUES (?,
    ?);"
prepared_statement = cursor.execute("BEGIN TRANSACTION;")
for i in range(10000):
    sensor_value = i * 0.5
```

363

```
    timestamp = f"2023-10-01 00:00:{i % 60:02d}"
    cursor.execute(stmt, (sensor_value, timestamp))
cursor.execute("COMMIT;")
connection.close()
```

This approach minimizes the memory footprint by reducing the amount of repeated parsing and compilation that occurs during batch inserts.

The use of in-memory databases is another strategy for managing memory usage effectively. SQLite allows for the creation of databases that reside entirely within system memory using the special :memory: identifier. In scenarios where temporary datasets are processed or when conducting unit tests on large data computations, an in-memory database offers significant performance benefits because it eliminates disk I/O entirely:

```
import sqlite3

# Create an in-memory SQLite database
connection = sqlite3.connect(':memory:')
cursor = connection.cursor()

# Create table and perform operations entirely in memory
cursor.execute("""
CREATE TABLE temp_data (
    id INTEGER PRIMARY KEY,
    value REAL
);
""")
cursor.execute("BEGIN TRANSACTION;")
for i in range(5000):
    cursor.execute("INSERT INTO temp_data (value) VALUES (?);", (i *
    1.2,))
cursor.execute("COMMIT;")
connection.close()
```

While in-memory databases dramatically reduce latency and improve performance, they are volatile in nature. Therefore, they are best suited for temporary data processing where persistence is not required. For applications that require long-term data storage, the in-memory

364

database may serve as an intermediate step before transferring the processed data back to a disk-based database.

Another aspect to consider when managing memory usage is the careful handling of large BLOBs (Binary Large Objects) and extensive text fields. Storing large files directly in a SQLite database can lead to significant increases in memory usage during read and write operations, especially when these objects must be loaded entirely into memory. One effective strategy is to store only references to the file locations, keeping the actual data outside the database. This design keeps the in-memory footprint of the database lower and allows the system to manage file access separately.

Memory fragmentation is another issue that can arise when handling large volumes of data over extended periods. Frequent allocation and deallocation of memory, especially from transactions that involve temporary objects, may lead to inefficient memory usage. One approach to mitigate fragmentation is to design the application to perform periodic maintenance. This might include re-indexing tables or vacuuming the database to reclaim unused space. The VACUUM command compacts the database file and optimizes memory usage, although it must be run when the database is not under heavy use:

```
VACUUM;
```

Careful scheduling of such maintenance operations during periods of low activity helps maintain an optimal balance between performance and memory usage.

In addition to these techniques, developers can utilize SQLite's built-in memory diagnostic features to monitor and manage memory consumption. The SQLite C interface includes features that allow applications to query the current state of memory allocation and usage. Although direct usage of these features typically occurs in lower-level programming environments, understanding their existence is useful for design-

365

ing systems that can adapt dynamically to memory pressure. For instance, monitoring tools can be integrated into the application to track metrics such as cache hit ratios, temporary storage usage, and the size of the in-memory cache, thus allowing for adjustments in real-time.

The interplay between the operating system and SQLite can further influence memory management. Scheduling and resource constraints imposed by the operating system may limit the amount of memory available to SQLite processes. Developers should architect applications with awareness of these constraints, possibly employing system-level monitoring tools to ensure that SQLite does not exceed available resources. This may include setting limits on the maximum memory allocation or restructuring queries to run in smaller increments to avoid spikes in memory usage.

Memory optimization is also an iterative process that involves profiling and testing under realistic conditions. Profiling tools can help identify memory-intensive operations, such as expansive join queries, deep recursive operations, or large batch processes. Once identified, these operations can be refactored to use more efficient algorithms or be split into smaller queries that are easier for SQLite to manage concurrently. In some cases, redesigning the data model or introducing additional indexes can reduce the amount of data that must be loaded into memory during a given operation.

Through the combination of SQLite configuration settings, efficient query design, the use of in-memory databases when appropriate, and leveraging diagnostic tools, developers can significantly improve memory usage when handling large datasets. Each strategy, from adjusting the `cache_size` and `temp_store` settings to systematically refactoring memory-intensive queries, contributes to an overall architecture that is resilient and efficient under heavy workloads. The cumulative effect of these techniques is an SQLite implementation that can manage substantial data volumes without compromising system performance or stability.

Utilizing these strategies not only improves immediate performance but also contributes to the long-term scalability and reliability of applications relying on SQLite. As data grows and application demands evolve, the techniques for managing memory usage become increasingly vital. Balancing in-memory operations with disk-based storage, dynamically adjusting settings, and continuously profiling performance provide a robust framework for effective memory management in SQLite.

9.6. Indexing Strategies for Large Datasets

Advanced indexing techniques are essential for maintaining query performance on extensive datasets in SQLite. As table sizes increase, scanning datasets and performing join operations can become prohibitively slow. Indexing provides a mechanism to reduce query execution time by creating lookup structures that the SQLite engine uses to locate rows quickly. However, the design, selection, and maintenance of indexes require careful consideration, as improper indexing may not only fail to yield performance gains but might also degrade performance for write operations.

A foundational concept in indexing is the creation of indexes on columns that appear in WHERE clauses or are used in join conditions. At its simplest, an index can be created on a single column using the following SQL command:

```
CREATE INDEX IF NOT EXISTS idx_customer_id
ON orders(customer_id);
```

This index accelerates searches filtering by `customer_id`. However, larger datasets often benefit from composite indexes that cover multiple columns. Composite indexes are especially useful when queries

367

filter on several fields simultaneously, as they combine multiple search keys into a single index structure. For example, consider a table where queries filter on both `customer_id` and `order_date`. A composite index can be defined as:

```
CREATE INDEX IF NOT EXISTS idx_customer_date
ON orders(customer_id, order_date);
```

The order of columns in a composite index is critical. The leading column in the index should be the column most frequently used in query constraints. In this way, the index can be leveraged efficiently for range queries and equality checks.

Beyond simple and composite indexes, advanced indexing techniques in SQLite include the use of covering indexes. A covering index is designed so that all the columns needed by a query are included directly in the index, obviating the need to access the table's main body. This can greatly reduce disk I/O and overall query latency. For example, if a common query refers to `customer_id`, `order_date`, and `total_amount`, a covering index that includes these fields would appear as:

```
CREATE INDEX IF NOT EXISTS idx_covering
ON orders(customer_id, order_date, total_amount);
```

When this query is executed, SQLite can retrieve all relevant information directly from the index without having to perform additional lookups in the table.

Another advanced indexing technique involves partial indexing, available in recent versions of SQLite. Partial indexes allow the creation of an index on a subset of rows in the table, defined by a WHERE clause condition. This approach is beneficial when only a fraction of the data is frequently queried, thus keeping the index smaller and more efficient. For example, consider a scenario where only active orders need to be indexed:

```
CREATE INDEX IF NOT EXISTS idx_active_orders
ON orders(order_date)
```

```
WHERE status = 'active';
```

Partial indexes reduce the overhead in maintaining indexes during write operations and improve query performance for targeted queries.

Expression indexes provide another layer of sophistication in indexing techniques. They allow creation of indexes on computed columns or function results rather than raw column values. Expression indexes can be particularly useful when queries consistently involve a function of a column, such as the lower-case version for case-insensitive searching. An example of an expression index is as follows:

```
CREATE INDEX IF NOT EXISTS idx_lower_name
ON customers(LOWER(name));
```

This index enhances the performance of queries that use the LOWER(name) function, ensuring the expression is computed once during index creation rather than during every query execution.

Index maintenance is a crucial aspect when working with large datasets. While indexes improve read performance, they also impose an overhead on write operations due to the requirement to update the index whenever the underlying table data changes. One must therefore balance the need for fast queries with the cost of slower inserts, updates, and deletes. Regularly reviewing the query workload and examining the actual usage of the indexes is recommended. SQLite provides tools such as the EXPLAIN QUERY PLAN command to understand query execution details, allowing one to verify whether indexes are being used. For instance:

```
EXPLAIN QUERY PLAN
SELECT order_id, total_amount
FROM orders
WHERE customer_id = 123 AND order_date > '2023-01-01';
```

By analyzing the output, one can determine whether the appropriate indexes are accessed or if further refinements are necessary.

For very large datasets, index fragmentation can become a concern. Over time, as data is inserted, updated, and deleted, indexes may become less efficient due to fragmentation. Periodic maintenance procedures, such as reindexing, can defragment the index and improve performance. The reindexing operation in SQLite is straightforward:

```
REINDEX;
```

Executing this command will rebuild all indexes in the database, and while it may be resource-intensive, performing it during maintenance windows can yield significant performance improvements.

When dealing with specialized query patterns, creating custom indexes may yield additional benefits. For example, if an application frequently performs full-text searches, SQLite's FTS5 extension provides virtual tables that include indexing mechanisms tailored for text search. By creating an FTS-enabled table, the engine builds an index that optimizes various text matching operations. An example of creating such an index is:

```
CREATE VIRTUAL TABLE documents
USING fts5(content, tokenize = 'porter');
```

FTS indexes are optimized for complex text queries and may include features like ranking and term frequency, making them indispensable for large text datasets.

Index selection must be closely tied to query patterns. Advanced techniques require an understanding of the specific analytical queries executed against the database. In many cases, it is beneficial to simulate the actual workload and iterate on your indexing strategy. Testing with representative data volumes under realistic conditions allows for empirical measurement of performance gains and identification of redundant or underutilized indexes. The decision to create an index should be justified by measurable improvements in query execution plans.

Beyond static indexes, dynamic query optimization approaches can also be considered. For example, periodic adjustments to indexes based on evolving query patterns could be automated as part of the database maintenance workflow. In environments where the data access patterns change over time, such adaptive indexing can ensure sustained query performance. This involves analyzing query logs, identifying frequently executed queries, and adjusting indexing parameters accordingly.

In distributed or high-availability systems where SQLite is used as a local datastore, one must consider the trade-off between the overhead of maintaining indexes and the speed of read operations. In scenarios where data is frequently written and seldom read, minimizing the number of indexes might yield better overall performance. Conversely, read-heavy systems benefit from aggressive indexing. Profiling the workload and resource constraints remains a best practice when designing the indexing strategy.

It is also important to consider the physical storage medium. When large datasets are stored on systems with high disk latency, the benefits of well-designed indexes are even more pronounced. By reducing the data that must be read from disk, indexes can help mitigate the performance impact of slower storage systems. Conversely, in high-speed memory or SSD environments, the relative benefit might be less dramatic, but proper index design still improves the overall efficiency of query operations.

Advanced indexing strategies in SQLite entail a blend of basic and sophisticated techniques aimed at accelerating queries on large datasets. From single-column and composite indexes to partial, expression, and full-text indexes, each approach serves a specific purpose in query optimization. Effective index management involves not only designing appropriate indexes but also maintaining them through regular analysis, diagnostics with the EXPLAIN QUERY PLAN command, and periodic reindexing operations. Understanding the cost-benefit balance of indexing in write-intensive versus read-intensive environments is critical. By continually refining indexing tactics based on real-world workload analysis, developers can harness the full performance potential of SQLite in handling extensive and complex datasets.

9.7. Partitioning Data for Performance

Partitioning data involves dividing a large dataset into smaller, more manageable segments in order to distribute the load and enhance query performance. Although SQLite does not provide native partitioning capabilities as seen in some server-based databases, effective partitioning strategies can still be implemented at the application level. By logically splitting the data across multiple tables or files, developers can restrict query searches to single partitions, thereby reducing I/O overhead and enhancing performance for selective queries.

One common approach is to partition data by a time-based column, such as date or timestamp. For instance, if a table recording transactions grows large over time, dividing it into separate tables by month or year can significantly reduce the amount of data scanned during queries that are limited to a particular time period. Consider a dataset representing daily transactions that needs to be partitioned by year. Instead of one giant table, individual tables such as transactions_2021, transactions_2022, etc., can be utilized. This strategy ensures that queries for recent transactions only access relevant tables, thereby reducing query latency. An example of creating a partitioned table for the year 2022 might look as follows:

```
CREATE TABLE IF NOT EXISTS transactions_2022 (
    transaction_id INTEGER PRIMARY KEY,
    transaction_date TEXT NOT NULL,
    amount REAL NOT NULL,
    customer_id INTEGER
);
```

In an application handling historical data, the selection logic can be implemented in the application layer. For example, when querying transactions for a particular date range, the application can determine which partitioned tables to target based on the dates specified. Such logic can be implemented in Python as follows:

```python
import sqlite3
from datetime import datetime

def get_partition_table(date_str):
    # Assumes date_str in 'YYYY-MM-DD' format
    year = datetime.strptime(date_str, "%Y-%m-%d").year
    return f"transactions_{year}"

def query_transactions(start_date, end_date):
    table = get_partition_table(start_date)
    connection = sqlite3.connect('financial.db')
    cursor = connection.cursor()
    query = f"SELECT * FROM {table} WHERE transaction_date BETWEEN ?
    AND ?;"
    cursor.execute(query, (start_date, end_date))
    results = cursor.fetchall()
    connection.close()
    return results

# Example usage:
results = query_transactions("2022-01-01", "2022-01-31")
for row in results:
    print(row)
```

In this example, the partition is selected dynamically based on the date range provided. By directing the query to a specific partitioned table, the number of rows processed is reduced, leading to improved performance even when the overall dataset is extensive.

Another effective partitioning strategy involves horizontal partitioning based on distinct data categories. For databases that manage multitenant applications or data segmented by geographical region, dividing the dataset into separate tables per category can be beneficial. Separate tables for different regions (e.g., sales_east, sales_west) isolate the

373

data in such a way that region-specific queries can run with greater efficiency. The advantage of this method is that writes and reads occur on smaller subsets, reducing lock contention and speeding up access times. For example, a table partition for eastern region sales data could be defined as:

```
CREATE TABLE IF NOT EXISTS sales_east (
    sale_id INTEGER PRIMARY KEY,
    sale_date TEXT,
    amount REAL,
    customer_id INTEGER,
    region TEXT DEFAULT 'east'
);
```

Application logic can then determine which table to interact with based on the region information associated with a transaction. This segmentation allows for parallel operations and minimizes the impact of large-scale writes on a single table.

Furthermore, partitioning can also include vertical partitioning, which involves splitting a table by columns. In scenarios where a table contains both frequently accessed columns and rarely used, large BLOB fields or verbose text fields, vertical partitioning helps in reducing the memory footprint during everyday operations. The frequently queried data is maintained in one table, while the less commonly accessed data is stored in an auxiliary table linked by a common key. Consider a table user_profiles that contains profile details along with large image data. By separating image data into its own table, queries that do not require images can be executed more rapidly:

```
CREATE TABLE IF NOT EXISTS user_profiles (
    user_id INTEGER PRIMARY KEY,
    name TEXT,
    email TEXT,
    date_joined TEXT
);

CREATE TABLE IF NOT EXISTS user_images (
    user_id INTEGER PRIMARY KEY,
    profile_image BLOB,
```

374

```
    FOREIGN KEY(user_id) REFERENCES user_profiles(user_id)
);
```

Vertical partitioning minimizes the amount of data loaded into memory and processed by queries where image data is irrelevant, thus enhancing overall system responsiveness.

When partitioning data, one must also consider the administrative overhead. Merging results from multiple partitions or queries that span partitions requires a well-designed methodology. For instance, while a user may need to see aggregated data across partitions (e.g., total sales over several years), the application must efficiently combine results. This can be achieved by executing queries on each partition and then consolidating the results in the application layer. A simplified example in Python might appear as follows:

```python
import sqlite3

def query_all_partitions(partition_tables, query, params):
    results = []
    connection = sqlite3.connect('financial.db')
    cursor = connection.cursor()
    for table in partition_tables:
        full_query = query.replace("{table}", table)
        cursor.execute(full_query, params)
        results.extend(cursor.fetchall())
    connection.close()
    return results

# Example: Sum of transaction amounts across partitions
partition_tables = ['transactions_2021', 'transactions_2022']
query = "SELECT SUM(amount) FROM {table} WHERE transaction_date
    BETWEEN ? AND ?;"
total_results = query_all_partitions(partition_tables, query,
    ("2021-01-01", "2022-12-31"))
print("Total Amount:", total_results)
```

This code snippet demonstrates querying multiple partitions and aggregating the results. Although this approach adds complexity to the application logic, it offers significant performance benefits when operating on a dataset that is too large for a single table to handle efficiently.

In addition to logical partitioning by date or category, file-level partitioning is sometimes applicable. SQLite allows applications to manage multiple database files, each of which can be treated as an independent partition. This is particularly useful if the total data volume approaches the file size limits imposed by the filesystem or the SQLite engine. Managing multiple database files requires a higher level of application orchestration, but it offers the benefit of separating workloads more distinctly. An application could maintain a directory of SQLite files, each named according to a specific partitioning scheme such as date ranges or regions. During query execution, the appropriate file is opened, and operations are performed on a smaller, localized dataset.

Effective partitioning also involves a strategy for maintaining data consistency and load distribution. When data is partitioned, factors such as how data is routed to the correct partition during writes and how updates or deletions are handled across partitions must be carefully planned. For instance, if an update involves changing the partitioning column (such as moving a transaction from one year to another), the system must perform a delete from one partition and an insert into another, ideally within a controlled transaction to maintain consistency. Sample pseudocode in Python for handling such an update may be expressed as:

```python
def update_transaction_partition(transaction_id, new_date):
    # Determine current and new partition based on the
    transaction_date column
    current_partition = get_current_partition(transaction_id)
    new_partition = get_partition_table(new_date)

    connection = sqlite3.connect('financial.db')
    cursor = connection.cursor()
    try:
        cursor.execute("BEGIN TRANSACTION;")
        transaction = cursor.execute(f"SELECT * FROM {
    current_partition} WHERE transaction_id = ?;", (transaction_id,))
    .fetchone()
        # Remove the old record
        cursor.execute(f"DELETE FROM {current_partition} WHERE
    transaction_id = ?;", (transaction_id,))
```

```
# Insert into the new partition
insert_query = f"INSERT INTO {new_partition} (transaction_id,
transaction_date, amount, customer_id) VALUES (?, ?, ?, ?);"
    cursor.execute(insert_query, (transaction[0], new_date,
transaction[2], transaction[3]))
    cursor.execute("COMMIT;")
except Exception as e:
    cursor.execute("ROLLBACK;")
    print("Error updating partition:", e)
finally:
    connection.close()
```

Dynamic partitioning strategies also allow for future growth. As datasets evolve, the partitioning criteria might need to change—such as moving from yearly to quarterly partitions if the volume increases significantly. This requires designing the partitioning scheme in a flexible manner, allowing for the addition of new partitions without impacting existing functionality. An adaptable partitioning system can incorporate metadata tables that track partitions, similar to a directory, which the application queries to determine the correct target for each operation.

The long-term benefits of data partitioning extend beyond query speed. By segmenting data into manageable chunks, maintenance operations such as vacuuming, indexing, and backup can be performed on individual partitions rather than the entire dataset. This not only reduces downtime but also minimizes the impact on system performance during routine maintenance tasks. For example, backing up a single partition is faster than backing up a monolithic database, and reindexing a partition may complete in a fraction of the time required for a large, unpartitioned table.

Overall, partitioning data for performance is a strategic approach that requires close coordination between database design, application logic, and ongoing maintenance practices. The effective use of logical and physical partitioning in SQLite can dramatically improve response times and system throughput, especially in environments where large datasets are frequently queried and updated. By implementing tailored partitioning schemes—whether by date, category, vertical separation, or even file-level distribution—developers can ensure that SQLite remains responsive under heavy data loads while also simplifying maintenance and enhancing scalability.

Chapter 10

Real-World Applications and Case Studies

This chapter examines SQLite's diverse applications across indus-tries, highlighting usage in mobile apps, web development, IoT, and gaming. It includes case studies showcasing e-commerce platforms and data analysis applications leveraging SQLite for efficient data management. Additionally, strategies for transitioning from other databases to SQLite are discussed, illustrating its adaptability and efficiency in real-world scenarios.

10.1. SQLite in Mobile Applications

SQLite has emerged as a preferred database engine for mobile appli-cations due to its lightweight design, serverless architecture, and efficient performance under constrained system resources. Mobile app development consistently requires robust, reliable data storage solutions that can seamlessly operate across various platforms including iOS, Android, and cross-platform frameworks. SQLite meets these demands by offering a self-contained database engine that resides locally within the application, reducing dependency on network connectivity and complex server architectures.

Mobile devices impose specific constraints such as limited memory capacity, processing power, and storage availability. SQLite is optimized for these conditions with its minimal setup and low overhead. Its file-based storage system ensures that the entire database is stored in a single file, a property that simplifies backup, deployment, and portability. This characteristic is particularly beneficial in mobile development environments where applications frequently need to safeguard user data across updates and system events.

A core advantage of using SQLite in mobile applications is its simplicity of integration. Given that SQLite can be embedded directly into the application, developers avoid the overhead of managing a separate database management system (DBMS). Instead, the SQLite engine is directly linked with the mobile app, allowing for direct access to data operations via standardized SQL commands. This direct integration reduces potential points of failure and enhances the robustness of data management functionalities.

In mobile architectures, the database file typically resides in a secure, application-specific directory. On platforms like Android, for example, the database is stored within the application's private data directory, ensuring that only the application can access its contents, thereby enhancing data security. Additionally, mobile operating systems provide sandboxing mechanisms that prevent unauthorized access to these files by other applications.

Data synchronization emerges as a vital feature when applications support offline use-cases. SQLite's compact size and efficient query processing make it well-suited for local caching of data that can later be synchronized with remote servers. Developers can implement strategies to queue user interactions or transactional data under offline conditions and later merge these changes with remote databases. This approach requires careful management of concurrent updates, versioning, and conflict resolution mechanisms. The inherent transactional properties of SQLite simplify these synchronization tasks by ensuring that the database remains in a consistent state even when interrupted by failures or network issues.

The transactional integrity provided by SQLite allows developers to wrap data modifications in atomic transactions. This is particularly useful in mobile applications where user interactions must be reliably recorded, even if the app unexpectedly terminates. Consider the following Python code snippet, which illustrates basic database operations using SQLite integrated into a mobile application context:

```python
import sqlite3

def initialize_database(database_path):
    connection = sqlite3.connect(database_path)
    cursor = connection.cursor()
    cursor.execute('''
        CREATE TABLE IF NOT EXISTS user_data (
            id INTEGER PRIMARY KEY AUTOINCREMENT,
            username TEXT NOT NULL,
            email TEXT NOT NULL UNIQUE,
            last_login TIMESTAMP DEFAULT CURRENT_TIMESTAMP
        )
    ''')
    connection.commit()
    connection.close()

def insert_user(database_path, username, email):
    connection = sqlite3.connect(database_path)
    cursor = connection.cursor()
    try:
        cursor.execute('''
            INSERT INTO user_data (username, email)
```

381

```
            VALUES (?, ?)
        ''', (username, email))
        connection.commit()
    except sqlite3.IntegrityError as error:
        print("Error inserting data:", error)
    finally:
        connection.close()

# Example usage within a mobile application context
db_path = 'mobile_app.db'
initialize_database(db_path)
insert_user(db_path, 'alice', 'alice@example.com')
```

This code example demonstrates initializing a database, creating tables, and executing insert commands in a manner that is easily inte-
grable within a mobile application's backend. The simplicity of the
SQLite API supports seamless embedding in mobile runtime environments where resource constraints necessitate optimized performance.

Error handling and performance optimization are also critical considerations when employing SQLite in mobile development. Mobile applications often demand a responsive user interface where long-running
database operations can lead to application unresponsiveness. In such
cases, developers may choose to execute database transactions in background threads or asynchronous tasks. As part of a well-designed application architecture, employing asynchronous execution models prevents the main application thread from blocking while waiting for data
operations to complete. Modern mobile platforms frequently incorporate frameworks that facilitate asynchronous data handling, making
SQLite a natural fit for these paradigms.

Memory management also plays an essential role when using SQLite
on mobile devices. Developers must consider the impact of database
caching, query complexity, and concurrent access on the available
memory resources. SQLite provides pragmas and configuration settings that allow fine-tuning of its memory usage. Adjusting these settings can mitigate the risk of performance degradation in low-memory

382

conditions typical in mobile operations. For example, adjusting the cache size via SQLite pragmas can offer a balance between query performance and memory consumption.

Concurrency in a mobile environment requires careful handling since simultaneous access to the SQLite database from multiple application components might lead to locking conflicts. SQLite employs file locking mechanisms to coordinate access, and developers should design their database access patterns to minimize contention. In scenarios where concurrent writes are expected, techniques such as batching transactions or designing an optimistic locking procedure are recommended. The efficient resolution of data conflicts and contention is crucial for maintaining the consistency and integrity of user data within the mobile application.

Beyond local data storage, SQLite supports various advanced features that enhance its applicability in mobile apps. Features like full-text search (FTS) extensions allow developers to embed sophisticated search functionality within the mobile application, enabling users to perform extensive queries on locally stored data. Such features expand the range of applications, from note-taking and logging utilities to content management systems, all built into mobile platforms.

Mobile development using cross-platform frameworks like Flutter or React Native further benefits from SQLite integration. These frameworks often provide native plugins or libraries that encapsulate SQLite functionality, allowing developers to write platform-independent code for database operations. The standardized SQL interface across these plugins contributes to code maintainability and avoids platform-specific discrepancies, streamlining the development process. Consequently, developers can target multiple platforms while ensuring consistent database behavior across diverse mobile operating systems.

The role of SQLite in mobile applications extends to security considerations as well. Since mobile devices are vulnerable to physical theft
and unauthorized access, protecting sensitive user data is paramount.
SQLite databases can be encrypted using extensions such as SQLCipher. Encryption ensures that the database content is secure even if
the underlying storage is compromised. While the integration of encryption introduces additional computational overhead, modern mobile processors typically handle these operations efficiently without
compromising user experience. Developers must balance the trade-
offs between enhanced security and performance impacts based on
application-specific requirements.

Designing a robust mobile application database system involves planning for scalability and future growth. Although SQLite is well-suited
for lightweight applications, scenarios with complex data relationships
or extremely large datasets may require additional strategies such as
data partitioning, indexing, and query optimization. For instance, indexes can be implemented on high-read tables to reduce query latency,
a factor that directly influences the perceived speed and reliability of
the application. Developers may also consider implementing version
control for the database schema, enabling smooth upgrades as the
application evolves. Database migrations should be designed to be
backward-compatible, ensuring that updates do not disrupt existing
user data or the overall responsiveness of the mobile application.

Mobile applications commonly benefit from user-friendly synchronization mechanisms that interface local SQLite databases with remote
servers. This integration allows applications to offer offline capabilities while ensuring that data generated during offline use is seamlessly
uploaded once connectivity is available. Synchronization strategies
must be designed to resolve conflicts in data updates, ensuring that
user actions are represented accurately after synchronization. Techniques such as timestamp tracking and differential data replication can

be employed to ensure that only changed data is transmitted, optimizing bandwidth usage and reducing synchronization times.

The application of SQLite extends to scenarios involving analytics and logging within mobile applications. In addition to storing user credentials and content data, SQLite is often used to record application events, user interactions, and error logs. These databases, though lightweight, provide a persistent record that can be invaluable for debugging and performance monitoring. The compact size of SQLite databases ensures that even extensive logs remain manageable and can be efficiently queried for analysis on the device or after being exported for remote diagnostics.

The integration of SQLite in mobile applications reinforces the importance of well-structured database design and careful consideration of platform-specific limitations. The comprehensive support provided by SQLite—from transactional integrity and efficient performance under low-memory conditions to its adaptability for offline synchronization and secure data storage—has made it an indispensable tool in the mobile developer's toolkit. This unified approach, leveraging SQLite, ensures that mobile applications effectively address the challenges of localized data management, synchronization, and scalability while maintaining high performance and robust security measures.

10.2. Web Application Development with SQLite

Web applications benefit from lightweight, self-contained database solutions, making SQLite an attractive choice when design constraints such as ease of deployment, minimal administrative overhead, and efficient performance are critical. Developers leverage SQLite's file-based database system in web environments where simplicity and portability are prioritized over the scalability offered by larger client-server database systems. The integration of SQLite into web applications reflects its robust support for SQL standards, straightforward setup, and compatibility with multiple programming languages and frameworks.

SQLite is commonly used as the default database for lightweight web projects and prototyping environments. This adoption is influenced by its zero-configuration nature, where the entire database is maintained within a single file. This greatly simplifies the deployment process— there is no need for an external server installation and configuration— and it permits quick migrations between development, staging, and production environments. Furthermore, SQLite's embedded architecture results in reduced maintenance, as the database engine requires only minimal tuning and administration.

An essential aspect of web application development with SQLite is its simplicity in integrating with server-side frameworks. Languages such as Python, PHP, and Ruby provide seamless support for SQLite through their standard libraries. In the Python ecosystem, for example, the `sqlite3` module offers a robust and easy-to-use interface for interacting with SQLite databases. Web frameworks such as Flask and Django come configured by default to use SQLite during the early stages of development. This lean configuration allows developers to focus on application logic without being burdened by complex database configurations.

Below is an illustrative Python example showcasing how SQLite can be integrated in a Flask-based web application to manage user data. In this example, a simple Flask application is set up to serve web pages and responses while interacting with an SQLite database. The code demonstrates database initialization, query execution, and data retrieval:

```
from flask import Flask, request, jsonify
import sqlite3

app = Flask(__name__)
DATABASE = 'webapp.db'
```

386

```python
def get_db_connection():
    conn = sqlite3.connect(DATABASE)
    conn.row_factory = sqlite3.Row  # Enables column access by name.
    return conn

def init_db():
    conn = get_db_connection()
    cursor = conn.cursor()
    cursor.execute('''
        CREATE TABLE IF NOT EXISTS users (
            id INTEGER PRIMARY KEY AUTOINCREMENT,
            username TEXT NOT NULL UNIQUE,
            email TEXT NOT NULL UNIQUE,
            created_at TIMESTAMP DEFAULT CURRENT_TIMESTAMP
        )
    ''')
    conn.commit()
    conn.close()

@app.route('/users', methods=['POST'])
def add_user():
    data = request.get_json()
    username = data.get('username')
    email = data.get('email')
    conn = get_db_connection()
    cursor = conn.cursor()
    try:
        cursor.execute('''
            INSERT INTO users (username, email)
            VALUES (?, ?)
        ''', (username, email))
        conn.commit()
        user_id = cursor.lastrowid
        response = {'id': user_id, 'username': username, 'email':
    email}
    except sqlite3.IntegrityError as e:
        response = {'error': 'Username or email already exists.'}
    finally:
        conn.close()
    return jsonify(response)

@app.route('/users', methods=['GET'])
def list_users():
    conn = get_db_connection()
    cursor = conn.cursor()
    cursor.execute('SELECT * FROM users')
    users = cursor.fetchall()
    conn.close()
```

```
    users_list = [dict(user) for user in users]
    return jsonify(users_list)

if __name__ == '__main__':
    init_db()
    app.run(debug=True)
```

This code leverages SQLite's convenient data storage properties and integrates them within a web API using Flask. Requests to insert and query user data exemplify common web application patterns such as RESTful design, where endpoints handle distinct operations on the dataset. The use of SQLite in this context ensures that the application remains lightweight and is easily portable.

In addition to basic CRUD (Create, Read, Update, Delete) operations, web applications often require complex transactional management. SQLite provides full ACID compliance, ensuring that even in environments subject to concurrent interactions, database integrity is preserved consistently. The transactional properties allow multiple operations to be grouped into a single transaction block, guaranteeing that either all modifications succeed or none are applied. This mechanism becomes particularly important in web applications that handle multi-step processes where partial updates can lead to data inconsistencies. The following example demonstrates the use of transactions in a Python context:

```
def transfer_funds(sender_id, receiver_id, amount):
    conn = get_db_connection()
    cursor = conn.cursor()
    try:
        # Begin transaction
        cursor.execute("BEGIN TRANSACTION;")
        # Deduct funds from the sender
        cursor.execute("UPDATE accounts SET balance = balance - ?
    WHERE id = ?",
                       (amount, sender_id))
        # Add funds to the receiver
        cursor.execute("UPDATE accounts SET balance = balance + ?
    WHERE id = ?",
                       (amount, receiver_id))
```

```
    # Commit the transaction
    conn.commit()
except Exception as e:
    # Rollback in case of error
    conn.rollback()
finally:
    conn.close()
```

Using explicit transaction control helps maintain a consistent state, a critical factor for applications dealing with financial transactions or any critical data operations. Whereas larger database systems provide complex transaction management tools, SQLite's simplicity and reliability render it sufficient for small to medium-scale web applications.

Another notable advantage in web scenarios is SQLite's support for advanced features such as full-text search (FTS). Web applications that include search functionalities often need efficient mechanisms for indexing and querying textual data. SQLite's FTS extensions allow developers to create virtual tables specially tuned for text search, enabling efficient querying over large volumes of text directly within the local database file. This capability speeds up the delivery of search results to end-users and can be easily integrated into web applications that demand rapid filtering and text analysis.

Scalability may impose limitations for high-traffic web applications; however, SQLite is ideal for projects where the workload is moderate and the primary focus is on rapid development and minimal operational complexity. It is particularly well-suited for prototyping and small-scale deployments where rapid iteration is required. Web developers often begin with SQLite during the development phase and later switch to more scalable systems for production. Nonetheless, for many applications, SQLite's performance characteristics, including fast read operations and adequate write performance when concurrent write operations are limited, provide a balanced solution without the need to transition to a dedicated server-based database.

Another emergent trend is the deployment of SQLite directly on cloud platforms where microservices architecture is implemented. In many cloud-based deployments, each microservice encapsulates its own small database, and the file-based nature of SQLite fits naturally into containerized environments. When combined with tools such as Docker, SQLite's simplicity ensures that container images remain lightweight and easy to manage. Moreover, when used alongside caching layers and content delivery networks (CDNs), SQLite can serve as the backend persistence mechanism for numerous microservices simultaneously.

Web applications that target rapid prototyping benefit from the agility associated with SQLite's integration. Developers can design database schema and iterate on application logic rapidly without the structural overhead or complexity associated with larger relational database management systems. SQLite's built-in functions and support for a variety of SQL standards allow developers to experiment with complex queries, indexing strategies, and performance tuning without administrative burdens. For example, a simple command to create an index on a frequently queried column in a user table is as straightforward as shown below:

```
CREATE INDEX idx_username ON users(username);
```

This command optimizes query performance by reducing lookup times for search operations, thereby enhancing user experience in web interfaces that rely on rapid data retrieval.

Error handling and debugging are also streamlined with SQLite. When web applications encounter database exceptions, SQLite's clear error reporting assists developers in diagnosing issues such as constraint violations or transaction conflicts. Coupled with comprehensive logging practices, these debugging mechanisms facilitate quick resolution of issues during both development and production stages. For instance, handling duplicate entries in a user registration process is managed efficiently by catching integrity errors, as shown in the earlier Flask example.

Security is a critical consideration in web development, and SQLite provides several mechanisms to secure data. File-level permissions on the database file, combined with HTTPS for data transmission and proper server configuration, help create a secure environment for web applications. Furthermore, when required, encryption solutions such as SQL-Cipher can be integrated with SQLite to safeguard sensitive information against unauthorized access. Although encryption may introduce some performance overhead, the trade-off is often justified by the enhanced security required for financial or personal data.

The advantages of SQLite for web application development are not limited to its performance and simplicity. Its portability also encourages a consistent development workflow across different platforms and operating systems. This uniformity reduces the risk of platform-specific bugs and fosters a development culture that prioritizes code cleanliness and modularity. Developers are able to maintain a single, standardized codebase during the transition from local development to production deployment without the need for extensive alterations in database interactions.

Web developers are encouraged to leverage the full spectrum of SQLite capabilities to ensure efficient data management. Appropriate database schema design, effective use of transactions, indexing optimizations, and supplemental features such as full-text search collectively contribute to a robust and responsive web application. The combination of these techniques allows web applications to retain high performance even when the underlying database is embedded within the application itself.

The integration of SQLite into web application development provides a powerful, cost-effective mechanism to manage data while retaining agility in the development process. Its capabilities dovetail with the requirements of modern web architectures, offering a reliable, self-contained database solution that simplifies deployment and ensures consistent performance across different environments.

10.3. Using SQLite in IoT Devices

The integration of SQLite in Internet of Things (IoT) applications addresses several challenges inherent to embedded systems, including limited computational resources, intermittent connectivity, and the need for minimal configuration. IoT devices often require local, reliable data storage that operates efficiently under power and memory constraints. SQLite offers a compact, serverless, and self-contained database engine that is well-suited for these requirements.

IoT devices typically operate in environments where network connectivity is not guaranteed. Many devices, such as sensors and controllers, must function autonomously and persist data locally until communication with centralized servers is possible. SQLite's file-based architecture enables persistent data storage in a minimal footprint. The database file resides on the device's internal storage or an attached medium, ensuring that sensor readings, system logs, and configuration settings are maintained even when the device is offline. This capability is critical for reliable IoT operations, where data loss can compromise system functionality or lead to incorrect event reporting.

The minimal resource footprint of SQLite makes it a strong candidate for embedded systems. IoT devices often have constrained memory and processing power, and the lean design of SQLite reduces overhead compared to more complex database management systems. The entire database engine is implemented in a few hundred kilobytes, which makes it possible to integrate SQLite into devices with limited flash storage and RAM. Embedded developers can thus rely on SQLite for data management without adversely affecting the device's performance or increasing power consumption.

Transactional integrity in IoT deployments is another significant benefit provided by SQLite. Many IoT applications involve critical operations such as controlling actuators or logging sensor data at high frequencies. In these environments, ensuring that data writes are complete and consistent is paramount. SQLite supports full ACID (Atomicity, Consistency, Isolation, Durability) compliance, which means that even abrupt power loss or system resets do not result in corrupted data. This robustness ensures that, once connectivity is re-established, the locally stored data accurately reflects the events that occurred during offline periods.

Integrating SQLite in IoT devices also simplifies the development process by reducing complexity. Developers can use SQLite without the need for a separate database server installation, which minimizes configuration and dependency management. This feature is particularly beneficial in production environments, where the complexity of managing multiple software components on an embedded device can lead to increased system vulnerability. The single-binary nature of SQLite means that the risk of misconfiguration is low, and developers can focus on ensuring that the core functionality of the IoT application is reliable and secure.

A typical IoT application might involve collecting data from various sensors, processing the data locally, and synchronizing it with a remote server when network conditions permit. SQLite can be used to store time-series data, configuration settings, device logs, and event histories. For instance, consider a scenario in which an IoT weather station logs temperature, humidity, and atmospheric pressure measurements. These measurements must be recorded locally and then transmitted to a centralized system for analysis. The following Python example demonstrates how SQLite can be used on a Raspberry Pi to store sensor data and later synchronize it when required:

```python
import sqlite3
import time
from random import uniform

def initialize_db(db_path):
    conn = sqlite3.connect(db_path)
    cursor = conn.cursor()
    cursor.execute('''
        CREATE TABLE IF NOT EXISTS sensor_data (
            id INTEGER PRIMARY KEY AUTOINCREMENT,
            temperature REAL NOT NULL,
            humidity REAL NOT NULL,
            pressure REAL NOT NULL,
            timestamp DATETIME DEFAULT CURRENT_TIMESTAMP
        )
    ''')
    conn.commit()
    conn.close()

def log_sensor_data(db_path, temperature, humidity, pressure):
    conn = sqlite3.connect(db_path)
    cursor = conn.cursor()
    cursor.execute('''
        INSERT INTO sensor_data (temperature, humidity, pressure)
        VALUES (?, ?, ?)
    ''', (temperature, humidity, pressure))
    conn.commit()
    conn.close()

def simulate_sensor_reading():
    temperature = round(uniform(15.0, 35.0), 2)
    humidity = round(uniform(30.0, 90.0), 2)
    pressure = round(uniform(980.0, 1050.0), 2)
    return temperature, humidity, pressure

if __name__ == '__main__':
    db_path = 'iot_weather_station.db'
    initialize_db(db_path)
    # Simulate periodic sensor reading logging
    while True:
        temp, hum, pres = simulate_sensor_reading()
        log_sensor_data(db_path, temp, hum, pres)
        print("Logged sensor data: Temp =", temp,
            "Humidity =", hum, "Pressure =", pres)
        time.sleep(10)
```

394

The above example illustrates how sensor data can be periodically logged into an SQLite database on an embedded device. The simplicity of the SQLite implementation in Python allows developers to quickly integrate local storage capabilities while ensuring that data remains persistent and secure. This example also highlights the importance of modular design in IoT applications, where individual components, such as data logging and data synchronization, can be developed, tested, and maintained independently.

Data synchronization with a remote server is an essential aspect of many IoT deployments. When devices operate in remote or mobile environments, network connectivity may be intermittent or unreliable. In such cases, SQLite enables an IoT device to continue functioning autonomously by caching data locally and synchronizing it when a stable connection is available. Synchronization mechanisms typically involve querying the database for unsent data, transmitting the data securely to a central location, and then marking the data as synchronized. Implementing robust synchronization protocols ensures that vital information is not lost and that the central system receives accurate and complete datasets for analysis.

The management of data storage in an IoT context requires consideration of potential constraints, such as limited storage capacity. Developers must carefully design the database schema to ensure efficient use of disk space. Strategies such as data aggregation, archiving older records, or using compression techniques can be applied to maintain manageable database sizes. Additionally, the periodic purging of obsolete data, based on pre-defined retention policies, can help prevent the exhaustion of available storage. Utilizing SQLite's lightweight design, embedded systems can continuously operate without the overhead associated with managing large or unwieldy databases.

Security is a significant concern in IoT applications, where devices are often deployed in environments susceptible to physical tampering or unauthorized access. SQLite supports various mechanisms that contribute to overall data security. File-level permissions can restrict access to the database file, ensuring that only authorized processes can read from or write to the file. For applications requiring enhanced security, integrating encryption libraries such as SQLCipher with SQLite protects sensitive data by encrypting the entire database file. Although encryption introduces a slight performance overhead, it provides an additional layer of protection critical in scenarios where devices handle confidential or regulated data.

In many IoT applications, efficient data indexing plays a vital role in ensuring that query operations can be performed rapidly. Given the limited processing capabilities of embedded systems, optimized queries and strategic indexing reduce the computational burden on the device. For example, if an application frequently accesses sensor data based on time intervals, creating an index on the timestamp column can significantly speed up query execution. A sample SQL command to create such an index is provided below:

```
CREATE INDEX idx_timestamp ON sensor_data(timestamp);
```

This command helps ensure that queries filtering sensor readings by time execute efficiently, which is particularly useful when generating reports or performing real-time analysis on the device.

The reliability of SQLite also comes into play when devices experience abrupt power losses or system crashes. The durability guarantees provided by SQLite ensure that once a transaction is committed, the corresponding changes remain intact despite unexpected interruptions. This behavior is crucial for IoT devices that operate in harsh or unstable environments, where interruptions may be frequent. Developers benefit from the confidence that the locally stored data accurately reflects the true state of the device's operations, thereby simplifying the task of error handling and data recovery in post-failure scenarios.

Another consideration in IoT applications is the periodic update of device firmware and software. Database schema migrations are often required during these updates, and SQLite provides mechanisms for smooth transitions between schema versions. When implementing schema migrations, it is important to design migration scripts that handle alterations such as adding new columns or modifying table structures without disrupting ongoing data collection. A typical approach involves maintaining version control on the schema and executing migration scripts during the device's initialization phase. This strategy minimizes the risk of data loss and ensures continuous operation even as the software evolves.

The scalability of SQLite within IoT applications, despite its lightweight nature, should not be underestimated. Although most IoT devices handle modest data volumes, the cumulative data produced by a large fleet of devices can be considerable. In such cases, SQLite's design promotes effective data partitioning and incremental backups, which are essential for managing and transferring data to centralized systems. Techniques such as rolling databases, where new files are created after reaching a size threshold, can be employed to simplify data management and facilitate efficient synchronization processes.

By serving as an embedded database engine that conforms to industry standards, SQLite supports the modular architecture that is common in modern IoT solutions. Architectures that employ distributed microservices or edge computing can utilize SQLite as a local data store, thereby reducing latency and offloading non-critical data processing to the device level. This distributed processing approach complements centralized analytics and decision-making, ensuring that high-level operations are informed by reliable, edge-collected data.

The role of SQLite in IoT development encompasses not only robust data storage and management but also an emphasis on developer simplicity and reliability. Its seamless integration with popular programming languages and minimal configuration requirements allow embedded developers to focus on optimizing device functionality rather than managing complex database interactions. The comprehensive support for SQL standards and advanced features such as full-text search or custom functions further extend SQLite's utility in scenarios where more sophisticated data queries are necessary.

Utilizing SQLite in IoT devices reinforces the principle of minimal yet robust design inherent to embedded systems. By concentrating data management locally and deferring synchronization until network conditions allow, IoT deployments leverage SQLite to maintain data integrity, secure storage, and efficient performance. This approach ensures that even in the absence of continuous network connectivity, the embedded system operates effectively and reliably, contributing to the overall stability of the IoT ecosystem.

10.4.   Case Study: E-commerce Platform

This section examines an e-commerce platform that leverages SQLite to manage both product catalogs and user data. With the increasing complexity of online commerce, managing product information dynamically while ensuring high availability for user interactions is essential. The case study explores how SQLite, with its self-contained design and transactional integrity, serves as a backend data store for operations fundamental to the system, including product management, user account handling, and order processing.

At the core of the platform, the product catalog holds information about items available for sale, such as product identifiers, descriptions, pricing, stock levels, and images. The product catalog is a dynamic dataset with frequent updates due to inventory fluctuations, seasonal promotions, and price adjustments. Given the need for rapid access and modification of product data, SQLite offers a file-based solution

398

with minimal overhead that is easily integrated with web development frameworks. The decision to use SQLite was driven by its simplicity in deployment; a single database file encapsulates all the necessary product data, reducing the operational complexity associated with networked database servers.

User data management is another key component of the platform. User accounts contain sensitive information such as personal identification, payment details, and order histories. Ensuring data consistency and security in this domain is critical, especially as the platform scales. SQLite's ACID properties provide robust transactional support that guarantees consistency even during high-concurrency interactions. For example, when a user registers, the platform must check for existing records to prevent duplicates and then securely store the new user information. The platform implements these functionalities using SQLite's integrated capabilities for handling unique constraints and transactions.

In one module of the e-commerce platform, the product catalog is initialized and maintained through a series of SQL commands executed during system startup. The following Python code snippet demonstrates an initialization routine where product and user tables are created, ensuring that the system is ready to handle live transactions:

```
import sqlite3

def initialize_database(db_path):
    conn = sqlite3.connect(db_path)
    cursor = conn.cursor()

    # Create table for product catalog
    cursor.execute('''
        CREATE TABLE IF NOT EXISTS products (
            product_id INTEGER PRIMARY KEY AUTOINCREMENT,
            name TEXT NOT NULL,
            description TEXT,
            price REAL NOT NULL,
            stock INTEGER NOT NULL,
            creation_date DATETIME DEFAULT CURRENT_TIMESTAMP
```

```
        )
    ''')

    # Create table for user accounts
    cursor.execute('''
        CREATE TABLE IF NOT EXISTS users (
            user_id INTEGER PRIMARY KEY AUTOINCREMENT,
            username TEXT NOT NULL UNIQUE,
            email TEXT NOT NULL UNIQUE,
            password TEXT NOT NULL,
            registration_date DATETIME DEFAULT CURRENT_TIMESTAMP
        )
    ''')

    conn.commit()
    conn.close()

# Initialize the database for the e-commerce platform
db_path = 'ecommerce.db'
initialize_database(db_path)
```

Efficient querying is paramount in a high-traffic e-commerce environment. The platform uses indexing to accelerate common queries, such as retrieving products based on popularity or filtering items within specific price ranges. SQLite facilitates the creation of indices with minimal overhead. For instance, an index on the *price* column can significantly improve query performance when users sort products by cost. An example SQL command to create such an index is as follows:

```
CREATE INDEX idx_price ON products(price);
```

Transactional operations are critical to ensuring that the system maintains consistency across concurrent operations. When a customer places an order, it is essential to deduct stock quantities from the product catalog and record the order details in a manner that prevents race conditions. SQLite's transaction support allows the platform to encapsulate these steps into a coherent, atomic operation. The code below demonstrates how to perform an atomic update of stock levels during an order transaction:

```
def process_order(db_path, product_id, order_quantity):
```

```
conn = sqlite3.connect(db_path)
cursor = conn.cursor()
try:
    # Begin transaction for processing the order
    cursor.execute("BEGIN TRANSACTION;")

    # Check current stock level
    cursor.execute("SELECT stock FROM products WHERE product_id =
?", (product_id,))
    result = cursor.fetchone()
    if result is None:
        raise Exception("Product not found.")

    current_stock = result[0]
    if current_stock < order_quantity:
        raise Exception("Insufficient stock for product ID {}".
format(product_id))

    # Deduct order quantity from stock
    cursor.execute("UPDATE products SET stock = stock - ? WHERE
product_id = ?",
                    (order_quantity, product_id))

    # Insert order details into orders table (assumed to have
been created similarly)
    cursor.execute('''
        INSERT INTO orders (product_id, quantity, order_date)
        VALUES (?, ?, CURRENT_TIMESTAMP)
    ''', (product_id, order_quantity))

    # Commit the transaction
    conn.commit()
    print("Order processed successfully.")
except Exception as e:
    conn.rollback()
    print("Order processing failed:", e)
finally:
    conn.close()
```

The example provided emphasizes the importance of transaction control in scenarios where multiple table updates must occur in concert. This approach reduces the likelihood of inventory discrepancies and ensures that user data remains in sync with product availability.

Beyond transactional data management, the e-commerce platform also employs SQLite to support advanced search functionalities. Full-text search (FTS) capabilities, available through SQLite extensions, enable customers to perform rapid, keyword-based queries against product descriptions and specifications. By creating virtual tables that index textual data, the platform can deliver responsive search results that enhance user experience. This integration of SQLite's FTS module demonstrates how the platform leverages built-in features to extend functionality beyond simple CRUD operations.

The need to manage large volumes of data efficiently has led the e-commerce platform to implement techniques for data archival and partitioning. Although SQLite is optimized for small to medium-sized deployments, the cumulative data generated by product updates, user interactions, and historical order records necessitates regular maintenance. The platform incorporates scheduled tasks that archive old records and maintain current datasets for active transactions. Such maintenance routines ensure that the SQLite database remains performant over time and that backup procedures remain manageable.

Beyond performance optimization, ensuring data security and integrity is a fundamental consideration in this case study. With user data, including payment information and login credentials at stake, the platform adopts multiple layers of data protection. SQLite supports the implementation of unique constraints and encryption extensions, which are integrated into the application layer to safeguard sensitive information. Encryption of the entire SQLite database, using tools such as SQLCipher, is a strategy employed in the platform to prevent unauthorized access to both user data and product information, especially in the event of a breach or unauthorized file access.

From a systems architecture perspective, the decision to use SQLite for managing the e-commerce platform was influenced by several factors. The portability of SQLite means that the product catalog and user data can be easily moved between development, staging, and production environments without the need for extensive configuration changes. The platform benefits from decreased operational complexity, as the self-contained database eliminates the need for managing separate database servers. Furthermore, the read performance of SQLite is generally excellent for the types of queries common in e-commerce, such as product searches, filtering based on attributes, and displaying user profiles.

In terms of scalability, the platform is designed with the understanding that SQLite is optimally used for moderate workloads or as an initial solution during the early stages of business growth. As the platform expands, data management responsibilities can be partitioned, with inactive data archived locally and active data maintained in a lean SQLite instance. This partitioning strategy enables the business to scale organically while ensuring that performance remains consistent for day-to-day operations. In some scenarios, the platform employs replication techniques, where multiple instances of SQLite databases are maintained and synchronized across distributed components, ensuring that load distribution is achieved without compromising data integrity.

The case study of the e-commerce platform demonstrates that SQLite is not merely a lightweight solution for mobile and web applications but can also be effectively applied to complex, data-driven environments. Through careful planning of schema design, transaction management, indexing, and security, the platform achieves a high level of performance and reliability. This case study reflects how a simplistic, well-understood, and widely supported database engine can serve as the foundation for a modern e-commerce solution, delivering efficient and consistent performance across a variety of operational scenarios.

10.5. Case Study: Data Analysis Applications

The utilization of SQLite for data analysis and reporting is exemplified in a system designed to process extensive log data from a network of sensors and web services. The application demonstrates the effectiveness of SQLite as a lightweight repository for storing, aggregating, and analyzing data that originates from various sources. By integrating SQLite into the analytical pipeline, the system leverages a self-contained, serverless database engine that minimizes infrastructure requirements while maintaining robust querying capabilities.

The data analysis application collects raw logs containing timestamps, event types, user identifiers, and additional metadata. These logs are stored in a single SQLite database file that serves as the central hub for subsequent extraction, transformation, and report generation. The design prioritizes simplicity so that analysts can directly query the database using standard SQL commands. Moreover, the application accommodates both real-time reporting and historical data analysis, allowing stakeholders to understand usage patterns, detect anomalies, and derive business insights.

A typical workflow begins with the ingestion of log data into a table specifically designed for reporting purposes. To facilitate efficient querying and minimize latency, the table is optimized with appropriate indexing. For example, an index on the timestamp column accelerates temporal queries, while indexes on event types and user identifiers support rapid aggregation and filtering. The following SQL statements illustrate the creation of a suitable schema along with the necessary indexes:

```
CREATE TABLE IF NOT EXISTS logs (
    log_id INTEGER PRIMARY KEY AUTOINCREMENT,
    event_type TEXT NOT NULL,
    user_id INTEGER NOT NULL,
    event_value REAL,
    event_timestamp DATETIME DEFAULT CURRENT_TIMESTAMP,
```

404

```
        metadata TEXT
);

CREATE INDEX IF NOT EXISTS idx_timestamp ON logs(event_timestamp);
CREATE INDEX IF NOT EXISTS idx_event_type ON logs(event_type);
CREATE INDEX IF NOT EXISTS idx_user_id ON logs(user_id);
```

The application often requires running complex queries to derive aggregated statistics. For instance, one common analysis might compute the average event value for different event types over defined time intervals. This enables reporting on fluctuations in system usage or customer activity. The query presented below groups data by event type and hour, calculating summary statistics that inform decision-making processes:

```
SELECT event_type,
       strftime('%Y-%m-%d %H:00:00', event_timestamp) AS hour,
       COUNT(*) AS event_count,
       AVG(event_value) AS average_value,
       MAX(event_value) AS max_value,
       MIN(event_value) AS min_value
FROM logs
GROUP BY event_type, hour
ORDER BY hour DESC;
```

This approach demonstrates how SQLite's native support for date and time functions simplifies temporal grouping and aggregation. The use of the `strftime` function converts raw timestamps into a standardized hourly format, thereby consolidating events into manageable segments for comparative analysis.

A critical aspect of the data analysis system is its ability to integrate with visualization tools and generate automated reports. Python, together with libraries such as `pandas` and `matplotlib`, is used to extract data from SQLite and convert it into analytical models. The following Python code snippet shows how analysts can retrieve data from SQLite and subsequently process it using `pandas`:

```
import sqlite3
import pandas as pd
```

405

```
import matplotlib.pyplot as plt

def fetch_aggregated_data(db_path):
    conn = sqlite3.connect(db_path)
    query = """
    SELECT event_type,
            strftime('%Y-%m-%d %H:00:00', event_timestamp) AS hour,
            COUNT(*) AS event_count,
            AVG(event_value) AS average_value
    FROM logs
    GROUP BY event_type, hour
    ORDER BY hour DESC;
    """
    df = pd.read_sql_query(query, conn)
    conn.close()
    return df

db_path = 'analysis_logs.db'
data = fetch_aggregated_data(db_path)
print(data.head())

# Plotting aggregated event counts for a given event type
event_type_filter = 'click'
filtered_data = data[data['event_type'] == event_type_filter]
plt.figure(figsize=(10, 5))
plt.plot(filtered_data['hour'], filtered_data['event_count'], marker
    ='o')
plt.title('Hourly Event Counts for "click" Events')
plt.xlabel('Hour')
plt.ylabel('Count')
plt.xticks(rotation=45)
plt.tight_layout()
plt.show()
```

In this example, the data is extracted using a SQL query that aggregates events by type and hour. The data is then loaded into a pandas DataFrame, which provides analysts with the flexibility to further manipulate the dataset. Visualization using matplotlib transforms numerical insights into interpretable graphical reports, enhancing the decision-making process for system administrators and business stakeholders.

In addition to routine aggregation, the reporting system is capable of identifying trends and detecting anomalies. For example, a sudden in-

406

crease in the error event types within a short time frame might signal potential issues in upstream services or a security breach. To support such analyses, SQLite is frequently queried to calculate the moving average of specific metrics. Consider the following Python snippet that computes a moving average of error counts over a specified rolling window:

```
def compute_moving_average(series, window_size):
    return series.rolling(window=window_size).mean()

# Fetch error events grouped per hour
def fetch_error_events(db_path):
    conn = sqlite3.connect(db_path)
    query = """
    SELECT strftime('%Y-%m-%d %H:00:00', event_timestamp) AS hour,
           COUNT(*) AS error_count
    FROM logs
    WHERE event_type = 'error'
    GROUP BY hour
    ORDER BY hour;
    """
    df = pd.read_sql_query(query, conn)
    conn.close()
    return df

error_data = fetch_error_events(db_path)
error_data['moving_average'] = compute_moving_average(error_data['
    error_count'], window_size=3)
print(error_data.head())
```

By comparing the hourly error counts to their moving average, the system can flag anomalous deviations from typical behavior. These insights facilitate rapid intervention by engineering teams, ensuring that performance issues are addressed before they escalate into critical outages.

Data analysis applications often need to reconcile multiple datasets. In our case study, the primary log data is complemented by auxiliary tables containing user demographics and session data. Joining these datasets enables a more nuanced analysis that combines behavioral metrics with user profiles. For instance, to evaluate how different user segments interact with the platform, an analyst may join the `logs` table with a `users` table. A simplified version of such a query is provided below:

```
SELECT l.event_type, u.user_id, u.age_group, COUNT(*) AS event_count
FROM logs l
JOIN users u ON l.user_id = u.user_id
GROUP BY l.event_type, u.age_group
ORDER BY event_count DESC;
```

This join operation allows the system to produce reports that highlight the distribution of events across various demographic segments. The use of SQLite in this context provides a unified platform for data integration and analysis, ensuring that disparate datasets can be combined without necessitating complex ETL (Extract, Transform, Load) processes.

The adoption of SQLite in the analytical system is further bolstered by its ease of deployment and maintenance. Since SQLite databases are stored as single files, they can be readily backed up, transferred, and even version-controlled using standard file system utilities. This portability is particularly beneficial when data analysts need to share subsets of data with remote teams or when deploying the application across heterogeneous environments.

Another advantage of using SQLite for data analysis lies in its flexibility when it comes to handling both structured and semi-structured data. The platform leverages SQLite's ability to store JSON data within text fields, which can later be parsed and queried using built-in JSON functions. This capability proves useful when log entries contain nested metadata that does not conform to a rigid schema. Analysts can extract key-value pairs from these JSON fields using queries such as:

```
SELECT log_id,
       json_extract(metadata, '$.session_duration') AS
    session_duration,
       json_extract(metadata, '$.browser')
FROM logs
```

```
WHERE event_type = 'session_start';
```

The flexibility to operate on both flat and hierarchical data within the same analytical framework adds significant versatility to the application. This adaptability ensures that the data analysis platform remains capable of evolving with the changing needs of the business environment.

Performance considerations remain paramount in large-scale data analysis applications. SQLite's efficient indexing, in-memory caching, and query optimization techniques contribute to rapid query execution, even as the volume of stored logs increases. Regular maintenance tasks, such as vacuuming the database and updating statistics, are integrated into the system to ensure long-term performance stability. These operations are scheduled during low-usage periods to minimize disruption to ongoing reporting tasks.

The case study of this data analysis application highlights that SQLite's simplicity and robustness make it a viable choice for complex analytical workloads. By using SQLite, the system benefits from a streamlined architecture that supports both real-time and historical data processing, reduces operational complexity, and minimizes latency in generating critical insights. The application effectively demonstrates that a lightweight database engine can serve as the backbone for advanced data analytics and reporting systems in a variety of domains.

The combination of structured SQL queries, integration with data processing libraries, and support for modern JSON functions further reinforces SQLite's role as a powerful tool for data analysis. Stakeholders receive timely and actionable reports that guide strategic decisions, while analysts enjoy a flexible, maintainable, and portable platform. This case study underscores how leveraging SQLite for data analysis and reporting can transform raw log data into meaningful insights, ultimately enhancing operational efficiency and driving informed business strategies.

10.6. SQLite in Game Development

In game development, managing in-game data and user progress efficiently is paramount to delivering engaging and seamless experiences.
SQLite offers a lightweight, reliable, and cross-platform solution capable of handling a diverse range of game data, from player statistics and
configurations to dynamic game world states. Its self-contained nature
simplifies integration into game engines and standalone applications,
ensuring that in-game data operations perform with minimal latency
and system overhead.

Game development typically demands rapid read and write operations
as the player's actions are recorded continually. SQLite's architecture,
based on a single file database, allows developers to store in-game
data such as levels, inventories, scores, and settings within one easily
managed file. This encapsulation is particularly useful during development cycles, where iterative changes to game data schemas occur frequently. The embedded nature of SQLite means developers can update
the database schema alongside the game engine without the complexities associated with a client-server database model.

A critical component of many games is saving and loading user
progress. This includes not only high scores but also complex
game states that encompass character positions, achievements,
and game world modifications. SQLite provides ACID-compliant
transactions, ensuring that all changes to the player's progress are
recorded completely and consistently. When a game state is saved,
multiple aspects of the game must be updated simultaneously. In
such scenarios, encapsulating these updates in a transactional block
guarantees that either all parts of the state are saved successfully,
or none are, thereby preventing data corruption due to incomplete

writes.

The following Python code snippet demonstrates a simplified routine for saving a player's progress within a game. In this example, SQLite is used to store game state details such as the player's name, level, score, and inventory items:

```python
import sqlite3

def initialize_game_database(db_path):
    conn = sqlite3.connect(db_path)
    cursor = conn.cursor()
    cursor.execute('''
        CREATE TABLE IF NOT EXISTS player_progress (
            player_id INTEGER PRIMARY KEY AUTOINCREMENT,
            player_name TEXT NOT NULL,
            level INTEGER NOT NULL,
            score INTEGER NOT NULL,
            last_saved DATETIME DEFAULT CURRENT_TIMESTAMP
        )
    ''')
    cursor.execute('''
        CREATE TABLE IF NOT EXISTS inventory (
            inventory_id INTEGER PRIMARY KEY AUTOINCREMENT,
            player_id INTEGER NOT NULL,
            item_name TEXT NOT NULL,
            quantity INTEGER NOT NULL,
            FOREIGN KEY (player_id) REFERENCES player_progress(
    player_id)
        )
    ''')
    conn.commit()
    conn.close()

def save_progress(db_path, player_name, level, score, inventory_items
    ):
    conn = sqlite3.connect(db_path)
    cursor = conn.cursor()
    try:
        cursor.execute("BEGIN TRANSACTION;")
        cursor.execute('''
            INSERT INTO player_progress (player_name, level, score)
            VALUES (?, ?, ?)
        ''', (player_name, level, score))
        player_id = cursor.lastrowid
        for item in inventory_items:
            cursor.execute('''
```

```
                    INSERT INTO inventory (player_id, item_name, quantity
    )
                    VALUES (?, ?, ?)
                    ''', (player_id, item['name'], item['quantity']))
        conn.commit()
    except Exception as e:
        conn.rollback()
        print("Error saving progress:", e)
    finally:
        conn.close()

# Example usage
db_path = 'game_data.db'
initialize_game_database(db_path)
player_inventory = [{'name': 'Sword', 'quantity': 1}, {'name': '
    Potion', 'quantity': 5}]
save_progress(db_path, 'HeroPlayer', 3, 7500, player_inventory)
```

This example illustrates the process of creating necessary tables and executing a transaction that saves a new progress record alongside the associated inventory. The transaction ensures that if any part of the saving process fails, the database remains in a consistent state, avoiding scenarios where a partial game state is recorded.

Beyond saving game states, SQLite is equally effective in managing dynamic in-game data. Many games feature evolving worlds where data must be updated on the fly. In massively multiplayer online games or procedurally generated adventures, elements such as player locations, non-player character (NPC) states, and environmental changes need to be simultaneously read and written. SQLite supports concurrent read operations with robust locking mechanisms that prevent data conflicts. While write operations are serialized to maintain consistency, careful orchestration and the use of separate threads or asynchronous patterns can mitigate potential performance bottlenecks in action-intensive game environments.

In addition to transactional integrity, the ability to perform complex queries using standard SQL can be leveraged to enhance gameplay. For instance, leaderboards, mission statistics, and achievement tracking systems can all be implemented using SQLite's querying capabilities. Consider a scenario where a game engine retrieves the top scores to display on a global leaderboard. The query might involve sophisticated filtering and sorting operations that are executed efficiently by SQLite. The following SQL query is an example of how one might retrieve a sorted list of high scores:

```
SELECT player_name, score, last_saved
FROM player_progress
ORDER BY score DESC, last_saved ASC
LIMIT 10;
```

Such queries exemplify how SQLite can serve as a critical component for real-time analytics within games, allowing developers to provide timely and competitive feedback to players.

The simplicity of SQLite also translates into ease of deployment. Game developers often prefer self-contained solutions to avoid dependencies that complicate deployment across multiple platforms. Whether deploying on PC, mobile, or console, an SQLite database does not require a dedicated service or additional setup. This portability simplifies distribution and ensures that the game experience is consistent across various hardware configurations. Moreover, the single-file design allows for straightforward backup, version control, and patching of game data, which is especially useful in distributed game environments where data integrity is a move toward persistent world continuity.

Performance optimization is another critical aspect of deploying SQLite in game development. Games, by their nature, are sensitive to performance issues due to strict frame-rate and responsiveness requirements. SQLite offers several configuration parameters and pragmas that can be adjusted to boost performance in scenarios with heavy read-write cycles. For example, modifying the cache size or temporary storage settings using SQLite pragmas can reduce disk I/O latency. A sample pragma command to optimize the cache is shown below:

```
PRAGMA cache_size = 10000;
```

In this context, tuning SQLite's performance parameters can lead to noticeable improvements in the responsiveness of in-game data operations, ensuring that game logic and rendering processes remain unaffected by backend database performance.

Another feature of SQLite beneficial for game development is its support for custom SQL functions. Game engines often require unique calculations or transformations applied to game data. Developers can extend SQLite by registering custom functions that perform specific operations, such as computing in-game physics parameters or analytics metrics. This extensibility reduces the need to export data from the database for external processing, allowing complex calculations to occur within SQL queries.

The integration of SQLite within game development extends to both single-player and multiplayer contexts. In single-player games, where the client manages all game data locally, SQLite ensures that user progress is stored reliably and without reliance on external services. For multiplayer games, SQLite can serve as an in-memory cache or a fast-access datastore to manage session data and transient game states, significantly reducing latency in network communications. Although a more comprehensive client-server architecture may be used for persistent global data, SQLite still plays an essential role in managing local state and providing immediate feedback to the player.

Furthermore, the ease with which SQLite is integrated into various programming languages and game engines fosters rapid prototyping. During early development stages, team members can experiment with different game mechanics and data models without investing significant resources into heavy database infrastructure. As the project matures, the proven reliability and scalability of SQLite can be maintained,

414

or the database can be migrated to more sophisticated architectures if necessary.

The application of SQLite in game development is multifaceted. It supports the storage of user progress, dynamic game state management, performance-critical querying, and the provision of in-game analytics such as leaderboards and achievement tracking. Its transactional integrity, ease of deployment, and adaptability across platforms make it an invaluable tool for modern game development. Through the use of SQLite, game developers are able to focus on creating engaging gameplay experiences while trusting that underlying data operations are robust, secure, and efficient.

10.7. Transitioning from Other Databases to SQLite

Migrating from a traditional client-server database management system to SQLite requires careful analysis of schema compatibility, application design, and performance characteristics. The migration process begins with a thorough evaluation of the existing database structure and the application's data access patterns. Often, legacy systems may utilize features that do not have direct equivalents in SQLite or require adjustments because SQLite emphasizes simplicity and minimal resource consumption. Consequently, a preliminary step in the transition is to review the current schema, stored procedures, triggers, and transactional requirements to identify areas that need redesign or conversion.

A primary consideration is the difference in architecture. Client-server databases typically allow for high levels of concurrency and centralized management, which might lead to the use of advanced features such as user-defined functions, complex joins, and partitioning. SQLite, on the other hand, is a file-based database engine that does not rely on network protocols and manages concurrency through file locking mechanisms. In transitioning, developers must ensure that the workload of the application—especially write-heavy operations—is within SQLite's capabilities. Applications that require frequent concurrent writes may need a redesigned access pattern. For example, batching writes or using asynchronous processing can mitigate the challenges posed by SQLite's serialized write behavior.

Schema translation forms a critical part of the migration process. This involves translating data types and constraints from the original database to those supported by SQLite. While many common data types such as INTEGER, TEXT, REAL, and BLOB map directly, more complex types and behaviors might require redefinition. Consider a situation where a database employs a BOOLEAN data type; in SQLite, this is typically represented by an INTEGER with values 0 and 1. Similarly, handling date and time values may involve transitioning to SQLite's recommended strategies such as using the ISO-8601 date format, or applying the built-in date and time functions like strftime. The following code snippet demonstrates a Python routine that migrates data from a source database to an SQLite database, highlighting how data transformations are implemented:

```
import sqlite3
import mysql.connector  # Example using MySQL as the source database

def migrate_data(source_config, sqlite_db_path):
    # Connect to the source MySQL database
    src_conn = mysql.connector.connect(**source_config)
    src_cursor = src_conn.cursor(dictionary=True)

    # Connect to the SQLite database
    sqlite_conn = sqlite3.connect(sqlite_db_path)
    sqlite_cursor = sqlite_conn.cursor()

    # Create a table in SQLite with a schema matching the source
     database
    sqlite_cursor.execute('''
        CREATE TABLE IF NOT EXISTS users (
```

```
                user_id INTEGER PRIMARY KEY,
                username TEXT NOT NULL UNIQUE,
                email TEXT NOT NULL,
                is_active INTEGER NOT NULL,
                registration_date TEXT
        )
    ''')

    # Retrieve data from the source database
    src_cursor.execute("SELECT user_id, username, email, is_active,
     registration_date FROM users")
    rows = src_cursor.fetchall()

    for row in rows:
        # Transform date or boolean fields if needed
        registration_date = row['registration_date'].strftime('%Y-%m
    -%d %H:%M:%S') if row['registration_date'] else None
        is_active = int(row['is_active'])
        sqlite_cursor.execute('''
            INSERT OR IGNORE INTO users (user_id, username, email,
    is_active, registration_date)
            VALUES (?, ?, ?, ?, ?)
        ''', (row['user_id'], row['username'], row['email'],
    is_active, registration_date))

    sqlite_conn.commit()
    src_cursor.close()
    src_conn.close()
    sqlite_cursor.close()
    sqlite_conn.close()

# Example configuration for the source MySQL database
source_config = {
    'user': 'db_user',
    'password': 'db_password',
    'host': 'localhost',
    'database': 'legacy_database'
}

sqlite_db_path = 'migrated_database.db'
migrate_data(source_config, sqlite_db_path)
```

The above example reflects one aspect of migration: data extraction, transformation, and loading (ETL). It is important to verify data integrity after each migration phase. Automating tests that check row counts, data values, and constraint validations can ensure that the new

417

SQLite database is a faithful representation of the original dataset.

Another important consideration during migration is managing application-level logic that was previously implemented within database-specific functionalities such as stored procedures or triggers. In many traditional databases, business logic is embedded within the database itself. SQLite supports triggers, but its capabilities in this area are more limited. Consequently, some elements of business logic may need to be migrated to the application layer. For instance, if the original database system relied on triggers to enforce business rules (such as automatic updates or cascading deletions), similar functionality can be implemented in the application code or by using SQLite triggers with simplified logic. An example of setting up a basic trigger in SQLite to update a timestamp field is shown below:

```
CREATE TRIGGER update_timestamp AFTER UPDATE ON users
BEGIN
    UPDATE users SET registration_date = datetime('now')
    WHERE user_id = NEW.user_id;
END;
```

This trigger example illustrates how SQLite can perform automatic updates; however, more complex procedures might require rewriting logic within the application. Migrating such logic to the application layer involves identifying all stored procedures, rewriting them in the application's programming language, and thoroughly testing to ensure that business rules remain consistent after migration.

Performance tuning is also critical when transitioning to SQLite. Unlike dedicated database servers, SQLite runs in the same process as the application, which can lead to different performance profiles. Developers must consider tuning SQLite's PRAGMAs to optimize performance for the new workload. For example, adjusting the synchronous setting can improve write performance, especially in use cases where the risk of power failure is minimal:

```
PRAGMA synchronous = NORMAL;
```

418

Such adjustments should be tested extensively to balance write performance with data integrity. Other PRAGMA settings such as `cache_size` and `journal_mode` can also be tuned based on the specific requirements and hardware characteristics of the deployment environment.

Another migration strategy involves running SQLite in a hybrid mode, where the new system uses SQLite in parallel with the existing database during a transition period. This allows for side-by-side comparison of data, making it easier to verify correctness and performance before fully decommissioning the old system. Techniques such as dual writes—where the application writes to both the legacy database and the new SQLite database—can facilitate a gradual migration. During this period, discrepancies between the two databases are analyzed, and corrective measures are implemented before the system fully transitions to SQLite.

It is also essential to consider the implications of SQLite's file-based architecture on backup and recovery strategies. Traditional databases often benefit from robust backup mechanisms that involve continuous replication and transaction logs. SQLite databases, being single files, require a different approach. Developers need to implement regular file backups coupled with checksums or incremental backup strategies to ensure data is not lost during file corruption or hardware failure. Many backup solutions integrate seamlessly with SQLite by simply copying the database file while ensuring that no write operations occur during the backup, or by using SQLite's online backup API.

Furthermore, documentation and training should be part of the transition plan. Developers and database administrators accustomed to the traditional database system need to understand SQLite's fundamental differences. Training might cover public API changes, new performance tuning tactics, and debugging practices specific to SQLite. Additionally, documenting the migration process, including any code

419

changes and rationale behind data transformations, ensures a smooth transition and provides a reference for future migrations or audits.

Finally, after migration, a comprehensive testing strategy is crucial to validate the new setup. End-to-end testing, including stress testing and evaluating concurrency under realistic workloads, helps to identify any lingering issues. Monitoring tools that track database performance metrics and error reporting should be integrated into the application environment. The transition to SQLite often results in a reduction of operational complexity; however, it is critical to verify that this benefit is not offset by unforeseen performance bottlenecks or data inconsistencies.

Transitioning from other databases to SQLite can significantly simplify application deployment and reduce operating costs. Leveraging SQLite's simplicity, portability, and efficient performance allows applications to operate in environments where managing a full-fledged database server is impractical. By following a methodical migration process that includes schema conversion, application logic adaptation, performance tuning, and robust testing, developers can successfully structure an application to rely primarily on SQLite. This approach ultimately leads to systems that are easier to maintain, deploy, and scale in scenarios where lightweight, embedded data storage is advantageous.

Through a deliberate and well-documented transition plan, the migration to SQLite proves to be a viable strategy for modernizing legacy applications and streamlining data management. The integration of careful schema mapping, transactional consistency, and targeted performance optimizations enables developers to harness the inherent benefits of SQLite while maintaining operational integrity and application responsiveness.